The Castle We Called Home

Our Living, Breathing and Emerging with Autism

Simone Brenneman

authorHOUSE®

AuthorHouse™
1663 Liberty Drive
Bloomington, IN 47403
www.authorhouse.com
Phone: 1-800-839-8640

First published by AuthorHouse   05/13/2011

ISBN: 978-1-4520-9857-9 (sc)
ISBN: 978-1-4520-9858-6 (e)
ISBN: 978-1-4520-9856-2 (hc)

Library of Congress Control Number: 2010918419

Printed in the United States of America

"*S*ensory issues continued to intrigue and baffle us. Hayden "kissed himself better" frequently and obsessively. If he bumped his head (a part of his body that he couldn't reach to kiss), he would kiss his hand and then touch his kissed hand to his head. It was very bizarre; but it did serve as an *emotional barometer.*

In other words, I could often measure the degree of *underlying, brooding stress* in him by noting the frequency of these "self-stimming behaviors." It was clear that he and his body was so wary and threatened by the world around him, that he literally had to soothe it when he came in contact with "the world around him."

On the days when Hayden was, for whatever reason, feeling exceptionally threatened and unable to withstand the force of the world, the need to "kiss himself better" increased, often to ridiculous, almost non-stop levels.

It was just so odd: people don't do that sort of thing. *At least not people who don't have autism.* But if you think about it, really what Hayden was presenting to us was exactly what autism is: a mind, a body and a sensory system that is unable to effectively process incoming sensory information. It is then overwhelmed and bombarded by the world around it. And what Hayden had created really, was a pretty *logical* coping mechanism: *if something hurts your body, you kiss it and make it get better.* With his own little body and his oddly intelligent mind, really he was telling us exactly what was wrong.

It was very powerful messaging, to those of us who were insightful enough to be interpreting it. *To me, it spoke volumes!*"

The Castle We Called Home

Our Living, Breathing and Emerging with Autism

Simone Brenneman

To

Justin Hayward

I write from a place,
I *live* from a place,
That was brought out by you.

And to all of the other
Moody Blues
John Lodge   Graeme Edge   Ray Thomas   Mike Pinder

and to

Karyn

To be read with jeweled glasses....

And, to

Glen Davies

Foreword

It was honored when asked to write the foreword for Ms. Brenneman's delightful first book, *Effervescence*, and doubly honored now to write a foreword for her second book *The Castle We Called Home*. Whereas *Effervescence* primarily tells the story of her daughter Genevieve's life and emergence into a joyful, capable, and creative young woman with autism, *Castle* follows the more arduous journey with her son Hayden. This journey is made more arduous by the nature of his condition plus the exponential complications from meeting the needs of two very different children with autism, within a single family.

Most of us can hardly imagine the challenges, practical and emotional, that parents with an autistic child face in raising their beloved child and moving heaven and earth to help them reach their potential. The challenges facing parents raising *two* children with autism are unimaginable. Add to this that Genevieve and Hayden represent the opposite ends of the autism spectrum for severity, personality, interests, and most other dimensions of this disability.

I have had the privilege of knowing this family professionally for 15 years. I have watched with awe as Ms. Brenneman rose to these unimaginable challenges and through remarkable energy, insight, and creativity has taken her family beyond 'coping' to flourishing. Her two unique children with autism have truly flourished, each in their own way, and so have their older brother and sister.

Castle is Hayden's story but even more than in *Effervescence* the reader gets a glimpse of the whole family: living, loving, struggling, learning and thriving. It is a more challenging story because Hayden is a more challenging child, but Ms. Brenneman writes with the same passion, enthusiasm, and "refreshing outlook" that impressed Temple Grandin. This is a book that will speak strongly and practically to families dealing with autism. But it is also a well written and inspiring story of the human spirit that will appeal to a much broader audience.

Dr. Glen Davies, Ph.D.,Psych.
Director, ABLE Developmental Clinic Inc.
British Columbia, Canada

Author's Note

When our son Hayden reached the turning point of moving from elementary to junior high school, I knew it was time to repeat the same process I'd felt compelled to follow a few short years earlier, with his sister Genevieve. It had been a colorful tale of autism, a depiction of who she was and what her complex challenges and gifts were. But in picking up a pen, I could feel that *this* story would be very different from hers. I couldn't put Hayden as the focus as simply as I had done with Genevieve in *Effervescence*. And it wouldn't be a tale, it would be an epic. It wouldn't be pink and fluffy, with twists and turns, as her story had been.

Even as I began to write the first few sentences, I could literally feel the familiar stone walls going up around me, and around the five people I loved. I could feel the turmoil that existed from *within* those walls, as well as from *beyond*. In our home, it often felt like the world was pushing in on us. I needed to be on guard at all times, to keep the six of us safe and thriving. Hayden's would not be a tale about an adorable boy with wavy red hair and the cutest dimples, who gave hugs like no one else. The presence of Hayden in our lives had been so pervasive, so profound and yet so sweet, often to the point of emotional overload, that our lives had been turned upside down, inside out and contorted in ways few people could even imagine! This would be an *epic* about an amazing place, a *real* place, *and* a state of mind; it was a complex, captivating place that had weathered incredible changes and exasperating times. It would be about a home, the castle that *we* called our home.

The story would be about our "castle" which was our reality and our existence. It was where the six of us lived as individuals and as a family. It was strong like a fortress, often separating us from the rest of the world, sometimes because we wanted it to, sometimes because we had no choice. Often the drawbridge was up and we kept to ourselves. Sometimes it was down, allowing us to leave. At times we tiptoed cautiously, other times we frolicked playfully, and sometimes we ran to escape!

I knew that anyone involved in Hayden's life, on any level, needed to be aware of the castle in which we lived. My epic story was my way of opening the door, so that each person involved with him or with us, could peek inside. I filled close to one hundred pages with complex and colorful bits of information; but it was barely enough to scratch the surface. You now are holding the extended, fuller version in book form and even it could be much longer; there are chapters and chapters I could be including.

At this moment, I hope that you are feeling just a little bit apprehensive, but intrigued and curious enough, to come on in and take a peek!

The reality is though, that's it's not enough to just *peek* inside. You have to come in and *feel* it. You need to *walk around and feel* each room and each person who lived here. At times you may feel overwhelmed and really, *how could you not?* But my hope is that you'll feel what I feel: *fascination and awe!* Look at the bigger picture. By stepping inside, you're becoming a part of something important and unique. You'll see the world through very different eyes: through the eyes of our two autistic children and the eyes of the four of us who are blessed to have them in our lives!

Table of Contents

Part One: A Fortress Unfurls..1

Part Two: An Honored & Altered Life..........217

Part Three: Epilogue...261

Part One

A Fortress Unfurls

Chapter 1

ayden. Hayden. H-a-y-d-e-n. How is it possible that one little name, six letters simply lined up on a page, can make my mind and my entire body react in so many ways, and in so many directions? *How is that possible, and why?* At this moment, I smile, a beautiful smile, really; the kind of smile that comes as you shake your head and say: "Wow."

What a complex "guy." What an amazing individual! And what a complex journey it's been. Honestly, it was a bizarre existence for him and for the five of us, those who love him and know him the most. I *almost* wish, as I unfold his story for you, that I could tell you the ending first! Then I know you'd keep on reading, assured that the ending *will be* well worth all of the twists and turns and contortions that abound throughout the pages....Oops, that tells you that you *are* in for quite a story, and there *will* be times when you're going to want to toss this book aside and say: "Oh my God...." But you *will* keep on reading. Of that I'm certain. Hayden, and his complex, troubled but very precious heart, will draw you in. You'll need only a few pages, maybe even paragraphs, to see that his story is one to be told, to be heard and to be immeasurably inspired by!

But be forewarned: don't let yourself fall into the trap that's happened too many times during our journey with Hayden. This story, this epic tale as I've presented it, is not just about Hayden. This epic is *equally* about the six of us, because we are all so deeply entwined and uniquely impacted upon, by his challenged body and mind. We are all forever altered and war-torn, and yet enlightened, enriched and forever blessed to have him in our lives. This *is* Hayden's story, but it is as much *our* story. It's his existence and ours, in our castle: the castle *we* called home. *Welcome!*

3

You may have already read *Effervescence: A True-Life Tale of Autism and of Courage,* which focuses on Hayden's sister Genevieve, and *her* remarkable journey. That was my original intent: to have her story unfolded and shining in your mind *before* you embark on this even-more complex story; but it's certainly not essential. Each tale stands uniquely on its own. It may even be some timely twist of fate that brought this tale into your hands first.

Regardless of which story you begin with, I'm betting that you'll anxiously seek out the second. *How could you resist slipping into the worlds, the minds and the bodies of both Hayden and Genevieve?* Each is so different from the other and yet with startling, incredible similarities. In other words, as *different* as Hayden and Genevieve are from each other, is how oddly *similar* they are. It's uncanny, really. Each tale and its hero or heroine, is separate and distinct and yet totally entwined with the other. That is *our* world: our effervescent/fortress world, maybe not quite so much now, but for many, many tumultuous yet exhilarating years!

Picture in your mind images of pink, fluffy clouds and "feet that don't quite touch the ground," contrasted by dungeons and draw-bridges and solid stone walls. *How did those worlds come to be and how did they mesh to become who we were?* It *is* quite a story! The place to start is with our little family, as we were, when our beautiful Genevieve fluttered into the world and into our eagerly-anticipating lives.

Chapter 2

When Genevieve was born, we were the "perfect family!" Sydney, our daughter, so sweet and mature was three and Kobe, our rough, tumble and intense son, was one and a half. They were both deeply connected to the other and they were so easy to love. As parents, all we had to do was love them and respond with lots of attention and patience and they flourished, bright, happy and delightful. Like us, they were grateful and absolutely spellbound by newborn Genevieve! With her soft red curls and perfect rosebud lips, she was the calmest baby I'd ever seen.

Juggling the needs of our three babies was a challenge, but a delightful and invigorating one that I couldn't get enough of. Though we had little money to spare, we had boundless creativity and magic, interlaced with frequent family adventures, parties and social activities. It was absolutely amazing what we could pull together to devise captivating theme parties and events, with nothing but creativity and "little kid wonder" to motivate us. *Every single day in our home was an adventure!*

But by the time Hayden came along, when Genevieve was two, much had changed. It was a *dramatic transformation*, really. She had swept from being a frolicking little munchkin, who had an amazing perspective on life, to being incredibly temperamental, wild and volatile. *It was disconcerting, confusing, ridiculously stressful and yet immeasurably fascinating.* During her many magical moments, it was as though she was on a completely different wavelength from the rest of the world. She frolicked through it, casting a captivating spell on us and everyone around us, by her humor, her sparkle and her sheer effervescence! But those moments were contrasted by horrendous, inexplicable and sometimes bizarre and concerning behaviors. *Life in our home had somehow transformed from the "perfect life" to a nightmare.*

Not every minute was a nightmare; that was part of what made Genevieve and her behaviors so incredibly baffling and hard to deal with. *And it was what saved us.* But many of her behaviors *were* bizarre, and our *existence was bizarre.* She and her odd behaviors were like a "museum of fascination" for those of us who were a part of her life. *But living with her became more complex, stressful and all-consuming, than any parent of a typical child can even begin to comprehend!* Autism, in full bloom, was running rampant through our house; we just didn't know it at the time.

Genevieve's complex and intense need for princess dresses, the spinning in circles, the screaming, the echolalia (echoing words that she heard), the tuning out and the isolation....all were contrasted by the captivating energy, sparkle and effervescence that could only be described as *Genevieve.* As parents, Nolan and I were physically and emotionally fried. The screaming was so hard to endure. But when Hayden came along, though we were exhausted and stressed, beyond *anything* that could be considered remotely "livable," we were filled with newborn wonder and excitement. There was magic abounding throughout our home. For me, it was my dream come true: four children, all five years old and younger. Most people shuddered, but I thought: "What could possibly be more exciting, more fun or more fulfilling?" I knew it *would* be an adventure and I was up for it!

Despite the extreme challenges of Genevieve's behaviors, everyday was exciting, watching our four little miracles interact, each of them so unique and captivating in their own way. They were intrinsically drawn to each other like a litter of puppies. *So much innocence, sweetness and wonder filled every inch of our home!* Ours was a home of cribs and diapers, of puppets and toys, of paints and fabric, of endless creativity and boundless love. But it was also a home that was captivating and curious one moment, then intense and bizarre the next.

What had happened to us and why? How could there be such variances in temperament, abilities and talents amongst us? And how much screaming and "walking on eggshells" to ward off more screaming, could one home endure?

As it would turn out, those early days were the tip of the iceberg!

Newborn wonder....that should have been enough to offset the sweeps in Genevieve's behaviors, and our nightmarish existence; and to some degree, it did. Even Genevieve was sometimes drawn into Hayden's loveliness, well enough to leave her ever-growing world of isolation. She even surprised us by presenting to Hayden a new dimension of her complex personality: a maternal and protective side. It was unexpected and precious. But the addition of Hayden's presence in our home and the growing bond that entwined Sydney and Kobe around their baby brother's life, made it all the more easy for her to slip into her own glorious little world of isolation.

And not all of Genevieve's world was glorious. She was an autistic child and for someone with an autistic mind and body, the outside world could be an extraordinarily frightening, overwhelming and difficult place to be. It's no wonder, looking back now, knowing all that we do know about autism, that she responded the way that she did, by tuning out or by reacting horrendously!

It *was* a curious and complex world we found ourselves living in: too much stress, too much that was odd and bizarre; and yet so much that was fascinating and purely magical! But aside from the wonders and oddities of Genevieve, there was one other flaw that marred the newborn magic of Hayden. *It was Hayden himself.*

I would never have guessed that Hayden's birth was about to open up another world of complex wonders. Like the rest of us, I was just so overjoyed and grateful to have him! He was, and is, a miracle. He was born healthy, big and robust and we all fell deeply in love with him. But within weeks, something nagged away at me....it told me to keep an eye, and I started documenting. At that point it was just notes in a journal, but I was watching and thinking and pondering. *I was consciously documenting.*

You'd probably be surprised how many people (even people I've never met before), have asked me over the years, if I suspected with Genevieve and Hayden's pregnancies that anything was "different." When you have a child with autism, it seems that people lose their sense of tact, and you and your history become some "communal right to know." It's very odd. With Genevieve's pregnancy, she definitely did feel "different" from the others. It was *the way* she moved within me, and *how and when* she moved; it was like she was uniquely playful but just couldn't stay comfortable in her own surroundings. It was definitely noticeable and intriguing.

By contrast, with Hayden I can't say much was different, except that for the first few months, I barely felt pregnant. But his delivery was different and curious in the sense that it felt like he *wasn't leaving.* It felt like he wanted to stay and that he had little desire to join the outside world. Having a history of ridiculously quick labors, I was mortified of being home alone with the kids when it happened, so he was induced two days early. Even then, it seemed that the safety of being contained within me was the place he most wanted and needed to be; and it took a lot of coaxing to get him to leave.

Hayden was really bruised at birth, literally black and blue, especially his head. Once the bruises went away, no one in the medical community seemed to give them a second thought or ponder if the injuries had been superficial or not. (Many years later, an insightful doctor, definitely brought them into question). But despite the bruises, Hayden was beautiful, sweet and responsive and he wrapped himself around our hearts. Sydney and Kobe couldn't walk past him without stopping to hug and kiss him; and Kobe could hardly wait to offer his brother his favorite blanket, an honor even his beloved Genevieve wasn't allowed to share.

But something *was* different and odd, right from the very first weeks. At three weeks I remember vividly, taking Hayden with me to a restaurant for dinner with friends. He was oddly miserable and ill at ease; it gave me a strange feeling and something in my heart told me that this wasn't right. Over the months that followed, it became a frequent practice to remove Hayden so that it would be just me and him; otherwise he was agitated and unsettled. But by contrast, he often had lots of smiles and responded when looked at and spoken to. He squealed loudly when excited and was mesmerized by Sydney, Kobe and Genevieve and he loved their attention.

The bond that Hayden had with me was very intense, and even separating from me for a nap was enough to make him squeal with delight to see me again when he awoke. It was lovely, but disconcerting. Gradually there were other reasons for concern. By eight months, he was big and solid but seemed to lack muscle tone. Nights were increasingly wicked as Hayden would wake up screaming. Night after night, he would frantically grab my hair while pounding his head into my chest, or biting my collar bone relentlessly. At the time, we attributed it to teething and ear infections; but now looking back, knowing what we know, I'm convinced otherwise. There was an *intensity* in these behaviors that was extremely alarming. By then I was documenting avidly and what I found was that there was a *lack of rhyme and reason*, as to when these episodes happened. There seemed no patterns that made any sense.

Hayden swept from being incredibly sweet, loving and excitable, to being unbearable to be around. He screamed so much of the time. At one point, he screamed for three days, with no apparent reason. Yet when he was happy and content, he was adorable. I'd never heard a baby laugh so whole-heartedly as Hayden, especially at Sydney and Kobe and the antics they would dream up to amuse him.

Hayden's laughter was wonderful, but it felt *different*, like he was on a very different wavelength. And he was more fascinated by his hands than with toys and clearly, he needed a tremendous amount of physical stimulation through hugging, snuggling or the feel of fabric, which did not feel "typical." He had an insatiable need to bite and often, he made a B-line for my toes!

By one year, Hayden was still doing the "army crawl" and there was no language other than the occasional "duh" when he saw something he liked. The frequent screaming bouts continued, contrasted by "loveliness." All day long, he literally held on to me, almost constantly, either with both arms or with one while the other explored and played. Occasionally he'd separate himself from me, only to crawl back every half a minute or so, to hug me and then venture off again. He frequently made strange with family and friends. Often he pushed even his dad away, shaking his head, as if indicating "no," while heading straight back to me.

Like Genevieve, Hayden had no sense of danger. In fact, both seemed intrinsically drawn to lie in dangerous places, like under the sundeck railing, on the very edge looking down. Genevieve continued to be horrendously difficult to deal with and she rebelled against structure of any kind and, she "paralleled" us, with few real interactions. It was like she sometimes wanted to be with us, but really didn't know how.

And Genevieve stuck to me like glue! I was unbelievably grateful that at least she felt the need to include me and connect with me, physically and emotionally; but it made the constant juggle with Hayden and his intense bond with me, even tougher to deal with.

Chapter 3

y eighteen months, quite out of the blue Hayden took his first steps and within five weeks he was walking almost constantly. What a relief…. maybe then all would be right with the world! And he was surprisingly bright at putting objects and concepts together, like the plug in the bathtub. He had amazing determination and recall of things he'd seen or experienced; yet he had almost no interest in toys or books. Essentially, all Hayden really wanted to do, was to spend his time snuggled on the couch with his bottle and me. And when he did that, his spare hand absolutely and obsessively *had* to feel my face,· my hair and his blanket.

Hayden's frequent and intense screaming continued, and often for no apparent reason. Most nights also continued to be horrid. On one, he lashed out and scratched my eye so deeply, that in the morning I had to go into Emergency. *That was how I spent Mother's Day that year.*

It would take several years for my eye to heal completely; but in trying to find something positive from that terrible experience, I saw it as a good "physical" and *constant* reminder to me that there were serious concerns with his development and that I needed to not "lose sight" *or the courage* to address them. An EEG showed no irregularities or particular reason for his sleep issues. It seemed obvious to me, that over-stimulation, bombardment and feelings of insecurity during the day were to blame. Even *positive* events could bombard and over-stimulate him.

Hayden and Genevieve were like fire and water! Neither understood about sharing, taking turns or the emotions of others. Between her screaming and his, the stress level was, most of the time, *unbearable.* Each day we swept from intense contrasts between heart wrenching to intensely sweet and magical. That was our norm.

Though Genevieve was strangely protective of Hayden, she had enormous animosity towards him. She had autism and because of that, she had almost no capability of understanding him or of having empathy for him. And the similarities between Hayden and how Genevieve had been at that age, were really scaring me. The wild, volatile behavior, the screaming, the unpredictable mood swings and the lack of language were alarmingly reminiscent of her. And yet, on so many levels, he was a *complete contrast* to her.

Where they differed most, was that Genevieve was so uniquely attached to me, yet she existed so much in her own isolated world, with me as her stepping stone. But with Hayden it was like even in childbirth, he had never detached himself from me and that didn't lessen once he was born.

Both children had such an unusual need for sensory stimulation. Genevieve craved spinning in circles and submerging herself in mud. The tiniest mud puddle was an adventure in submersion to her (physically and emotionally). Hayden needed sensory stimulus from fabric, hair and people's skin; predominately, it needed to come directly from *me*. *He lapped up and consumed sensory stimulation from each of us, like it was an addictive drug; and then in the blink of an eye, he would lash out, sometimes even at me.* It was all incredibly complex. And *unlike* Genevieve, he *hated* to be alone.

All of our kids were snuggly, even Genevieve in her own interesting way. But with Hayden it was on a whole different level, from anything I'd ever seen before. There was an intense need, almost a *rapture* that was unique, and to be honest, alarming. One day, for example, after teaching a very sweaty dance class and yearning for a shower, I had to decline because Hayden was having an exceptionally rough and clingy day; I couldn't leave him unattended for even a minute. I opted for plan B which was a bath, so that he could at least join me. It was *utterly fascinating* because he stood in the water for a solid ten minutes, with his arms wrapped around my neck. Occasionally he'd reach out and touch a bath toy, but essentially, he stood there the entire time, extraordinarily relaxed, happy and content. It was like he was *inhaling* that close physical contact with me. It filled him with a profound and wonderful sense of peace and security that we almost never saw in him.

How do I even put into words how unique this experience was, and how *telling* it was of *who* my baby was and *how* his body worked? I'll never forget it; and I think that those moments and that experience forged a new path and a new understanding, somewhere in my mind. It struck me as amazing but bizarre how any child, particularly one as volatile and unpredictable as Hayden, could become so at peace from a *"sensory fix."* We'd seen "sensory oddities" with

Genevieve, but this was very different from what we saw in her. This was *people,* this was *skin.*....this was very different from her!

Chapter 4

As Hayden neared his second birthday, he was still perplexingly clingy and he adhered to me like a shadow. If I wasn't physically holding him, he wanted to putter at my feet, literally all of the time. He couldn't keep himself occupied with toys; yet in many respects, he was smart and obviously *watched us* very closely, though like Genevieve, he didn't *appear* to. Hayden had an interesting sense of humor and would laugh uncontrollably at simple things, like dropping clothes down the laundry chute. He clearly experienced things on a unique level. When he was happy, he would absolutely squeal with delight....*that was what saved us!* And, that was what motivated us, especially Sydney and Kobe, to keep him happy.

The tricky part (well, one of the many "tricky parts"), was that Hayden didn't initiate play and he needed us nearby constantly, to engage and amuse him. Once he gained more mobility and a little more dexterity, he developed obsessive habits, like putting lids on things and closing doors and drawers. If they weren't open, he would open them so that he could close them, both at home, and even more obsessively and compulsively, when we were out.

These behaviors were very strange; but from our point of view, at least he was finally doing something on his own! But it was alarming that he filled so much of his time that way. Likewise, he often would reach up and grab things, spilling or knocking them over, compulsively. His behavior was becoming even more volatile and erratic; he bit and pinched if he didn't get his way. Often, he bit and pinched for no apparent reason at all.

Socially, Hayden was exasperatingly unpredictable! At his second birthday party, he did well and was surprisingly less clingy than usual, *and* he was remarkably sweet and gentle with his infant cousin. Yet, in "Toddler Gym" class, he would push over other children, often biting them, leaving deep teeth marks on their sweet baby skin. Most times, these "attacks" appeared *totally unprovoked*. At times Hayden seemed threatened by the other toddlers; other times there seemed *no reason* at all.

Gym class was an absolute nightmare and we had to stop attending. That was a turning point and truly a heart-wrenching nightmare. Sydney had been the original participant in that gym class years before, and all of our kids had followed in her footsteps there. We were well-known and loved by the staff; but how could we continue on with our little family legacy, when we were leaving deep teeth marks imprinted on baby skin?

As for speech, it really wasn't happening for Hayden. He could say:"Hi Dada!" and utter a few sounds to indicate some of his needs, but it didn't move much beyond that.

Hoping that food allergies were to blame for at least some of Hayden's behaviors and lack of speech, we removed wheat and dairy products for two weeks. We'd seen dramatic improvement in Genevieve's life the year prior when we'd adjusted her diet, so our fingers were crossed. We tracked his behaviors and noted that he was happier, gigglier and more responsive. He was still clingy, but it seemed sweeter and less suffocating. He was a little more outgoing and better able to occupy himself with toys. Hayden actually seemed to accomplish *more* little milestones in those two weeks than in the two months prior.

When we increased Hayden's wheat and dairy intake, behaviors worsened, giving us incentive to carefully limit and structure his diet. But as we'd seen with Genevieve, his behaviors were so overwhelming and complex, that the food sensitivity improvement was barely a drop in the bucket!

Chapter 5

The Christmas season that year, when Hayden was two and Genevieve was four and a half (and Sydney and Kobe were seven and five), was a time to be *endured*, rather than enjoyed. Both Hayden and Genevieve screamed most of the time, like they didn't know if they were coming or going. The lack of routine, the anticipation, the "stress" of gifts, the chaos and the family socializing were all too much for *both* of them. Nolan and I worked ourselves beyond the point of exhaustion to shower Sydney and Kobe with attention, to help undo the damage. But it was worth the effort. Somehow we survived "the festive season" and there were enough glimmers of happy, calm and beautiful moments with Genevieve and Hayden, that *the magic of Christmas* stood out most in Sydney and Kobe's minds.

But for me, it was the saddest Christmas ever, because it was on Christmas Eve, in my parents' home that I knew for sure "about Hayden." It all came crashing down on me.

Ironically, as with my "revelation" about the seriousness of Genevieve's transformation a couple years prior, we were again with my sister Charlize and her boys. Like me, she now had a fourth child, a son Jeremy, who was just two months older than Hayden. Watching the two baby boys in the room together, amongst the Christmas Eve splendor, was beyond painful; it made it all indisputably and poignantly clear, how *different* Hayden was.

> But it wasn't just that Hayden and Jeremy were miles apart developmentally. *It was the fact that I had to spend almost all of that Christmas Eve, tucked away in a separate bedroom, to keep Hayden's siblings and cousins safe from him!* It wasn't just the screaming we had to stifle, it was his intense lashing out. He couldn't handle the people and the Christmas festivities in the rest of the house. They were pushing him over the edge.

This was serious; this was pervasive. This was my baby.

Alone, in a separate room, me and Hayden against the world....that was how Hayden and I spent most of Christmas Eve. He was happy to be alone with me, and I was in tears, because I knew that he had autism, and that this was very different from "the autism" and the world that was Genevieve. I was scared, really, really scared.

On that Christmas Eve, in that moment of truth, I can't honestly say I was filled with the same conviction and resolve that I had been in my moment of truth about Genevieve. This *was* different.

And this awareness came just three months after the blow about Genevieve's diagnosis. You have to know that with Genevieve, she truly was an effervescent, albeit complex soul, but she had such shining and sparkling potential. With her, it *had* been like finding the missing piece to a curious and complex puzzle; but still it was overwhelming and it did hurt. But the revelation about Hayden hit deeper. His behaviors were even more complex and disturbing than hers, and the level of aggression was much more intense. And as a family, we were already stressed, exhausted and pushed to ridiculous limits dealing with day-to-day life with Genevieve. *Now we had Hayden.*

And to me, Hayden was the fourth baby I never thought I'd get to have. I thought he was going to do all the little things that Genevieve hadn't. That Christmas Eve, many of my tears were because I knew in my heart that he was even more pervasively challenged and disabled than her. Many of the things that she *could do*, I didn't believe then that Hayden would *ever do.*

Even Hayden's lack of speech was so different than hers had been. Echolalia (an autistic trait of echoing or of simply repeating word for word what is heard) was *not* a problem with him because at that point, his speech was at a standstill; *he couldn't say enough words to be echolalic!* And I'd done the reading: statistics at that time said that fifty per cent of people with autism reportedly never speak. If Hayden *did* have autism, I had a terrible feeling that he was going to be one of those fifty percent, because speech just wasn't happening.

That Christmas Eve, how I pulled myself together at the end of that night, hiding the devastation and the anguish from my kids and relatives, I have no recollection. But I'm quite certain none of them knew. But I *do* remember walking out the door and leaving; I can see it in my mind and I can feel it. It was like taking steps into a world that was no longer the world that I knew. It was forever changed.

The next morning was glorious Christmas Day, but I don't remember a single thing about it.

Chapter 6

s I re-read the past couple of chapters, scrutinizing as if reading through *your* eyes, I can see how confusing this story must be. On one hand, you're likely thinking: "For God's sake, this child was leaving teeth marks on baby skin; he had no speech....how could they have not known?" What you have to remember is for one, back then, autism was still considered to be very rare and relatively little was known about it. To my horror, even the psychologist who had diagnosed Genevieve admitted that he knew little about it, but was "willing to learn." But what added to the confusion and the "mystery of Hayden" was exactly the *same* thing that had happened with Genevieve: Hayden was *adorable*. He was *beautiful* and he was *captivating*. As odd and difficult as he could be, he could be *equally warm, loving, intelligent and absolutely our sunshine!* It wasn't that we were blind or lacking insight. And don't forget, he was only two. Just as it had been with Genevieve, Hayden was extraordinarily complex and perplexing!

Well, if "Life is a Journey", we already had two distinct journeys underway. One: to find answers for Genevieve and all of the complexities of her life. Two: to meet the needs of Sydney and Kobe *and* to undo the damage of their siblings. Now, we had a third journey, and its severity made it take the spotlight, despite our intentions of moving full speed with the first two.

Looking back, I must have been oddly suspended in a place that teetered between anguish, and sheer motivation. The brutal "Christmas-time revelation" *was* overwhelming but I was once again instantly propelled into "mission mode." I knew that the next two years would mean an onslaught of assessments and appointments with therapists for both Hayden and Genevieve, *and* that both Kobe and Sydney would need as much attention and support as we could possibly give. Changes needed to be made, and ASAP. Basically, any extra events over and above fun activities that could *directly* benefit any or all of our four kids, were put on hold indefinitely. To the disappointment of my dance classes, I abruptly canceled the morning classes I'd operated for years, to help free up my time and energy. I kept only my evening classes, more for my sanity than anything else (and thank God I did). Once Nolan was brought up to speed with my extreme concerns about Hayden, he stepped up his role and increased his involvement with Sydney and Kobe and their activities.

On one hand, Hayden *was* so young, just barely two years old, and certainly not the first child to have delayed speech. But there were so many concerns, things that were just plain odd, some of them bizarre. I went through my notes and journals. I compiled a list of all of the oddities and the areas of concern: there were *thirty-one items.* Had I been asked to compile a list for my typical kids, I wouldn't have been able to find even two. A list of thirty-one *was* scary; but at least I had ammunition!

Off to our family doctor I went. She was a warm, caring and intelligent woman, who was still "licking her wounds" after Genevieve's recent diagnosis and her not taking me seriously, when I'd brought those concerns to her attention. Genevieve's diagnosis *should* have given me some clout, but it was the complete opposite. This doctor outright stated that I was now "simply being paranoid."

I was *exasperated* and finally made it clear that I was not leaving her office, because I was not waiting *another minute* to see if Hayden improved. At last she agreed to refer me on to a pediatrician. Moments later, as my kids and I got up to leave her examining room, she undermined *all* that I thought I had impressed upon her, by stopping me, turning and saying: *"Just try really talking to Hayden."* She followed with her recommendation that if he "wasn't talking by the age of four or five*, then we'd start worrying."* Can you imagine? I could have slapped her!

Seriously, picture this: there I was, an experienced mom of four (in addition to raising a younger brother affected pervasively by Down syndrome), sitting in her examining room, with my four kids......Genevieve was engrossed in her own little autism world, spinning in circles chanting: "Teeka, teeka, teeka, teeka"......Hayden was impulsively opening and closing the cupboards and drawers, and pushing buttons (this trait was bad enough at home but in confined spaces like a doctor's offices, it was even worse)......this behavior alternated between his screaming and pinching fits.......meanwhile, my two "typical" kids calmly took it all in, because to them, these were everyday occurrences! *This was our norm.*

We knew something was wrong. We'd learned to accept and embrace it; but we needed help and insight, *and* a diagnosis!

Was that what this doctor, this trained professional actually thought? Was I just *not talking enough* to my child?

Chapter 7

The pediatrician was even worse. Armed with my list of thirty-one concerns, I sat and listened as she stared blankly back at me and said: *"Lots of kids are clingy; lots don't speak or walk until they're older. I don't really think we should be all that concerned. If things haven't improved when he's four or five, then we'll take a look..."*

Did these doctors seriously think that with all I juggled, I had nothing better to do with my time than make up things about Hayden to make him look bad? And I wasn't talking "clingy", for instance; I was talking: "he couldn't survive without being physically attached to me!"

I had a list of *thirty-one* concerns; *didn't they understand how precious time was?* Both doctors were terribly intimidating. I will admit: had it not been for Genevieve's recent diagnosis, I *would* have backed down. They *would* have talked me out of it. I would have raked myself over the coals for not having more faith in my child and for not being a better mom. Hayden *was*, as they said, very young. For all I knew, maybe they were right; maybe he just needed more time. Did we, as parents, *have the right* to put numerous people through the time and expense of testing and assessing our child?

But all I had to do was relive Christmas Eve in my parents' home, and I didn't back down.

The *only* thing that sparked the pediatrician's attention was the fact that my sister was schizophrenic and she thought there might somehow be a connection. (That was an indicator of how far off she was: in all of the years to come, no other doctor or therapist would ever link Hayden with any reference to schizophrenia). Reluctantly, after numerous waste-of-time appointments, she referred us on to a specialist at a leading Children's Hospital.

I think there may have been a look in my eyes that told her I wasn't leaving until she did.

Finally, the wheels started moving. The specialist was guarded, but was clearly intrigued and concerned about our family's link to both autism and schizophrenia. She was equally intrigued and concerned about the uniqueness of

Hayden's behaviors and development. As parents, we didn't know whether to be grateful or horrified that he warranted so much of her concern and fascination; but at least she was listening and *she* was extremely eager to get moving. With only her referral, we were almost instantly connected to a new level of social services and waitlists for assessments and therapy. Thank God!

During the months when I struggled to be listened to and to be taken seriously by our doctor and pediatrician, I *did* thank God for the staff at Turning Point Preschool. That was where Genevieve was attending. This preschool really was a turning point in her life, because of the staff's skill and comfort level with children who had behavioral and developmental challenges. Rather than treating me like a paranoid parent, they *encouraged* me to listen to my instincts. They had seen the work that I'd done with Genevieve and they had seen enough of Hayden's behaviors, to recognize, understand and validate my concerns.

The Turning Point director immediately put Hayden's name on their waiting list for the following fall. Her decision, and the emotional support from her and her staff, truly helped change the course of his life.

How can I possibly stress the importance of early intervention? That time is so incredibly precious and can alter a child's potential dramatically. Those teachers were a gift to us. At that point, I was so driven, yet pulled in too many directions. And I was exhausted. I don't believe for a minute that I would have been strong enough to push the way I did, without their support. *Not once did they utter the words: "Let's wait until he's four or five."* They didn't want to waste a minute and they reassured me that if it turned out that Hayden would prove us all wrong and magically become a "typical" kid, we'd all be happy and still say it was time and energy well spent.

What a gift these people were!

ven today as I write these words, there is so much uncertainty and speculation as to exactly what the causes of autism are; back then, there was much more mystery and very few answers. Even the diagnostic and assessment procedures were limited and the medical community seemed to scramble for whatever bits of information or clues they could use to determine, if the child was, in fact, autistic. As is still the case today, there was no "conclusive blood test" that universally indicated autism; but the one blood test that could, in some cases, confirm a diagnosis of autism, was a test for Fragile X.

That was one of the first steps that the Children's Hospital specialist requested, and wow, did that shed new light and cast a new shroud of complexity over our Hayden.

Both Genevieve and Hayden were tested for Fragile X. After six agonizing months of waiting for test results, a bombshell was dropped on us. Though neither child had Fragile X, genetic abnormalities were found in Hayden's blood work. They were significant ones. He had an array of inversions and translocations that had never been seen before. There was no specific name for it and the only information the Cytogenetics team could offer us, was confirmation that anyone with those abnormalities would definitely have a very significant mental disability. Beyond that, there was nothing more that they could tell us.

The genetic report was frightening, devastating news. At least if it was a known genetic abnormality, there could have been some predictions as to the level of disability we could anticipate, or if there were other related health concerns. But this news opened up a whole spectrum of questions, concerns, uncertainties, and unknowns.

And it was, to be honest, creepy and unnerving. I say that, I think because at least with behavioral or psychological challenges and variances, you feel that you have some degree of being able to alter and modify. But it seemed like "blood is blood" and you can't change what is flowing through someone's body or how their cells are made. This was a lot to take in and to deal with. And we were already pushed far beyond our breaking points......

Chapter 9

*A*ppointments, appointments, appointments…they became our norm, and our everyday activity. As Hayden had no speech and his behaviors were even more complex and intense than Genevieve's, his list was even longer than hers. Month after month, I met almost daily with professionals ranging from psychiatrists, psychologists, speech therapists, occupational therapists, physiotherapists, behavioral therapists and social workers. And the thing that you need to keep in mind, is that we're talking about two children with autism. One of their greatest challenges was "transitioning" from one activity to another. *We didn't glide in gracefully from one appointment to the next!* I could make your hair stand on end to describe some of our finest moments, even our "average moments" for that matter.

As "the mom" and the orchestrator, the whole process was mind-boggling to me, as each professional needed very specific information about our past, about our present, about which child did what and when, all of that. I needed to be sharp, as their time and insight was precious. *But I also needed to reserve time, energy and brain power to do what had come so naturally for me to do, and what continued to be so important: observing, documenting, analyzing and contemplating behaviors.* And it wasn't just Genevieve and Hayden's behaviors that needed to be scrutinized. Sydney and Kobe were both enormously affected by the chaos that filled their lives; they too, needed full-time attention and scrutiny. *Journals were my necessity and my sanity.*

It was my pleasure, but also a deep necessity that I kept myself constantly "in the heads and bodies" of all four of my kids, literally at *all* times. Obviously, seeing the world through Genevieve and Hayden's eyes was most crucial. I needed to know what strategies were working and which were not. Above all, I had to maintain that all-important link and intense level of trust that I had built with them. Even *with* that bond, there were times when they both tuned me out and pushed me away. The fear and the potential of loosing them loomed over me: the literature was there, reports of young autistic children, who, for no apparent reason, completely isolated themselves and pushed their families away, even their moms. They then retreated into their own unique world of isolation.

That potential loomed over me constantly. I had worked so hard to build relationships and a deep connection with both Hayden and Genevieve and be damned if I was going to lose them! I knew I could withstand almost anything in life, but I didn't know if I would be able to withstand that.

It was a grueling schedule we kept, sometimes two appointments in a single day, and all of that in addition to Sydney and Kobe's school, dance and sport commitments. Each appointment meant another transition that almost always led to tantrums and meltdowns. Sometimes, by the time we arrived for an appointment, Genevieve, or Hayden, or sometimes both of them, would be so strung out that we couldn't even participate and had to leave. But we persevered and did what we could.

Despite the chaos and the madness that was *us*, I think pretty much every therapist we have ever encountered, picked up on the love, the absolute acceptance that abounded amongst us, and the *magic* that was *us*, and they in turn, fell just a little bit in love with each of us. And I'm betting that most of the time, because of that, we got their very best. (Well, there *were* just a couple of exceptions, that you'll hear about later).

As Hayden's speech was pretty much non-existent, except for the occasional "uh-huh." we focused on sign language. I practiced constantly because I was *desperate* to communicate meaningfully and reciprocally with my son. He responded well and quickly learned several basic signs like "more" and "help," which reduced his frustration. Sydney and Kobe were wonderful at teaching him. But because his eye contact was limited, we often had to compensate and hold our hands directly in front of his face to "talk" to him. That was an additional challenge.

Many speech therapy sessions went well and there was slow but fascinating progress. At that point, we weren't really working on actual speech, but more in teaching Hayden signs and giving him an understanding about interacting and communicating.

I remember those sessions vividly. They were all done through play, and because Hayden was so attached to me, I would work and "play along with him and the therapist. *Always* our work was done through his chosen theme: a mommy and a baby. It didn't matter to him whether it was through dolls, dinosaurs, animals or even simple cut-outs; as long as it was on that theme, he was receptive. "Mommy and baby" was something that he understood and could relate to; it was what he felt safe with. *It was how he saw the world, and how he approached it.*

Much of that therapy time really was precious and enjoyable time spent together. But, there were many times when I feared the speech therapist must have thought I was the worst mom, because so often I would fall asleep, literally mid-sentence. *I couldn't keep my eyes open.* I think it was the subconscious realization that there was another insightful adult present in the room, who could attend to Hayden. That allowed me to let my guard down just a little.... that was all it took, and I would nod off in the blink of an eye. Looking back, I think and hope she could see that I was really a pretty good mom; I was just *really* exhausted.

Chapter 10

I f I were asked to give advice to parents or to a family dealing with a young, newly diagnosed child with autism, it would be to accept that you can't do this all on your own. It's just too complex and too demanding. And it isn't just that you need the *insight* and *experience* of people who are trained in this field. You need to surround yourself with intelligent people who can also connect *emotionally* with you, who have some idea of the magnitude of what you're dealing with, as a parent *and* as a family. *You need their help and positive insight so that you can embrace autism and not fear it.*

I have to stop for a moment and focus on those two words: *autism and embrace.* To me, they go hand-in-hand, like one just glides into the next. By the time that you get to the end of this book, and definitely if you've already read *Effervescence*, you'll understand the passion that I have about joining these two words. It's the reason, during the months that followed the publication of *Effervescence*, that I poured my time, energy and personal funds into traveling and speaking to media and their viewers and listeners, about how important, and quite honestly, how *magical* the results can be. My family is a perfect example of that!

But for now, before I let myself go off on that tangent….*to reach any level of acceptance and to be swept up with the determination to meet the challenges of being an "autism parent or family," you do need emotional support, expertise and understanding.*

Friends and family may be well meaning, but the reality is that they simply cannot relate. Once you get moving and are confronted by the onslaught of therapists and appointments and therapy, you *will* be exhausted. You *will* be confused and overwhelmed. You *will* need to feel supported. That's just the reality, *so work with it.*

The thing is: as strong and as brave and determined as you as a parent may be, your friends and family will be hurting for you. At times, you may feel like *you* are supporting *them* through your child's diagnosis, and all that is to follow. They may *want* to help, but most won't know what to say. One day, for instance, I decided to let my guard down and let a close friend know exactly how intense and grueling my week of eight appointments had been (in addition to the usual array of bizarre autism behaviors). Her response was: "Oh, I know *exactly* what you mean. This week I had to take Moira (her typical child) to a doctor's appointment and then later in the week, to the dentist!"

I nearly lost my grip! These were not everyday doctor and dentist appointments that I was talking about; and these were not typical kids who could deal with transitions from one activity to another, without being severely affected by the sights, the sounds, the lighting, and the people of every different environment, much less the chaos of being in the car! Only two appointments in a week would have been a walk in the park for us.

A part of me understood that as a friend, she couldn't relate, nor could she let herself acknowledge what we were going through, because she felt bad for us. And that angered me, because we didn't want people to feel sorry for us. We had our challenges and life was incredibly stressful; but we still felt that we had so much to be thankful for. All we really asked for was acceptance of our situation and our children, and to feel supported and not judged.

Honestly, what *would* have helped me, would have been for this friend to let her heart wince for a moment, because she did genuinely care about us; but then shift and think to herself: "What would help me if I were in her shoes?" I think her heart would have said: "Don't pretend this is no big deal; be supportive and genuine." From that, she would have said: "Wow, that must be hard. But it's all going to be worth it." Or maybe: "You must be exhausted! Could you get a babysitter in so you can have a nap once in awhile?" *That* would have made me feel respected and validated.

Basically what I learned, time and time again was: "Keep it to yourself; they won't understand and they don't want to hear about it, because they can't handle it." And that can only make things build up counter-productively, deep inside you, which is never a useful thing. It's wasted energy.

Chapter 11

I definitely learned early on, that *invaluable* positive energy came from surrounding myself with people who validated our challenges, rather than downplaying them. Trust me, it's easier to gain momentum and feel that your exhaustion will eventually lead to better things, when it's acknowledged and maybe even held a little bit in marvel. When you're dealing with issues that are extraordinarily complex, unique and stressful, it's more empowering to hear someone say: "How do you do it?" than: "Oh, I know, we all do that."

One of the people that I surrounded myself with, was "plunked into our lives," surprisingly the result of a glistening brainstorm of someone within our government, who understood that *informed* and *supported* parents were an autistic child's single best resource. This person was Dr. Davina Nyles, a gifted and delightful psychologist. I can't say her name without smiling! She immediately saw that I embraced Genevieve and Hayden's behaviors with fascination, determination and insight. A deep connection was quickly forged between us; *she then opened a door and I stepped inside*. She opened my eyes to see, on new levels, the world the way my Hayden and Genevieve saw it. Most of all, she taught me to understand *why!*

I was a quick study, because it all made perfect sense to me. It was like filling in the blanks to a fascinating and almost deliciously perplexing puzzle, that I had already started piecing together all on my own. Davina didn't have all the answers. No one did at that time. And let's be real; as I write these words, years later, there are still *many* of the mysteries of autism yet to solve. But Davina had insight and intellect, joined with a sense of humor and a love for children who were "different."

Davina was there to offer insight and to offer support. Every hour with her was a gift!

24

Chapter 12

*O*f this was a fairy tale, I *should* be able to say that Davina cast a spell of knowledge and support that dissipated all of the chaos, the strain, and the sweeps that ravaged through our home, that made us feel happy, blessed and determined one moment, and then devastated, exhausted and worried about the plight of our family, the next moment. *On any given day, we experienced "lovely and amazing highs" and "devastating lows," with rarely anything "average" in between.*

But this is an epic after all, not a fairy tale. And there are many, many chapters left to unfold!

One of the issues that we had to meet head-on was the news of Hayden's genetic abnormalities and all of the uncertainty that those results held. It *was* devastating, unnerving news; I can't deny that. But it was also a mixed blessing. I *can* say, with serious honesty, that those test results also saved my sanity. *I mean that very literally.*

Genevieve's diagnosis of autism was one thing. She was affected in all aspects of her life, but she was so beautifully effervescent. There was sparkle and obvious potential. And she's proven to be a true inspiration and a true wonder! She is unique and extraordinary. Whether you actually know her personally, or experience her through her art and literature, she is a captivating gift.

With Genevieve, I found it easy to focus on all that was *amazing* in her and to direct my energy more to the future *and how to get there.* Of course, when she was first diagnosed, there were times when I struggled with guilt. I questioned myself; I asked doctors if this was something that I was somehow responsible for. Had I *done* something, or had I *not* done something during her pregnancy?

But there was nothing to indicate that I was to blame. I lived an exceptionally healthy lifestyle and Genevieve's pregnancy had been uncomplicated. I really did see her diagnosis much more as a "missing puzzle piece." I think I was more *relieved and grateful than upset,* to get a diagnosis, though I wouldn't have guessed autism. But I knew that finally we could just get moving and that a diagnosis with something as pervasive as autism, would open doors and we'd get help.

But with Hayden's diagnosis, everything changed. With one child, I could say: "Wow, but okay, these things do happen." But with a second child, and to have that child heaped with other disabilities as well, it was just too much. *And now*

25

we had two children, both pervasively challenged, both with bizarre, complex and stressful-beyond-words behaviors.

Everything in our world changed and everything in *my thought processing changed.* Everything.

> I'd so desperately wanted to have a fourth child, to add to our litter of precious little beings, each with their own contributions to the world. I didn't think Nolan would even join me in my desire for more. Honestly, to me four was a minimum. And here we were, with Hayden, the one who would "round off" our family and "do" some of the things that we'd missed out on with Genevieve. And yet I knew in my heart that he was so much more challenged than her....and she had that sparkle, that effervescence....but with Hayden, at that point, his behaviors were so severe, so inexplicable and so aggressive, that it was difficult to see what potential lay within him....

> *How do I even write these thoughts in black and white for you to read? How do I let you in and see where my thoughts were? This isn't easy.* But there *has* to be honesty for Hayden's story to make any sense. And there *has* to be honesty because there *are* other parents, and there will be many more, who have or will have children like Hayden placed into their lives.

> *It is for you, and for your beautiful children that I don't hold back during the pages of this book....*

The guilt that I felt was unbearable and I was consumed by it. When I looked at all of the day-to-day behavioral issues of both of my kids: the screaming, the biting, the pinching, the spinning in circles, and then witnessed the strain and impact on Sydney and Kobe, on Nolan and myself......to have this happen twice, to two of our four children; *how could it not be something I had done?*

Maybe it would have been oddly easier to accept if there had been developmental issues with Sydney or Kobe; but they were exceptionally healthy, bright, happy and intuitive children. And to complicate things, I *did* have a personal health history that now filled my *every* thought: when I was three months pregnant with Genevieve, it was as if someone had "flicked a switch within my body," and in what seemed to be literally overnight, I developed severe immune system issues. I became violently reactive to literally *all* but two foods (rice and potatoes), and many, many inhalants.

Thank God, the peak of severity of these reactions came *after* Genevieve was born, but it lasted until the first third of Hayden's pregnancy. And in between pregnancies, and for years after Hayden was born, there were times when even rice and potatoes were not safe, and perfume and chemical inhalants were brutal. There were times when I was, quite literally, starving. Many nights I cried myself to sleep, because I was just so hungry and there seemed no end in sight.

It was a terrible feeling, to be surrounded by the love, sweetness and innocence of four amazing kids, being so affected by this condition, and doctors really not knowing what was wrong or what to do about it. At that time, the discovery of AIDS was filling every newspaper and basically, I *had* acquired an immune system deficiency. It was terrifying, watching my babies, wondering if I had some unknown strain of AIDS.

Obviously, I didn't have any form of AIDS, but that didn't alter the severity of the health issue I faced everyday. And it didn't alter the glaring reality that I'd had two healthy, happy "normal" kids; then developed a severe immune deficiency, and then had two kids diagnosed with autism. *The possible link filled my every thought, month after month.*

How could that not be the reason? Even back then, nineteen years ago, there was lots of literature linking autism with food sensitivities. Donna Williams' book *Nobody Nowhere* had just hit the book shelves and there she made frequent references to her autism and probable links to food sensitivities. Even in our own home, I had altered Genevieve's diet before she was even diagnosed, thinking food sensitivities might have been the cause and culprit of her odd and severe behaviors. Though it turned out to be "drop in the bucket", there had been no denying that her diet was tied in with her behaviors and we saw a startling improvement within *one* day.

> *The writing on the wall leered at me: to have two exceptionally healthy and happy children; then have some weird immune deficiency overtake my body, and then have two children with autism....I was to blame.*

> *The guilt was unbearable.*

I wasn't thinking rationally. I was intelligent and well educated; I was an experienced mom. And I was someone who's entire life had pretty much revolved around people with disabilities. I had a brother with Down syndrome, who I'd been like a mother to. I had a brother who had become a paraplegic as a teen; I had a sister who was schizophrenic. I had another sister who had died as a small child from polio and a large family who'd struggled to pick up the pieces. *I had learned that good could be found from almost anything; that lives can be different from the norm and still be meaningful and important.*

But the guilt that consumed me and the impact of the chaos that I saw *each and every day* in our home, *distorted everything.*

Even when I was in the safety of my dance classes, I was dangerously close to quitting because I was so filled with guilt and self-blame that I couldn't look them in the eye. I was convinced that they too blamed me for what had happened to both of my children. How do you connect with people if you can't look them in the eye? How do you teach the personable kind of classes that I did, if you don't invite them to look in to who you are? How do you ask them to create images and movement from their bodies, when *your* body is in torture?

> My classes were no longer my safe reprieve. Finally, I had to make the choice, to either leave or confront them and tell them that it wasn't me, that I wasn't to blame. It took every ounce of courage that I had…. to my surprise, they looked back at me in shock….didn't I know that they never could have blamed me….in fact all that they saw when they looked at me, class after class, was an inspiration and a role model of strength and conviction, and an amazing mom….

It was an important step, reaching out to them. It helped. They were and are my angels.

Chapter 13

It isn't just that parents and families need support and understanding when their child is diagnosed, *and* that there needs to be an absence of blame. What I'm talking about now, starts *long before* a child is diagnosed, it's even before they're born. It's that double-edged sword of "healthy pregnancy / healthy baby" promoted amongst the medical community.

In my case, I was healthy, I was fit, I "did" everything right. Yes, during parts of each pregnancy I struggled with foods but I took supplements and I lived healthy. To have two "normal" kids, and then have two with such pervasive challenges, no matter what I told myself, the reasoning that had been pumped into me through every pregnancy, shouted out at me: "If they turn out to be 'not healthy' then it must have been something unhealthy that I had done. I must have been somehow responsible."

Everywhere I turned, the signs were there, literally. At the doctor's office, at the health unit where we went for therapy...constant reminders on the walls and in pamphlets, promoting and promising that a healthy pregnancy means a healthy baby. This concept and this assumption were and are wrong. It needs to be re-phrased and re-approached.

Of course I understand that we want to educate pregnant and nursing women on the importance of living healthy; but it is irresponsible and damaging to draw such clear cause and effect images.

Sometimes it just happens. It happened to us, and I wasn't to blame; yet it consumed me and the rational was all around me. Consequently, I punished myself in countless ways. Then, just as I'd start to feel stronger, trying to put it all behind me, I'd walk into an office or a bookstore to look at books with my kids, and there would be a new book displaying the same concept. Instantly I would be in tears, quickly gathering up my gang, scrambling to cover up my emotions so that my kids wouldn't know. We'd dash home, leaving me unable to leave the house for days afterward. At least at home, where it was just us, I could shut out the world and its judging eyes.

This pattern lasted for months. Honestly, I had enough to deal with, just getting the six of us through each day. I didn't need this on top of it all.

⸙

Finally, I stopped beating myself up. *I forced myself* to recognize that even if I *had* inadvertently done something "wrong," *I hadn't meant to. I forced myself* to recognize that I needed to focus my energy on all that I *had* done for my kids and all that I knew that I *could and would* do for them. Soul searching helped; counseling helped, and the wonderful, supportive and non-judgmental staff at Turning Point Preschool helped. But it wasn't enough.

What I needed the most was *concrete* proof that I was not to blame. That's what Hayden's genetic test results brought. They forced me to accept, once and for all, that no matter what I did or didn't do, I *couldn't* have done that to him.

29

And during the six months we spent waiting for those test results, it reinforced in my mind that no matter what was wrong with my Hayden, or how seriously he might be affected, I didn't care. *I just wanted him anyway that I could have him.*

And the test results *immediately* did open doors. *Suddenly our list of thirty-one concerns was taken very, very seriously!*

Chapter 14

At this moment, I'm wondering if you're shrugging and asking: "How were Sydney and Kobe through all of this?" How did they weather the torrential downpour and ravaging storms of autism that seemed to fill the walls and the world around them? *In a word, they were simply amazing.* What the two of them have endured is almost incomprehensible. But that is definitely not to say that they didn't both pay high prices, at this time or later on in their lives.

But if you were to look at either Sydney or Kobe today, you would see their bright eyes and eager souls. You would see two extraordinary people, at this moment, aged twenty-four and twenty-three. I'd love to side-track and give you "snapshots" of who they are today; but that's part of this epic, and part of the mystery. Their roles have been intrinsic and fascinating, each of them uniquely entwined in the lives of both Hayden and Genevieve.

Parts of Sydney and Kobe's personal stories *will* unravel throughout the chapters of this book and they'll be part of the reason that you'll want to take in every word, until the final page! Neither Hayden nor Genevieve would be who they are today, without the roles that their brother and sister have played, and continue to play to this day. *If Hayden and Genevieve are to be considered the hero and heroine of these tales, as they truly are; then both Sydney and Kobe deserve almost equal acclaim!*

I like to think that both Nolan and I deserve a piece of the credit in our "typical" kids' successes, because we really did work hard to smother them with love and positive attention. It was through sheer determination, especially in the earlier years, that we were driven to not let their needs go unaddressed. But it would be blind and naïve to say that there weren't times when they missed out on activities, or on getting our full attention, or that the stress level in our home wasn't seriously damaging. *But many parts of our home life were wonderful!*

In our home, there was always something going on that was fun and creative. We had the kids' sports, dance, and school events; we had my dance classes and Nolan's work and sports. We had "little kid" artwork and projects. *Much of the chaos in our home was absolutely magical!*

Through our own creative forces, we soared and we grew! We added to that, the creative powers of "the master" himself, Walt Disney. We used it to the hilt! Flip through *Effervescence* if you want to see how the "magic of Disney" entwined brilliantly with Genevieve's emergence and evolution.

But that magic didn't stop there. Our world had become very much a kingdom all of its own and many of those classic Disney movies and stories oddly reflected the way that we had come to live. And "all that is Disney" offered a wealth of positive role modeling and rich characters who helped both Hayden, and more impressively Genevieve, *to understand how to communicate.* They helped them to understand *people, relationships, emotions and interactions.* Those are the things that are most difficult for any autistic child!

For us, *Fantasy* held the key in working with both of our autistic children. I saw that long before Genevieve was even diagnosed. *It was what I saw when I got inside her mind and her body, when I looked at the world through her eyes and felt it through her body.* And the world of Disney fit perfectly into my plan! We learned to animate *everything,* for both Genevieve and Hayden. It wasn't just that it was fun and magical; it was also a way of providing a "buffer" between them and us. That way they didn't have to deal directly with us and they felt safer. The world made more sense.

Here's just a little example: I would never say to either Genevieve or Hayden: "Go get your shoes." Instead, it would be: "Shoes, where are you?" It worked like magic, but for reasons far more complex than you might imagine. That's autism!

"The magical world of Disney" probably holds levels of meaning to us that most families wouldn't really understand. *Disney and all of his magic were tools, fabulous tools.* They were a part of us. Each of us wrapped that beautiful world around us, using their stories, their movies and their characters like a shroud of safety and absolute inspiration.

31

But the reality was, life wasn't just castles and kingdoms, and plights and conquests. We *had* become unique characters in a castle, but definitely, not all was magic and pixie dust!

Desperate to have "normal" time with Sydney and Kobe, and to undo the damage, Nolan and I stole precious moments whenever we could. Both kids complemented each other so well, and they adored each other. Both were mature and wonderful to be with. Time spent with them was all so *easy*; there was harmony. The bond between them was strong and they innately supported each other. I drew so much strength from them and wrote pages and pages in my journals about the little ways that they connected and supported each other. One of the loveliest was the day Sydney got her ears pierced. Kobe, the intense athlete who lived for every game and practice, dashed in from his soccer game with one concern, and one concern only: to see how the piercing went and how her earrings looked. They were a pair!

Both Sydney and Kobe had an amazing maturity and perceptiveness that allowed them to look far *beyond* the screaming and bizarre behaviors. They saw the captivating little souls, who were their sister and brother. But that didn't mean it wasn't a near-impossible way to live. They got such mixed signals from Genevieve and even more seriously, from Hayden. It *was* bizarre, the complex, abusive relationship that they shared with him. He would sweep from being loving and sweet, and then in the blink of an eye, terribly aggressive and volatile.

Both Sydney and Kobe, and sometimes Genevieve, bore scratches and teeth marks on their arms, legs and faces. They rarely had friends over as they felt awkward because of Hayden's aggression and unpredictable behavior. Sydney remarked, when I asked her about it: *"We're weird."*

One day we had a little going-away party for Sydney's best friend. Even with our best of intentions and our skills at being *the* master party-givers, it was a disaster. Hayden was a terror and responded by running around wildly, screaming and biting Sydney's school friends. As most of these girls were new to us and had no knowledge of our history, they were unprepared and shocked. Even Genevieve, in her innocence and literal way of thinking, set the tone for a night *not* to remember. She ran up to one little girl, who was of East Indian descent, peered into her eyes and said: "Hi little brown girl!" And as if the little girl was not shocked enough, Genevieve repeated it again: "Hi little brown girl!"

On the bright side, at least Genevieve was being unusually social that day!

Both Sydney and Kobe met frequently with Davina Nyles, the psychologist who was becoming so well versed in the wonders of our family. She was *very* impressed by their ability to articulate their challenges, their perceptiveness *and* their worries. And she was equally impressed how they both challenged themselves, to assist their siblings with all of their pervasive challenges.

Both kids were deep thinking and realistic. One day I overheard Sydney remark, after Davina had conveyed her personal belief that in a few years Hayden would settle down, that she wished for "life insurance" just in case, so that there would always be people to help him out. Sydney, very much an "old soul," was a very realistic eight-year-old at the time.

As the coming years would prove, despite Davina's insight and optimism, Sydney's prediction about Hayden's future would prove to be much more accurate.

Davina wasn't the only one who saw amazing qualities in both Sydney and Kobe. John, the behavioral consultant assigned to us, often watched them with eyes wide open and a glowing heart. Though he didn't typically involve the siblings in his therapies and in-home strategies, in our case he could see that they were a huge asset. Sydney and Kobe *wanted* to be involved; *to them, as it was to me, it was like breathing.*

And John did his part in offsetting the stress that they were under, by bending his company's rules and spending one on one time with each of them, hanging out at Dairy Queen or McDonald's to let them vent, conspire with him and dream up new strategies.

Sydney and Kobe offered Nolan and me a lovely contrast and reprieve, from the intense and complex interactions that we had with Hayden and Genevieve. Yes, both Sydney and Kobe were indeed deep and gifted, but they were still *children*, and they showered simplicity and magic over us! For me, it was usually when I needed it most. One time, Kobe said the sweetest thing that meant the world to me, because it not only showed how big and innocent his heart was; but it proved to me that despite all of the chaos and the juggling, there *was* enough of me left over for him:

Kobe: "Mom, do you see stars in my eyes?"
Myself: "Yeah Kobe, I see little twinkles there."
Kobe: "Do you think I have stars when I look at Sydney or anyone else?"
Myself: "I don't know Kobe; do you?"
Kobe: "No, just you!"
Later that night, at bedtime:
Kobe: "Mom, don't forget what I told you today!"

I'm not sure that there are many moms who've had as much stress and chaos thrown at them, and yet as much love, wonder and sweetness, as I've had. I'm very blessed! Today, Kobe is six foot five, a big, strong and mature man and I know those stars are still there.

Chapter 15

Over and beyond the beautiful and glorious pictures I could paint of Sydney and Kobe's lives, there were less than glorious ones as well. Our complex home was taking its toll. I watched and documented their behaviors along with Hayden and Genevieve's.

It was fascinating but alarming to see how both Sydney and Kobe expressed guilt that they didn't "teach Hayden enough." They were only children and we made it clear that any involvement that they had was optional and on *their* terms, but their compassion and love always took over.

Sydney swept from being sweet and helpful, to sulky and wild. Kobe bounced from being happy to aggressive; he cried easily and suffered frequently from frightening nightmares. Even with Davina's support, his behaviors became increasingly bewildering. He had a terrible rash over most of his body, blended with the frequent scratches and teeth marks from Hayden. Often at bedtime, he would fall to pieces, especially if Hayden was acting up. Several times he cried *hysterically* about concern he felt for his Uncle Erland, my brother who is affected by Down syndrome. It seemingly made no sense, as Kobe rarely saw Erland and he knew that his uncle was living happily and was well cared for.

Each of those bedtime episodes was heart-wrenching and confusing, and I scrambled to console Kobe and settle him down. But I was not a psychologist, for God's sake. I wasn't trained in this! And I was already so burnt out, so exhausted and pulled in so many directions.

….By bedtime, I just didn't have just much left…but Kobe was so precious, with talents and perspectives well beyond his young years, and yet so innocent….a child, and he was *my* child….and this *was* fascinating….I *had* to find it within myself to push everything else

34

away....I had to hear and see *only* Kobe, only his body, his images and his tears....then and there, in those hysterical, bedtime moments, I had to put myself and my head in a place where it was just Kobe and me, and my beautiful Erland, and feel things I'd felt in raising Erland when he was little.....*and then when I analyzed the state of Kobe's body and of his behaviors and the words and images he made with reference to Erland.... it was obvious to me that his depth of emotion and of concern, showed that this really wasn't about Erland at all. This was all about his brother.* These were fears and concerns that touched him so deeply that his body and his mind couldn't access them. Instead, they were transferred, almost like a weird misfiring and redirection. It *was* complex and heart-wrenching.

But once I was able to acknowledge and see in my mind and register how Kobe, my child, was now so clearly transferring all of his images on Erland.... Kobe and I could connect and I could help him to see *in his mind and feel in his body*, the transference that was going on. He could then let me in to a place where those concerns could take form through words. We talked about the parallels in my life and now his, with both of us having disabled siblings and extraordinarily complex lives.

It helped; I think it helped a lot. But the sad reality remained that even though Erland was very challenged by Down's, Kobe was well aware that Erland was a gentle soul who did not have the long history of complex and aggressive behavior that his brother did. And Kobe also had Genevieve and all of her issues and challenges to complicate the picture. *He had every reason to have had so much concern, fear and anxiety tucked away inside of him.*

The impact of our existence manifested itself in other ways in Kobe. He was six, grade one, very bright and very articulate; and yet he was stuttering. At home we were almost as frustrated listening to him, as he was, in trying to talk and get his point across. He complained endlessly about school and claiming that he had no friends. None of it made any sense. He'd always been a natural-born leader, a charismatic child, always surrounded by "adoring and loyal fans." And the stuttering; what was that all about?

Desperate for help and input, I met with Kobe's teacher, a wonderfully talented and experienced teacher. My heart almost stopped when she looked back at me, with curious but compassionate eyes and said: "What are you talking about? I've *never* heard Kobe stutter. And as for friends, he's the most popular kid in the class!" She described how he always had an entourage around him and could be endlessly counted on to dream up new games for them to play. "Come take a look!" she said. We peeked out the window at the playground and there he was, laughing and playing, bigger and taller than the rest, and as charismatic as ever.

I was relieved, but mystified!

Back to Davina I went, with my observations. She and Kobe dug a little deeper, helping him to access more trapped emotions. *The biggest one was guilt: guilt at getting angry at Hayden for being so aggressive and abusive; and guilt for thinking he wasn't working hard enough to help his brother. What a precious soul. And what a lesson in seeing how even children, intuitively take so much upon themselves.*

Suddenly, it was like someone had literally tapped a magic wand. The stuttering "miraculously" stopped and Kobe was much more jovial. He raved about the fun he was having playing with his friends at school. *He had needed to get all of that guilt off of his chest.* He had needed to have his concerns and challenges *validated by someone in a professional capacity, who really understood the magnitude and seriousness of his home environment.*

My hero Kobe is one of the driving forces behind writing this book, and in asking him to let people peek inside *his* world. For a complex family like ours, you have to remember, we are just that: *a family.* All of us were and are affected, profoundly. When I witnessed how complex Kobe's behaviors had become, that was the moment when I began making it very clear to anyone involved with us that we were *not* to be seen as a family with *two* special needs children. *We were a family with four.*

That wasn't looking for pity or being melodramatic. It was an important recognition and it ultimately became one of the reasons for our high level of success. Trust me; it wasn't being melodramatic. It was being accurate and realistic. Sydney and Kobe needed and deserved that distinction. I can't write another page without making that clear.

The thing is, once that distinction was made, many people could make that connection. They *wanted* to help. Many people, like teachers, were quick to respond and we got their best. We got their hearts and we worked as a team. It helped!

The stress and guilt also weighed heavily on Sydney. Like Kobe, she worked with Davina and was able to express similar feelings of guilt. She questioned and analyzed her role with both Genevieve and Hayden, wondering if she had only played more with Genevieve or had tried to talk more with Hayden, if they would both be acting more "normally" now. *Oh the pervasive power of guilt!*

Technically, Sydney was better able than Kobe to distance herself from what she considered to be her responsibility, and what she felt was realistic to give. She struggled more with the intense frustration of the screaming and the bizarre behaviors. Above all, she feared for her own personal safety. And she feared what she saw happening to her family. In particular, she worried about what it was doing to me.

Like Kobe, Sydney was very intelligent and agile with abstract thought processing; she was perceptive far beyond her years. She was very quick to make the connection between her own challenged family and the highly-dysfunctional family that I grew up with. She saw how shattered my family had become, because my family had had too much serious crisis to deal with and parents who didn't handle it well. *She was mortified that we would repeat the pattern.*

It became a reoccurring theme that she and I would explore countless times: she needed to know that much of *my* insight and determination came *from* seeing what had happened to my family. I was *not* going to let that happen to us. My parents chose not to communicate about our complex issues or to set goals or find strategies. Nolan and I had a very different plan.

I encouraged Sydney to reach for some of the tools that I reached for, like keeping a journal. She took to it immediately. She said that when she wrote, it was "like all the darks clouds lifted and a rainbow appeared!"

To really understand how complex our world had become, I think you, the reader of this epic tale, could use a lovely and clear visual, an image of Genevieve and even more potently, of Hayden. No two characters that I could possibly create in my mind to be the hero and heroine of my two books, could be more "breathtakingly beautiful" and adorable than these real-life embodiments:

Genevieve had perfect rosebud lips and beautiful, long, wild and curly red hair. In the sun, it glistened with a hundred different shades of red, as if every strand was of its own unique tint. Her eyes, on the odd occasion when she would be drawn to make eye contact with you, showed themselves as green, a gorgeous, light shade. She had slightly chubby cheeks and lovely skin. So far beyond that, she exuded what can only be called, yet again: effervescence. Despite her challenges, she saw life with sparkle and humor, constantly flitting from our world to hers, sometimes in torment, often in complete rapture. To quote *Effervescence:* "When she walked she giggled, like life was the funniest thing. She appeared to experience life on a whole different level than the rest of us!"

And then there was Hayden. He too had red hair, though wavy, not wild and curly. It was a lighter shade than Genevieve's, an important distinction in *her* mind, as she wanted no parallels to be drawn between the two of them, especially on something as intimately a part of her as her hair. He had *the* cutest dimples and a cleft chin, very blue eyes and beautiful skin. His cheeks were sprinkled with just enough freckles to be captivating, almost like they were hand-drawn to be placed in such a way as to *pull you into his unique little being,* even further!

He was so different from her. When she was calm and happy, she was aloof and flitted back and forth into our world and into our attention. But Hayden was the exact opposite. Genevieve drew people to her because of her beauty, her effervescence and the uniqueness of her soul. Hayden drew people to him because he was absolutely adorable and because he reached out and *grabbed* them!

He had this way, and this is what you need to know to understand how complex and confusing it was to be living with him....it was like he just had this way of reaching out and grabbing our hearts and wrapping himself around them. He just had this way of demanding, but more of *enticing* our attention and our hearts. And he *did* draw us in; he did it continuously, despite his bizarre and aggressive behaviors. The problem was: *he couldn't handle* our love and our attention. Something in his body would react. *What was it? Why?*

This beautiful little boy, still a baby of three....we loved him, we adored him....he drew us to him, absolutely lovingly and melting into us one moment and then the next, reacting fiercely to us, scratching our faces, our eyes....often it was literally in the blink of an eye and without *any* warning or apparent reason.

Kobe was affected the most, because he was *drawn in* the most. He was such a "family guy" and above that, he had dreamed of having a brother. That bond and that role was one he greeted with intensity and open arms. No wonder he bore the greatest brunt, emotionally and physically.

But there was something in Hayden's eyes. I'm not so sure we saw it at the time; we were probably too distracted trying to keep him calm and entertained. Maybe we didn't or *couldn't* let ourselves see it. But I see it captured in photographs and portraits of him back in those early years.

It's like in those beautiful blue eyes there was a *seething energy, a resistance to the world*.

There's one portrait, actually, that I recently had to tuck away, hidden. It's a shame because the lighting was perfect and his hair, his dimples, his freckles....all *so* beautiful. But *his eyes* jump out at me, and I see who he was at that time. I *feel* that seething energy and that resistance, and it's painful; it's disconcerting. It *needs* to be left behind, to be left hidden.

I can't even believe I am revealing this to you now; but you need honesty. *And I am telling you this now, because I no longer see that in Hayden's eyes. It's not captured in photographs or portraits anymore, because it is no longer there.*

That seething energy and that resistance to the world, is no longer there.

In *my* eyes, there are tears at this moment, because I do want you to follow this book, my epic tale, right to the very end. Then you'll know that it *is* okay that I tucked away my child's portrait; and that my knowing it's there hidden, and me glancing to it occasionally in my mind, *not* in my vision, reinforces to me how far he's come, and how worth the journey he has been.

Chapter 16

The last chapter: there was a lot to tell....insight into Hayden, into Genevieve, the impact on Sydney, on Kobe, the intense soul-searching bedtimes with Kobe.... *But not all days, and certainly not all bedtimes, were laced with deep, soul searching and chaos!* Some were magical, if only for moments.

One night, Genevieve, who usually did her best to keep the world and even me at arm's distance, took my breath away! I think she had a goal somewhere in her mind to never let us feel like we were of any importance to her; but often at bedtime, she would at least let me crawl in and snuggle with her. On this one magical night, when she was almost asleep, she very uncharacteristically whispered: *"Mommy, you're my very best friend!"* I knew it was probably a line from a movie, but she knew what it meant, and it meant the world to me. It gave me sustenance and it filled me up!

I thanked God for the glimmers when Hayden and Genevieve were delightful. I seized moments like bedtime as fabulous opportunities. I gave each of our four kids their own lullaby and snuggle time, even though they were probably too old for lullabies. Bedtime was a long process, often up to two hours each night; but I loved it. I needed that time to connect with each of them, so that no matter how rough the day had been, it ended on a positive note, each of them feeling warm and some degree of "safe."

Nolan thought I was spoiling them. I thought I was spoiling me!

Chapter 17

Life with Hayden and Genevieve was so different than it had been just a few years earlier with Sydney and Kobe. Back then, even when they were just little, I could take them anywhere and everywhere and we'd talk and talk and talk. But with Hayden and Genevieve, it wasn't like that, even when they were calm.

Everything had to be taught. With the first two kids, *all* aspects of life were wonderfully in sync; but with the other two, *life seemed to be either in parallels or in odd opposition.* Genevieve was aloof and distanced herself from us and the world; whereas Hayden was strangely dependent on physical and social stimulation. But he couldn't handle either of those two things and they constantly pushed him over the edge.

At age three, it was still prevailingly "me and Hayden against the world." Physically, he just couldn't get close enough to us, especially me. I was still his favorite toy, one of the very few toys he had any interest in. He constantly pulled my sweaters down so that he could feel my shoulders, and he often did the same to Sydney. Even more strangely, he would literally slide his body under my sweater so that his stomach would be against my back and his arms overtop of mine, right under the sleeves of my sweater. *It was very sweet but very bizarre!*

Hayden swept from giving *the* most melt-into-you hugs and caresses, to lashing out violently and unpredictably. He loved and *craved* active, physical play with Sydney and Kobe; yet it was his greatest downfall. In the blink of an eye, he'd push them away, biting and kicking and hitting and pinching them. It was horribly confusing. And he did not make the connection when being reprimanded. He rarely even responded when his name was called. *It was very much* like his sister!

In the playground, we had to watch Hayden like a hawk! As he had been with his toddler gym class, he was unpredictable but most times, terribly aggressive. I or Nolan literally stood within a foot of him at all times. At his cousin's first birthday party, Hayden scratched her face, marring her perfect, flawless baby skin on that milestone day. He also pinched her one-year-old friend. *Another nightmare event!*

It was so sad because Hayden "looked normal" and so people expected him to "act normal." I'd been made sick to my stomach many times when adults treated him like he was mean and cold-hearted. They didn't see the beautiful side that we saw. At least once he started learning sign language, I made a point, *whenever* we were in public, of signing to him to tip people off that he was disabled. My hope was that they'd respond with a little more patience and understanding. It definitely helped.

With Hayden, we had to go right back to basics, as we had done with Genevieve. There was so much that he just didn't understand. We had to *teach* him emotions, because it made no difference to him if I pretended to laugh or cry when he acted out against me. All he knew was that when he acted out, he got a reaction. He didn't see more beyond that. (Well, I write those words, but I know they aren't completely true. There were "those eyes" back then. There *were* times when he knew exactly what he was doing and he *fed off of it*. There *were* times when there was malice).

Hayden wanted so desperately to play with his siblings and he did whatever it took to get their attention. *It was tragic that he couldn't make the connection that they loved and adored him, and would have loved and adored him even more, if he would just stop hurting them!* Sometimes it was beyond his control. It was his body talking over.

By age three, Hayden really hadn't formed much of a bond with his dad. Most times he preferred Sydney or Kobe over him. I was still his number one choice. He *knew* Sydney and me, by the *feel* of our hair:

> One oddly calm, family evening, while sitting on the couch watching a movie, he was playing obsessively and compulsively with my hair. It was a common activity, like he was literally trying to stuff it into his ear. After awhile, he reached over to play with Sydney's hair, his eyes glued to the TV. He fondled her hair lovingly for a moment, then abruptly stopped, realizing it wasn't Sydney's hair at all; it was Genevieve's. The look on his confused face was priceless, though the look of horror on Genevieve's was not. He matter-of-factly jumped off the couch, and onto the floor, to where the "real Sydney" was sitting. He casually resumed his hair stuffing with the real Sydney hair.

What a house of wonders we were!

There was next to no spontaneous conversation with Hayden, or with Genevieve. Neither played "normally" with toys and Hayden barely played at all. When left to his own devices, he hardly knew what to do with himself. We had to do most of the work to "play." Really, both of them needed to be "taught" *how* to play.

Some of it came naturally to Genevieve and she would typically tune into her own little world, playing there for hours in her unique way, rarely using toys the way they were intended. But Hayden would continue only if he were prompted and guided to sustain it. And they rarely played *together*.

One day, friends with two toddlers came over to visit. For me it was an immediate but painful reminder of how *easy* it was with typical kids, and how *natural and unintentional it was to have harmony*. When the little boy showed an interest in our toy bus, I surprised myself by immediately picking it up, flipping it over and showing him how the wheels could spin. *That* was what I would have done with Hayden or with Genevieve. We would have made it some little animated, bizarre adventure.

But this little boy just stared back at me, his eyes saying: *"Why are you doing that? That's not what buses are for!"*

Safety issues: that was a big one. Certainly by the time that Hayden was three and a half, it was painfully obvious that I could no longer take all four of my kids on outings unassisted. Despite my high energy level, a trip to Science World or an afternoon of shopping at the mall was so physically and mentally exhausting, I'd have to lie down when we got home, which could rarely happen.

There *were* serious safety issues. Neither Hayden nor Genevieve had any sense of danger. It was like they had no natural sense of perimeters. It made no difference to them if they walked on the sidewalk or down the middle of the street! Traffic meant little or nothing to them. Heights were of little consequence. When Hayden and Genevieve were in environments that were over-stimulating, it was even worse.

Outings had become dangerous. One evening at our favorite mall, in the blink of an eye, Hayden had pulled himself up and onto a railing. It was a miracle that I was able to grab him in time. A split second later and he would have dropped to the cement floor a storey below! That was the moment of truth when I knew that I could not possibly take the four of them out again, unassisted. *So much for our passion for frequent adventures!* That was tough for all of us to accept. And it hurt. Since the moment Sydney was born, I'd seen every day as an adventure, and it was just who I was, to pack up my gang and be off! But this had become serious.

And it wasn't just about safety; it went far beyond that, as if that wasn't enough. Born to shop as I was, malls were not a place that I could *dare* for us to be. Aside from the safety issue, Hayden was horrid in malls. He would scream and go after complete strangers, *anyone* who got in his path. Once in awhile we got lucky and he would do well; but there seemed no rhyme or reason as to the "state of mind or state of body" he would be in.

Even if it was just me and Hayden together in a mall, with me being attentive and focused on keeping it low key, he was unpredictable. Most times, he was terribly aggressive. He might manage going up and down aisles in his stroller....until we passed a child. Then he'd impulsively lash out, grabbing the child's face with his hands. *It was mortifying for me; I can't even imagine what it was like for his poor child-victims.*

Store merchandise wasn't safe from the wrath of Hayden. Often he broke or dismantled things. One of the most dramatic was a fabric store: within a matter of seconds, he had literally pulled down an entire wall filled with bolts of fabric. He was tiny, barely even three!

Sometimes I'd step back and wonder: at what point did my life shift from calm strolls through the malls, for hours at a time....my three small kids and my newborn in our very long, twin stroller....total strangers stopping me to marvel at how beautiful, playful and yet placid and well-behaved my children were....now we were in this place of madness.

Back then, everyday was an adventure! Then, seemingly like turning a page on a calendar, life turned into this nightmare existence where complete strangers would stop and stare....some would go out of their way to let me know that Hayden and Genevieve's horrendous tantrums and bizarre behaviors, were a result of my inadequate parenting skills....apparently it was my lack of discipline. Any idea how many times I've been told that if I just smacked them everything would be fine and all would be right with the world?

Our coveted twin stroller had transformed. It was no longer a vehicle for fun and frolic, through malls and parks; it was now a get-away necessity. If I was desperate, I could pile all four kids in our stroller, so we could get the hell out of there and leave the scene of the crime and the chaos we had created. We could escape judging eyes.

We still turned heads, but now it was for a completely different reason. When did this transformation happen and why?

It used to break my heart, knowing that often onlookers and even acquaintances misjudged Genevieve and Hayden, tossing them off as rotten kids. *In reality, they should have been admired for their ability to survive in a world that was overwhelming and foreign to them.*

Chapter 18

Through all of our experiences and adventures, the good and the bad, I don't think I've ever really felt embarrassed by Genevieve or Hayden's behaviors. I love them and I and understand them. *That opens the door for boundless compassion.* But I have felt intense frustration. And I have felt embarrassed and deeply hurt and misjudged, when outsiders thought it was all because I was not in control or able. Little did they know, I was *very able*. How many moms would have even attempted outings with behaviors like that? But that didn't make their comments hurt any less. *Sometimes it wasn't my children's behaviors that put me over the edge, it was the comments that people couldn't resist making.*

Maybe I was stupid or just plain stubborn, or maybe it was that even amongst all the stress and chaos of those outings, there were wonderful little "glimmers of normal life." Sydney, Kobe and I needed to have those to cling to: little everyday things that the world around us took so much for granted. *That* was what got the three of us through the chaos of those outings and adventures; and *that's* what we choose to remember the most, today when we look back.

And for me, over and above the nightmarish moments of those outings, *there were* captivating interactions amongst the four kids that were precious enough, that I *did* keep going back for more.

Outdoors, where there were no people or overwhelming buildings, activities, colors, scents and sounds, we did better. At the end of a rough day, we could take even a short walk and within minutes, *where it was just us*, we could push away the troublesome outside world, and our best side would shine through.

Our home *had* become a castle; there was no denying that. It contained us and it kept us safe from the outside world. And journeying *from* our castle in search of forests and trails, was where we did our best. *Leaving* those trails far behind and climbing through bushes and creeks was even better! The deeper we went, the more at peace we were.

We could be just us, with nothing but our imaginations and quest for adventure at hand. It was our private, glorious world.

But put us in a mall or a gym and......

Or put us at a family get-together: bizarre and stressful behaviors would run rampant! Easter dinner at the grandparents' that year was excruciating. Nolan and I had to stick to Hayden like glue, because his two year old cousin was there. It made us feel sick to think that we had to shadow our child so closely, so that he didn't hurt others. Hayden was hard enough work at home, but at least within the walls of our castle, there was a certain leeway. Our home was child-proof and to some degree "Hayden-proof." I knew all the sounds; even if I wasn't watching him directly, I knew where he was and had a good idea what he was doing.

And at least at home, it would be *our* kids he was biting or pinching or scratching. *(Oh my God, look at what I've just written. But that's where things were at that time).*

Easter dinner meant four hours of complete and draining focus. If you've read *Effervescence,* you may remember my Easter story of Genevieve at that same Easter dinner. She innocently and delightfully drew everyone's attention to the distorted images on our wine glasses. The contrasting and disturbing images I've just given you of Hayden at that same event, probably tip you off as to why I focused on Genevieve's presence so affectionately in her tale!

And yet, as delightful as Genevieve could be at events like Easter, you need to remember that she too, was autistic and swept from her own array of curious, bizarre and often stressful behaviors. In a nutshell, in social settings, she usually would be engaged for bits of time, and then tune out, by entering her own little happy world or by spinning in circles "crowing."

We were quite a menagerie of oddities, I am sure.

For *all* family and social events, we had to seriously limit Hayden's attendance. That came with a big price, because it also meant limiting my presence as well. *Every* outing and *every* event meant a decision, where we weighed out the pros and cons of taking Hayden. Would it be worth the price? Could *he* handle it? Could *we* handle it? Could *everyone else* handle it? None were easy decisions to make and each was painful to us.

When we first started this process of opting out of social engagements, I'd feel physically sick to not take Hayden. But at the same time, I was *equally* relieved at not having to deal with the trauma. And though most of our family and friends were accepting and did their best to deal with him, it was just too much for them. It was too much for us and most of all, *for Hayden.*

Very soon into "the process" I found that the path did become very clear: the flipside was that if I stayed home with Hayden, it wasn't just that I didn't have to deal with the trauma, or put others through it. The flipside was the sweetest reward of all: it was the emergence of the *true Hayden.*

This was the Hayden that I needed so desperately to see. This was the Hayden that his family and the world around him would need to see. One on one, with me and Hayden separated from the rest of the world, brought to light the adorable, the funny and the delightful little being that was Hayden. Sure, he would still have his odd sensory fixations and teetered between over and under stimulation, but he would just be so delightful and beautiful to be with. The contrast of who he was and who he became when it was just him and me, always made me fight back tears. *How could I mind being there, home alone with him?*

The pattern grew; the pattern was reinforced, time after time. The decisions got easier. Some events we deemed worthy of "enduring the trauma," and sometimes we were glad we did; sometimes we made mistakes. But overall, that became our pattern and how we operated. And it continued for many years, always surveying every situation and making a decision. We still do it today, for some events and occasions.

Because the reward of having precious time with calm and happy Hayden was so immediately reinforcing, and important to me, I can honestly say that I did come to accept it. Often, for those first few minutes when I would watch Nolan leave, with Sydney, Kobe and Genevieve all excitedly piling into the car, for whatever event it was....yeah, I would cry....just get it out....and then I'd shift gears. I'd look at my beautiful little boy and know that I had made the right decision, and that I had *work* to do.

My work was to figure him out, to try to understand him, to put him in a calm space. My work was to fill myself up with the fabulous Hayden, because God knows I needed it to sustain me the rest of the time with Hayden!

My only regret, really, was the assumption I made, that Nolan could handle this and see it the way that I did. The bottom line was that I felt grateful and happy to have this magical time with Hayden and to some degree, *I welcomed* the opportunities. And I was relieved to know that our other three kids could socialize without their brother's complex presence. To me, it was almost like a bit of "an adventure" that Nolan and I could share....this terribly challenged family, but these unique opportunities to just forget what typically parents would do, and to just respond to the needs and act upon them.

I *wanted* Nolan to feel guilt free, each and every time that he'd leave with the others. In my eyes, this was what *we needed* to do, and that was okay. Sure there were times when it was hard; but it had been my intention that he and I could just acknowledge that together, with a look or a touch that said: "This is hard, but it will all be worth it."

But Nolan was a sensitive person and he hurt for me. And I guess I have to remember that I grew up differently than most people: I had a higher level of acceptance and of adapting, than most people would have had in my shoes. This was all new to him. I don't think he ever got over the guilt that he felt. He couldn't let himself see that ultimately, I was okay with it, and so he *couldn't make it* an intimate moment between us.

A wedge was created.

Chapter 19

ocial events were one thing. They came and they went. Day to day life was quite another.

Weekends were the worst time of the week. They were certainly not the relaxing end-of-the-week reward that they used to be. On weekdays everyone, especially Genevieve and Hayden, responded better to the school and evening routines. And with Nolan, Sydney and Kobe away for the bulk of each weekday, there was less "social presence" and fewer bodies in our home. But that was thrown out the window on weekends. The lack of structure and the physical presence of the others impacted *both* Genevieve and Hayden. *Even being happy to have them home impacted them.*

And then there was the weekend influx of activity and flurry. Nolan, Sydney and Kobe were constantly in and out, juggling their sports and activities, adding more chaos. I tried to juggle the other two. It was terribly challenging because I was so limited with what I could do with them *and* I was so tired of tantrums and trying to stop them from constantly terrorizing each other. It was overwhelming and yet tedious. If I got lucky, sometimes we could watch a movie together, but that was about it. Though I frequently engaged a babysitter to take one or the other down the street to her house, often they would refuse to go.

As rough as days were, night-time rarely offered much reprieve. Generally, at least every third night, Hayden continued his pattern of screaming in the middle of the night, frantically holding my shoulders, pounding his head into my chest, like a wild animal. Tylenol helped to calm him down but it was horrendously exhausting and frightening for him, and for us. As for me, I rarely got any real sleep.

Davina, Dr. Nyles, suspected that over-stimulation during the day was a potential cause. I tracked and documented and found that both social and sensory stimuli had a serious impact on Hayden and affected his sleep. In other words, being around too many people affected his sleep, as did settings and activities that were loud and colorful.

Sometimes Hayden sank into what Davina referred to as "Nowhereland." It seemed it happened during the day, and even at night when he was sleeping. *Nowhereland was a place he would withdraw to and sometimes he would "get stuck there," like it was somewhere in between his world and ours and he couldn't get out.* It happened regularly at night. Observing and documenting his daytime behaviors led me to believe that it explained some of his horrendous outbursts during the day as well.

Nowhereland was becoming an alarming and very difficult phenomenon to deal with. It was overtaking our lives.

It's funny looking back now at the little habits Nolan and I adopted in response to the stressful, bizarre and often unexplainable behaviors that had become part of our everyday life: often at 10:00 or 11:00pm, once we had finally got the kids down for the night, we wouldn't say a word to each other; we'd both head straight to the kitchen cupboard. Nolan would munch senselessly on nachos and for me, it would be miniature marshmallows. I think there was something empowering about chomping down on those white, puffy, innocent little things. After a few minutes, the stress of the day would lift and we'd do what we could to recharge, knowing the whole thing would be repeated the next day.

Otherwise, we lived pretty healthy. Thank God we weren't smokers or drinkers!

Chapter 20

To quote *Effervescence*: the "war between Genevieve and Hayden raged on!" When Sydney and Kobe were at school, often Genevieve and Hayden were relentlessly at each other's throats, biting and pinching. Genevieve, who was typically a passive child, though at times self-injurious, rarely lashed out aggressively at others (except in severe temper tantrums). But she was *learning* behaviors from him; and much of the time, she was *responding* out of fear and frustration.

One day, for instance, Hayden picked up a glass and threw it at her. It shattered, leaving her hysterical whenever he was around. All of these experiences she internalized and pulled *into* her autistic body, as negative associations catalogued under *the file of Hayden*. Naturally, she distanced herself from him, and in the process, often distanced herself all the more from the world at large. It became a sad and entangling irony that as parents of an autistic daughter, we tried so hard to get her to spend *less* time alone and *more* time with us; yet her autistic brother was forcing her to seek refuge in her own safe world.

But *there were* glimmers: odd, curious glimmers of peaceful interactions between the two of them. Our backyard playhouse sometimes offered a reprieve, and strangely enough, so did our community playground adventures. That was such a bizarre irony because some of our absolute *worst* experiences with Hayden happened at playgrounds because of his unpredictable and severe aggression. *But there was, squeezed into those nightmare interactions between Hayden and Genevieve, room for fascinating work to be done!* Often in playground settings, and in our backyard playhouse, I was able to create what I would later call *The Autism Triangle*.

The Autism Triangle was a way of submerging Genevieve, Hayden and me into a world of fantasy. It just seemed to evolve, rooting from me being alone with them in our little playhouse…. the scent and the feel of the cedar walls around me….watching Genevieve….watching Hayden…. putting myself in *their* headspace and their bodies…. looking into my own heart….

….we would act out endlessly, scenes from fairy tales like *The Three Little Pigs*. All three of us would alternate roles and both Genevieve and Hayden learned to take the perspective of one character, and then do the whole thing over, as a different character. They were actually interacting *with* each other and with me.

Yes, to a large extent, they were "actors in roles" and that provided a certain wall of social buffering, but they *were* interacting and they *were* learning, on a multitude of levels.

Though Hayden was essentially non-verbal, through this activity he learned to alter his voice to act out different characters. In that way he could "feel himself climb down the chimney" as the wolf, or "stand below the chimney, looking up," as if he *was* one of the pigs.

I do believe these "theatrical adventures" did also help to enhance Hayden's ability *and* his desire to speak.

The three of us could maintain our "submersion" in *The Autism Triangle* for as long as we needed. Even Hayden, with his ridiculously short attention span, could be drawn in and captured, sometimes to the point of obsession, where we could have gone on forever. *The Autism Triangle* was a fabulous learning opportunity. *And* it was a time for me to relish that on some level, I could co-exist with both of my very unique kids! *And*, it was creative and fun, and that was where my heart so naturally glided. *It felt good. It felt like me.*

The Autism Triangle was *also* a critical survival technique. It was *essential!* We could "take it with us", to playgrounds and parks. If the three of us were at a playground (with or without Sydney and Kobe*), it was almost always essential that I kept Hayden away from the other children; and Genevieve would naturally tune them out anyway*. But at least by *submerging the three of us* into our triangle, we could co-exist *alongside* the other children. If Sydney and Kobe were with us, they could join us, or join the "land of the typical kids." *Usually they did a mixture of both; it reflected the way* *they directed their lives, jutting back from the outside world, to our inner and rather unusual autism world. That was very much who we were!*

On a personal level, *The Autism Triangle* was fascinating and wonderfully rewarding. The three of us did impressive work and the connection I felt with my two autistic children was *indescribable*. But having said that, I will admit that the process was very intense and it became very much a way of life, *changing who I was*.

The Autism Triangle led the way to what I called *submersion*. What I am talking about now, is what I call *Deep Submersion*. It wasn't just a tactic or strategy to help us co-exist amongst others in playgrounds. It wasn't a method of helping to build some semblance of a relationship between two autistic siblings, the way the *Autism Triangle* was. *Deep Submersion* was a personal process and my personal commitment to lower myself into their worlds, to *look at and to live* every aspect of their lives: how they fit in, or how they didn't fit into the world around them. *Deep Submersion was about pushing everything else away and seeing and feeling the world through their eyes and their bodies. It was about feeling, scrutinizing and responding.*

I need to focus on this because for you to really understand how extraordinarily a person with autism perceives, processes and responds to the world, means that you have to acknowledge how deeply the people who do *truly insightful work* with them, *need to understand them*. This isn't something that you stand at the sidelines and make observations about. This is the real thing. This is caring so much and loving so much, and acknowledging what is so amazing *in them*, that you not only allow, but you *welcome* your self to be taken over, to be let in; to let it happen. This is understanding that *they* are worth it. This is understanding that if you take this step, you will *not* be the same person. But you will become a *better* person.

In my case, I was submerged, literally twenty four/seven and ours was such a complex situation. The level of submersion was deeper than might be needed with a more "typical" autism family, but the concept remains the same: *you need to understand them and understand their world. You need to open yourself up to that.*

For you to really understand our castle and the way that we lived and the way that we evolved, I *do* need to continue focusing on *The Autism Triangle* and on *Deep Submersion,* and the way that they changed me:

> Back when Genevieve and Hayden were small, there was *not* a lot of information about autism. It was still considered to be extremely rare and having two in one family was almost unheard of. I *had* to find things out for myself. We wouldn't have survived otherwise. *Deep Submersion* became a place and a state of being; and for a number of years, I really didn't feel that I had a choice about it. Hayden's behaviors were so severe; there *was* no other choice. *I had to protect him and I had to protect the world.*

> And then there was Genevieve and all of her behaviors and reactions....

> But I *do not* want to sound like a martyr here. It wasn't *all* out of necessity. An *equal* part of it was my personality and my sheer fascination. Hayden and Genevieve drew me in because they were and are, precious. It was *because* of the wonder that *was* Hayden and Genevieve.

> For me, there was intense need *and* there was sheer desire; *that* was a powerful combination.

> *Deep Submersion*: once I let myself go to a very deep and profound way of perceiving Hayden and Genevieve's worlds, it all made such perfect sense to me. I was drawn in even more. I watched and I documented and I did whatever I could, to see and experience the world the way that they did. That was a complex challenge because there were many "common threads" between them and yet so much that was completely different. *But what remained most constant was that both children were so intrinsically at the mercy of their bodies, almost like their bodies were at war with the world around them. It was sensory; it was social; it was exasperatingly pervasive!*

"*Social buffers*" was the term I used to describe what both Hayden and Genevieve needed, to feel some degree of "safe" when they were around people. Usually it would be in the form of an inanimate object that would be the "middle man" between them and the outside world. Often that "outside world" included their immediate family, even me.

"*Social strings attached*" was my term to describe the effects and repercussions of social interactions and activities. Almost *any* interaction had social strings attached; social activities had even more. It would be immediately seen in Hayden and Genevieve's behaviors and usually it would be *stored* somewhere in their bodies, (even if we didn't see an immediate reaction). There it would be strangely catalogued *within* their bodies; and associations would likely be triggered at some point in the future. *In other words, they might react at that moment or it may simply remain hidden, almost lurking but held within their bodies, ready to pounce at some point down the road, when something would trigger a familiarity.*

The Autism Triangle was named that in my mind, because there were three of us. It was that continual image of maintaining a safe place for the three of us where we could interact, co-exist around others, and where I could teach them. But triangle or not, it was the *submersion* that was at the heart of the concept.

> My belief and my experience with Hayden and Genevieve, and with others that I've since worked with, is that the key lays in *your* ability to get them to *allow* you to step into their world. *They need to feel that you enjoy that world and that you are at home there. They need to feel that you value it. They need to feel that you are fascinated by them.* They need to see and feel that you are not asking them to step out and be like us; you just want to be there with them.

> *That's it; it all begins there.*

One of the key messages that I love to focus on in my writing and in the talks and interviews that I've done about my books and my kids, is this *phenomenal irony*:

> When you look at someone who has autism, it's staggering to realize that the things "we" take for granted, do not come naturally to them. People with autism need to be taught about emotions; they need to learn how to label emotions. They need to learn how to converse. Making eye contact is often so foreign to them, that it almost feels painful.

But the irony, and it *is* a beautiful, phenomenal irony that's important to recognize, is that though they may *appear* to be oblivious to what's going on around them, they *do* understand when someone feels comfortable with them. They may not even make eye contact with you, and they'll likely struggle to understand their own emotions, much less yours; but they *will* sense your comfort level: *they'll feel it and they'll see it.* No one will ever convince me otherwise. I've seen it and felt it countless times with my own children, and from a very young age with each of them. I've seen it in others. It *is* important to recognize.

Never underestimate the perceptiveness of a child or an adult with autism. Their peripheral vision is extraordinary and their ability to take in details in a simple glance, is not like yours or mine. And though their minds may have difficulty processing people and interactions, their bodies internalize *everything*. Associations are always made.

Chapter 21

he *Autism Triangle* and its basic concept could have been done had there been just one autistic child; it just wouldn't have been a triangle. But of course, as fate would have it, we were *not* a family with just one, we had two. To enable my kids to be able to survive in a world that was so frightening and overwhelming, *I needed* to submerge myself deeply in their world. But it wasn't just when we were at the playground or in the playhouse. *I needed, constantly and instantly, to train myself to instinctively survey every single setting that I put them in.* And I got good at it. In a matter of seconds, I'd make a mental note of sights, sounds, scents, and above all, other children and other adults, so that I could prepare Genevieve, Hayden, and to be truthful, myself. I needed to be able to *immediately* respond to their reactions to any given situation. *It was Submersion.*

I quickly became extremely skilled at it; I had to be!

But there were prices. *Submersion* and seeing and experiencing the world through the eyes and bodies of my children, did become so instinctive, that I *did* begin to loose myself in what had become my day-to-day reality. I know it probably seems hard to understand if you're reading this. But for me, as I write these words, it's as clear as writing down a grocery list.

If you've ever watched the movie *Wolf*, it would give you an idea of where my life was at that time. I remember thinking exactly that, as Nolan and I sat watching it one night, back in those early years of *Submersion*. The way that Jack Nicholson's character took on animal instincts paralleled where I was at that time. I related deeply to the character and how overwhelmed he would be, by having such heightened senses. At times he was grateful and captivated; other times, it was too much because he felt bombarded by the world. What I felt when I watched this movie also gave me new perspective, about how overwhelming the world must be for my kids and their unique minds and bodies.

Being submerged and being so tuned into my autistic kids and their worlds, *and our (the typical) world,* was a tricky way to live. It was a treacherous straddle. When the three of us were at a playground or even on the school swings after picking Sydney and Kobe up from school, I didn't chit chat with the other moms anymore. *How could I?* I had to be completely focused. Otherwise, the prices were too high and the behaviors from both Genevieve and Hayden were horrendous.

But it wasn't just the physical act of being focused that was so all consuming. *It was that I was, on many levels, retreating as well.* Why on earth would I *want* to talk to the other moms? I was so different and the things that they talked about and the challenges in their lives, was a piece of cake from where I was standing. A wall would always go up between them and me: *it was a solid, concrete wall. I could feel it and I could almost see it.*

But I found that at least by "staying on our side of the wall," I could connect and play and protect my kids in a way that meant the world to me. And it was *my* world, and in my world, I didn't feel judged.

Really, the topic of *Submersion* could fill chapters and chapters. It could be a book itself, as you've probably guessed; but you've probably got the picture. But I *do* want to expand to say that though it was *deep submersion*, it certainly was *not* full submersion. There was enough of me left over, to not let that happen. I had two typical kids and they had demands on my time and my attention. The wonderful influxes of "typical kid" obligations and opportunities *forced* me to stay connected and "come up for air."

And I had my dance classes....my glorious world where they knew a little, but they really didn't know all that much about our world of autism, and the "normal" world and how I straddled them both. They had glimmers of some of the tough stuff at home, but they didn't know the gory details. I wanted it that way for one, because I was *their* oasis and two, because I needed that reprieve, to be forced to have an hour, a couple of times a week, where I was *forced* to stay close to the surface. Often, the joy of music, muscles and movement and the joy of each person in my class, lifted me *miles* above the surface!

> But it was a struggle. It really was straddling two worlds, constantly. And most of the time, I was so far down into the other world. I loved that world; but I paid prices. "Little things" that weren't all that "little" were changing in me. Things like eye contact, that nemesis of autism, became one of *my* issues. It was like it rubbed off on me. It happens when you're submerged the way that I was, when you're constantly amidst little beings who turn their faces away from you, almost every time that you look at them or try to connect.
>
> I guess that's one of the reasons why I came to understand their worlds so well: *because I felt it.* Increasingly, almost any time I went to look at someone or speak with them, *a force literally turned my head away.* And it literally *was* a force; I can feel it right now as I retrace those days with these words. It was learned behavior; but it was also behavior that reflected what I felt towards much of the outside world: *disconnection.*

These were very real issues. When I came to realize how much my life was altering, I really had to *re-train and re-program* myself, to regain a comfort level with making eye contact. There are moments in my life when I *still* feel that discomfort, and my body instantly relives those years of submersion. I'm still working on it; but I'm close!

As to the intense level of submersion and training myself to be continually focused and on guard: the chapters to come will tell you how and why eventually that need lessened; but back then it was all so entrenched, that I literally *did* have to consciously re-train and re-program myself to leave it behind me. There came a time where I had to force myself *not to document* behaviors every single day, and to enjoy *being able to be less focused*. It was tougher than you might think! The trouble was that it was a tough balance because at any given time, I knew that I might need to slip into that alternative way of thinking and responding. Even today, years later, I sometimes have to consciously make efforts to *not* slip into the old ways and old patterns of submersion.

> Back then, when Hayden and Genevieve were so small and so overwhelmed by the world, I took their lead and I trained myself. It was out of desperation, so I was highly motivated. But it was also out of fascination. *In some ways, getting in and living in their world was the easy part. The tough part was getting out and reprogramming myself.*

But I truly do have no regrets. As I wrote in *Effervescence*, for all that I feel I've been able to teach my children, it's barely a fraction of what I've *learned* from them!

Chapter 22

Looking back at the years when Hayden was between two to four, it really is like a collage. It's pointless to try to describe it in organized, chronological, step-by-step order. Life for us *was* a collage of beautiful, sweet, bizarre and most prevalently, mystifying events and interactions. Often there was no rhyme or reason; *but within the realm of autism, much of it made perfect, amazing sense!* As bizarre as it may sound, when I transposed what I saw and felt, especially when I was in *The Autism Triangle*, there *was* an odd sense of harmony. But *outside* of that world, there were new dimensions that went far beyond mystifying; there truly was no rhyme or reason. *It was chaos, utter, and often merciless chaos.*

Between the reclusive way we had come to live and the overwhelming undertaking that each new day promised to be, I was plummeting. Energy had to come from somewhere and my mind could only be pulled in so many directions. I think we all were plummeting; but at least Nolan, Sydney and Kobe had many constant ties to the community and the outside world. *All I could think of was how to make us survive....how to make myself survive enough to get us all through the next day.*

My cherished dance classes had transformed from being my lifeline, to being just another source of demands on my time. I'd already dwindled down to just a few classes a week, but it was still too much. Before, they were precious hours a few times each week, where I could push away the stress and the chaos. There, I could step out of my "reclusivity" and connect with "normal" people, people that I loved and who loved me and the role that I played in their lives.

But something had to give and my classes seemed the only choice. Though it should have absolutely broken my heart to make the decision to leave, I felt almost nothing; nothing except numbness and the awareness that those classes were taking too much out of me, physically and emotionally. To teach the kind of classes that I taught, I had to give of myself. I had to take little trips into their heads, during each magical hour that we had together; that was the secret to how I operated. I loved it all: the dance, the choreography, the muscles, the sweat, the breathing. I loved my students, their issues and their energy. But it all just took so much out of me. I just had nothing left and what little I had, needed to go to my family. And so, I made the decision to leave. In my mind, it was carved in stone.

But something *was* at work. It was very real and I've learned to never take it for granted. Call it God, or a guardian angel or fate, or the universe unfolding, or whatever makes sense in your mind; but it was very real. I *was* being taken care of. I always have been; I just didn't always know it at the time.

In this case, at that moment, I was in no condition to make such an important decision; *but it was made for me.* It's a beautiful, little story and it's important because I really do want other parents like me to know, that you are never alone in a journey like ours. *You are never alone. You are never alone. You have to remind yourself of that. And I have to be able to tell you that:*

> *On the very night that I'd planned to announce that I was leaving (and in my mind I was fully packed up and ready to go), as they entered the room, I agonized, wondering how I was going to find the words....then in waltzed Virginia, one of my favorites and one of my role models. With her vibrant energy and the looks of a forty year old, her eyes sparkling, she said: "So what are you going to create to celebrate my sixtieth birthday?" My jaw dropped and I thought: "Oh my God, how do I tell her that I'm not going to be here?"*

At that moment, I looked in her eyes and I vowed to myself that I had to hold on for six months, that the moment her birthday class was over, I could leave forever. But I had to hold on until then; I had to find a way.

Long story short, this *was* a miracle. It's not exaggerating or romanticizing to say that. *It would have been a disaster on so many levels, if I had obliterated that precious part of my life.* I, and my family, would have paid the price and it would have been *a high price.* I needed to have that release and that creative outlet; and I needed to have my body physically in good shape to meet the stressful challenges of every day.

Ultimately, I did hold on and in turn, it helped to pull me out of the terrible place that I'd been in. We did have a fabulously fun and theatrical class, our little version of a Broadway-Fitness-Dance class, with Virginia highlighted as the star. She really was a star in my life, though at the time, she had no idea exactly why. Believe it or not, but ten years later, we'd celebrate this remarkable woman's seventieth birthday with another spectacular theme class.

At that event, I did take a serious moment to tell her and everyone there, the special significance of her sixtieth birthday and how it had been literally life altering for me and my uniquely-challenged family. It meant so much to me, and to everyone there who knew her, to finally be able to thank her from the bottom of my heart. She deserved to know; and I wanted each of them to know, that miracles in life really do happen. It's what I want *you* to know.

Chapter 23

Speech for Hayden wasn't happening. His understanding of emotions had only glimmers of happening; but multitudes of bizarre events and behaviors *were* most definitely happening. On many levels Genevieve, then in grade one, was doing well. But we still walked on eggshells around her. Her inability to share or to understand the perspectives of the people around her, was very difficult to live with, especially for Sydney and Kobe. She loved school and loved the concept of going to school; but she was often overwhelmed by it. Frequently she screamed and refused to go; it was just too much for her. When she did go, often she *appeared* to manage the day at school, and then absolutely fell into pieces the moment she got home. I called it *aftershock* and it was brutal. And she wasn't the only one who suffered from it.

Genevieve was adorable and effervescent but so complex; she alone would have been enough for one family to handle!

But as always, *fascinating* moments of wonder glistened brightly amongst our murk and chaos. In one lovely moment, Genevieve acted out the role of the "sister" character in a video designed to teach kids to "say no to drugs." It was important because what she was actually doing, with her autistic mind and body, was "trying on for size" what it was like to *feel* concern for her brother Kobe, and to express that fear to her parents, as the character had done in the movie.

In the same voice and inflection as the character on film, she expressed her "feigned fear" for her own brother. As Kobe didn't have issues with drugs like the brother in the movie, she made up a new "issue":

Genevieve: "Mom, I'm worried about Kobe!"
Myself: "Oh, why is that Genevieve?"
Genevieve: "Because he's slurping and burping!" (a love of Kobe's at the time).

"Slurping and burping"; big worries they were! But what Genevieve was doing, was some very powerful work in her own personal journey. She was exploring "our world" in a way that was safe to her. And, she was showing us that she did in fact, watch us all very carefully, even though most of the time she appeared to tune us out.

Inadvertently, through her character re-enactment, Genevieve was also giving me an invaluable reprieve from the storm raging around us. It was innocent and it was beautiful. And it was another example of how utterly fascinating she was, *and how hard she worked*. Her tale, *Effervescence*, is filled with examples of how brilliant and driven she was at teaching herself to navigate. *She had a "master plan" for her own emergence*. It began by the time she was barely four. She was and is amazing.

Our home, our castle, could be the most amazing place to be!

Often Genevieve would parallel us, engaged in the rapture of her own little world of capturing and exploring life through her drawings. Often when we would watch TV nearby, as soon as the commercials came on, she'd slip out of her world and dash in and join us. She was captivated by the commercials, only to slip back to her private world the moment they were over, and the TV show that captivated the rest of us, was on. It was all just so curious!

Even our darkest days had glimmers of loveliness. And there was nothing like the simplest of events like Mother's and Father's Day, where Nolan and I would wake up to the sounds of little bodies scurrying around, making us breakfast and gathering the treasures they'd made at school, or even more precious, on their own time. For all parents, those moments are unforgettable and delightful; for us they were treasured even more because they were scattered amongst the sheer chaos that filled each day.

No matter what, what Nolan and I will always remember more than the chaos, was the love and sweetness and innocence that filled every single day!

Chapter 24

peech therapy in the beginning had little to do with speech but everything to do with sign language. Hayden had always responded to our attempts to teach him to speak, by hitting or scratching our faces. Part of that was probably due to his frustration; and in his defense he had severe apraxia (a disability in the sequencing of speech sounds), and low facial muscle tone. But speech *is* largely a social activity and that was where he struggled. He had that innate autism barrier of discomfort. *But sign language was less obtrusive and less threatening. It did not have the same "social strings attached".*

Sign language was speaking with "his hands." It was him speaking to us *through* his hands. It was safer to him. *And* it could be taught through toys which provided that *social buffer*... and it could be taught and performed with *no* eye contact.

Sign language was hard work but it was wonderfully exciting! It helped Hayden feel more at peace with himself and with the world. It all started with the signs for "help, more" and just for pure fun: "pop." From there, a little history was made! Sign language was never seen as a substitute for speaking; the hope was that his frustration level would eventually decrease and his comfort level and desire to speak would increase. It didn't happen overnight, that's for sure. But it set the scene.

Ironically, last night, the night before I wrote this section, I happened to be walking our dogs near the gym of an elementary school near our home. The outside gym door was standing open. Adorable little boys were practicing soccer, so I peeked in. How could I resist? *"Wow!" I thought, taken aback by the sudden emotion. "There's a step back in time!"*

In a flash, vibrant images and memories flooded back into my head. I saw weeks and weeks, many years ago, of me in that very same gym, trying to focus on Genevieve's gymnastics class, while juggling my other three kids. I saw tiny Hayden and his wild behaviors, all the while my hands and my brain in a frenzy, trying intently to memorize and practice signs.

I was so desperate to "talk" to my baby, in whatever language he could handle; and I was desperate to make a difference in his behaviors. I needed to learn signs and I needed to teach them to him.

Most of what I remembered about being in that gym, was trying to stay awake! I was just so exhausted!

Chapter 25

By the age of three, it was obvious that someone needed to be with Hayden, almost constantly, and with focus. It wasn't only because of his aggression or his lacking sense of danger. It was as much because he would otherwise wander aimlessly, looking for trouble, putting objects of any type in his mouth or destroying things. Or even worse, he would park himself in front of the TV and slip into *Nowhereland.*

It tormented me. *Why couldn't I get more deeply into his head?* It was like standing in a corridor, a door ahead, locked and bolted shut....and me, hopelessly and frantically, fumbling with a mess of keys....none of them fitting.

Was it that I genuinely didn't possess the right key? *Or was it that I wasn't able to give myself the presence of mind to recognize the right key and then guide it into the lock?*

Or was the problem that there really just wasn't a key *anywhere* that would fit?

It truly tormented me because we were falling apart at the seams. *I had found the key with Genevieve.* I'd only had to think her and feel her and reach down from within. *With her it was all about getting into her head and her body and her world, and then letting her feel safe and accepted enough, to let me enter. From there, it was a matter of using tools that fit for her, like Fantasy.* But with Hayden, I didn't feel that I had that edge.

I couldn't help feeling that I had let Hayden down. Why couldn't I do the same for him that I had done for her?

Chapter 26

On our long list of goals for Hayden, number one was communication (and hopefully speech).

Number two was teaching him emotions. Emotions had been Genevieve's first goal; because at that age, she *could* speak, she just couldn't speak conversationally and she really didn't have much inclination *to* speak. *Like her, Hayden could see and acknowledge the transition from one emotion to another, but he didn't understand the emotion itself.* In other words, he could see that my expressions were different, but it didn't seem to register on him whether I was happy or sad, or why!

Hayden *felt* emotions; there was no doubt about that. He had a long range of emotions. And when he gave hugs, they were incredible, melt-into-you hugs. And when he would offer a kiss, he would reach out and pull your face to his and kiss so sweetly. His fascination with hair continued, and he was *almost always* touching hair, especially mine. It was like a blind person might, yet with a distinct intensity, *as if his fingers expressed his emotions and his needs.* As he got a little older, we let him grow a long "tail" so that he could "use" his own hair, at least some of the time. It was a little more "socially acceptable" than using mine, or even worse, using the pony tail of the little classmate sitting next to him in preschool.

Hayden's aggression exasperated us. Some days I could tell by the look on his face and the way he carried himself that it was going to be one of "those days." Sometimes it took us by surprise and there seemed no warning at all. Picture my thirty-sixth birthday:

> I spent it in my bedroom, held a prisoner, with tiny three-year-old Hayden. Nolan and I had recklessly invited our close friends, the Foxx family, over for the evening. In a perfect, or at least a typical world, it should have been a fabulously fun and entertaining evening: two vibrant and intelligent, fun-loving couples, with eight young kids between them. *And this was a family that spoke our language. They thrived on creativity and theatrics and little-kid wonder. They should have been a perfect match for us!*
>
> Or so you would think. But Hayden was immediately pushed so far over the edge. He was relentless towards all seven of the kids, most of all, the tiny little one year old boy. *It was terrible!* There was no choice but for me to slip off to my bedroom, with Hayden in my grasp, the door closed and the outside world safely pushed away.
>
> Beyond my bedroom, the evening adventure continued on, I think for a couple of hours. Nolan and our lovely friends, I guess had the awkward position of just continuing on and pretending that it was no big deal. It was just who we were; everyone knew that. But it *was* just odd; and

it *was* a trauma. It was one of many, and there would be many more in the years to follow. *It was who we had become.*

But this one was my birthday.

At least with the destructive force of Hayden removed from the picture, the other seven kids could delve into their worlds of play and make-believe and costumes (that world that I loved being a part of). On some level, of course Sydney, Kobe and even Genevieve felt the loss and our absence; it no doubt entered their bodies and their minds on some level. But thank God the magic of those special friends helped fill up the gaps!

As I sat in my bedroom with Hayden, I felt trapped, alone and scared. He was bombarded by the chaos, the people, the noise and the *socialness*. But the occasion was my birthday and I was spending it locked inside the private world of my bedroom, so that my child wouldn't terrorize the guests who had come to celebrate. *How sad was that?*

I had lots of time to think...it was just me and Hayden, alone in my room. And with the two of us separated from the world, he transformed into lovely Hayden, the Hayden who brought tears to my eyes, good tears. *I studied him, I studied the evening; I studied the guest list.* It wasn't just "the chaos, the people, the noise and the socialness." It was more specific than that. *It was Hayden seeing the little one year old boy.* With all of Hayden's limitations and disabilities, and his difficulty in understanding the world and people and his body and his emotions, *one thing that he did understand, was that he was different. I could see that.*

It was tough enough for him to deal with that in the presence of his siblings, and even with their friends. But there was something in seeing little one year old Logan....*I do believe that on some level, Hayden saw in Logan, a reflection of who Hayden was not, and that hurt him. It brought out his worst. Really, who could blame him?*

I know these aren't easy words to hear, and maybe some of you reading this will think that I was reading too much into the situation, but I can't agree with you. I remember being just a child, just nine or ten years old, and my beautiful Erland only a few years old. Despite his pervasive disabilities, *he knew* that he was different. I remember saying those words to myself: "Erland knows he's different."

I'd seen the same thing in Genevieve. *They know; and they know it at a very young age, whether they are consciously aware or not.* That's not necessarily a bad thing! *But it reminds us that we need to flood their lives with love and acceptance, right from the very beginning!* And it's one of the reasons where I simply do not understand and I just have so much difficulty relating to people, who are sworn to secrecy about their child's disability.

Whether it's autism or Down syndrome or whatever; *I just don't see it as a label. I see it as an explanation.*

A person shouldn't be defined by the fact that they are affected by something like autism; but *it is* part of who they are and how they respond to life. *Why would we not embrace that and then let them feel our acceptance and then just get on with things?* Feeling accepted can only help them motivate *themselves* to continually emerge and evolve, to be the best that they can be.

To me, it's as simple as that. That's my rant, my mantra.

But for now back to my bedroom, on my thirty-sixth birthday:

Being locked away there, and forced to recognize the severity and complexity of Hayden, it *was* like having a door slammed in my face. I was just so sad and the images of doors *literally* filled my thoughts.

Maybe it was just out of determination or sheer stubbornness, but I knew that no matter what, *every* closed room *had* to have a way out, even if it was hidden. This closed room and the closed state of mind, our castle really, *had* to have another way out....some little trap door. I just had to find it.

That night, I *did* discover a little trap door and I knew it could lead to a way out, if only a tiny step. The key *had* to be in finding a way to let people peek inside Hayden's world, to see who he really was. Their compassion would be what would open the world for him *to feel safe enough, and less threatened* enough, to venture out just a little.

Maybe then he would stop lashing out at the world as violently as he did.

67

I knew it would be a slow journey, that this was a *tiny* trap door. *It's probably a good thing I had no idea how long and winding a journey it would be!* But the start was so clear. I had to use what was within *my* hands and *my* capabilities to reach inside and formulate exactly *who* Hayden was and how to present him to the world. I needed to transpose all that I knew of him, into little roadmaps for him *and* the world to follow.

All I needed was a pen and a vision of who Hayden was, and who *I was,* all of those glorious moments when he and I were alone together.... all the times when he and I *had to leave* or *chose not to even go,* to events so that it could be "me and him against the world"....the times when he could feel safe and *himself.* That's what I would capture with my pen. Even his dad and own siblings only saw bits and pieces of the real Hayden, the one who was calm and completely at peace. The world around him saw even less. *That needed to change.*

Out of sheer respect for Hayden, I wanted to create pictures of his sweet and loving side. To do that, I knew I'd have to paint torrid, graphic pictures of the horribly challenging, nightmare side of Hayden, so that they could understand that his behaviors were *not* of his own making. His body, his wiring, and his genetic make-up were *not* of his own design and he had little control. *It's not like he had ever asked to have the body he was given!*

I also wanted the chance to let Sydney and Kobe shine! I wanted for the world around them to be filled *not* with sympathy, but with understanding and to be honest, awe. They deserved it. And I wanted for people to see how Genevieve's curious but complex world was intensified by Hayden; and yet she journeyed on, amazing soul that she was.

And so, from my "birthday-bedroom epiphany" the first story of Hayden was born. With beautiful photographs and carefully-chosen words, it showed how hard we worked with him, and how far he'd come. Most of all, it showed how deeply he was loved and the fact that despite the chaos and the aggression, he did have things to offer the world that were important, unique and meaningful.

My story answered some of the questions, at least the ones that we *could* answer, about Hayden's behaviors. And it helped to draw friends, family and professionals *into* his world. He was difficult to be with and to understand; but he was fascinating and he *was* precious.

This was a trap door. God knows we needed one. And it helped; it was another turning point.

Chapter 27

reschool was a mixed blessing. After a rough start in September, by October Hayden would wave to me as soon as he got there and run off and play. Most of his time he spent "paralleling" the other children, with limited interactions; but still, staff had good success in teaching and modeling social skills. And combined with his out-of-school speech therapy, *very* slowly speech was emerging.

Even with Hayden's limited signing vocabulary, more of his personality was shining through. One day, when crying hysterically about something, Nolan signed: "Crying finished!" Hayden immediately looked up at him and signed emphatically: "More crying!" By three and a half, he would sometimes say: "Mama, Dada, Ko (Kobe), Eee (Sydney), and hum (come)." His words were not spontaneous, but they gave us hope!

Surprisingly, preschool saw few acts of aggression. Likely the high teacher/child ratio helped, *and* the training of the staff helped to check behaviors before they got out of control. But staff also got the feeling that Hayden almost didn't feel "at home enough" with the other preschoolers to bite them. It was very odd.

Instead, Hayden saved up his aggression for when he got home. It was absolutely mystifying to us and to the Turning Point staff, that he could manage as well as he did, and then be *horrid* when he got home. We paid high prices for the two and a half hours he spent at preschool! He whined and screamed and his aggression and level of anxiety increased seriously.

To make matters worse, Hayden's time away from home, and the exposure to other children, increased his dependence on me dramatically.

Once again, we were in a tailspin. There were emergency team meetings, more scrutinizing of behaviors....but at least the complexity of Hayden was being recognized. We reduced his preschool time and I spent part of his sessions there with him. It all helped. But there was no denying: this *was* a complex child!

At the time, we were still learning about autism and I hadn't yet coined the term "aftershock"; but that was what was happening. Like Genevieve, it took *everything* Hayden had to survive the socially and sensory bombardment of preschool. It was mystifying, and hard to not take it personally. *Maybe it was just me?* Why else would he manage well and then fall apart when he was home with me? Maybe I was somehow bringing out the worst in him. I *agonized* about it, as I had done with Genevieve, who responded exactly the same way.

But I documented and scrutinized and looked for patterns. It kept coming back to the same thing: it wasn't that Hayden and Genevieve were reacting to me. It was more that once they saw the "safety of Mommy," all the stress of the day just came tumbling down, taking me and their siblings as victims. *It was terrible.*

Back then, people didn't recognize this trait in autism. That's improving now, thank God; but I'm certain that I'm not the only parent who questioned her abilities and impact, or was questioned by school staff, as we all scrambled to make sense of *aftershock*.

Changes had to be made and fast. And it wasn't going to happen by me simply attending part of Hayden's preschool session, or reducing his time there. The magnitude of his behaviors opened some doors and the Ministry of Children kicked in with a child care worker, to help us for ten hours a week, so I wasn't spread quite so thinly. At that point, I rarely left home except to teach a couple of classes or to get groceries. *I knew that the second I let up or lost my focus, something would happen and the stress level would soar.*

It helped having someone there to assist me; but ten hours spread out over a week, isn't a lot of time. And often I'd find myself upstairs washing dishes, while she was downstairs laughing and playing with my kids. I welcomed the break, but what I really wanted was to be the one down there playing!

And even with this helper, I still felt trapped. *The fear of Hayden going over the edge if I wasn't there loomed over me constantly!* You need to understand that it wasn't just because of the aggression and the severity of his behaviors. *We were dealing with autism.* Sometimes kids with autism just retreat. They push away the world, even their moms. *I don't mean for short periods of time like Nowhereland. Trust me; that was tough enough. I mean some retreat and they don't always come back.*

I'm not exaggerating when I say that this fear was very real and it loomed over me constantly.

The lack of harmony in our little kingdom was poignantly clear the day we had Genevieve's "Castle Party." With Nolan's craftsmanship and my eye for paints and imagery, we created a spectacular wooden castle in our basement. It was a playhouse to complement our ever-evolving costume room.

This event could have been subtitled: "Grab what's safe and meaningful to your autistic child and go with it"....this party was creatively but *strategically* designed to connect Genevieve's home and school, through fantasy and reality. By sculpting the concept of a castle party, making medieval invitations and themes, Genevieve and I could carefully let her entire kindergarten class and her teachers, into her home world. That was an important step. They would all be mesmerized and happy to join us, because our kingdom, and Genevieve's creative personality, could be captivating places to be!

For me, her two teachers felt "safe" to have in my home, because they didn't judge us the way outsiders did. I'd always felt respected with them and if anything, I think I, and we, were held in awe.

It was absolutely a dream for me to have our home filled with twenty five-year-olds, each bursting with sparkle and energy. But it tore at my heart to see how there was such a natural harmony amongst this group of typical kids. Those twenty were easier, and less mentally and physically exhausting, than my four. That was a glaring and rude awakening.

And then there was Hayden and how he responded to having to open up our castle doors that day and let them in....

Chapter 28

ydney, then in grade three, swept from being her usual happy, fun yet mature self, to spontaneously reacting with an exasperating attitude of total disrespect and disregard for everyone, *especially* me. She had become non-motivated, always dressed in black and often, seemed just so unhappy. It was explainable: the constant bizarre and stressful behaviors from both Genevieve and Hayden. But what cut her most deeply was realizing that her baby brother was never going to be like our toddler friend Logan, or any other baby brothers that she knew.

And her sister: Sydney longed to build on their relationship, but Genevieve was so aloof and often disconnected. It was a complicated life that Sydney led.

As for Kobe, then in grade one, I really was worried that I was loosing him. I don't mean in the autism way as it was with Genevieve and Hayden; but in my emotional and physical connection with him. He was high energy and adventuresome; he loved to be busy all of the time. I was pulled in so many directions and Genevieve and Hayden inhaled my time and attention. Often Kobe would get discouraged and run down the street to his friend's house. *I missed him!* I missed playing with him and I knew that much of the time he missed playing with me.

Often the littlest thing would have him in tears; often he was aggressive and unhappy. We had him allergy tested and discovered that he too needed to be on an extremely restricted diet. How much of that was caused by stress, I wondered?

To offset Sydney and Kobe's feelings of neglect, I did what I could to capture magical moments with them, sometimes surprising them and their classmates with little bits of theatrics in class or teaching dance classes for their whole school (they were pretty proud!). Nolan and I made a point of using respite funding for the four of us to go cycling or hiking. *We were always absolutely amazed at how wonderfully easy and uncomplicated it was, when it was just the four of us.* We couldn't help but laugh (and with some resentment) at our many friends with typical children who always seemed barely able to keep on top of things. *They had no idea how simple every single one of their days was!*

Those outings only lasted for a few months. As much as the four of us loved them, we always felt like something was missing. Our hearts were so entrenched with the two that we left at home. It was all just so complicated.

Both Sydney and Kobe continued to be close and connected. Watching *Aladdin* together, they would sit on a pillow, as their magic carpet. Kobe had taken to crawling into Sydney's bed with her, as he'd been struggling with intense nightmares, and she was always ready and willing to offer her protection.

They were an amazing pair and people around us often commented. Their experiences and home life gave them insight and worldliness, but still they were precious and innocent. At age seven, for instance, Kobe was convinced he'd seen the tooth fairy and emphatically gave us a detailed description of her. Sydney loved him too much to burst his bubble with the truth.

> Love and sweetness oozed throughout our home and I was "the queen" of all of that loveliness. I was the one who got to experience it the most. It was an exhausting role but I was *always* rewarded. One special night, at the end of a very long day when I still had the long bedtime routine to fulfill, I climbed up to Kobe's top bunk for lullabies. I found that he'd already proudly set aside and puffed up his pillow for me, leaving for him only a stack of stuffed animals to use instead.

> *How could I want to be anywhere but right there, in that home, in that castle, at that very moment? Everything was worth this!*

I remember those nights so well. Yet by contrast, I also remember the mornings. I'd wake up feeling completely overwhelmed, walking around the house, pacing and wringing my hands together, asking myself: "How the hell do I get us through another day?"

Chapter 29

This must be the oddest story! Your head must be spinning. Here's another one, another example of "the contrasts":

Nolan and I knew we had to carve out some changes; that was clear. But we had to do it carefully and strategically. Out of desperation to have some *uncomplicated* time with Sydney and Kobe, I left the other two with a respite worker. The three of us went out for dinner and a movie. I'll never forget it because it was just so lovely and so uncomplicated!

Even Hayden and Genevieve did well at home that night. It even seemed to help build their relationship a little.

Thinking that we were on a roll, a couple of days later, Nolan took all four kids and our respite worker, to a park event. The main idea was to give me a rare day off. Surprisingly everything went well! *It was glorious.*

But by the following morning, everything unraveled. Genevieve was a wreck and screamed hysterically when it was time to go to school. Hayden responded by waking from his nap, screaming. *He would not let me or anyone near him.* When I tried, he kicked me in the stomach and scratched and pinched. In contrast, awhile later, he clung to me relentlessly *and wouldn't let me go.*

This was all aftershock. It was a high price to pay.

I wish I could say that it happened only that one time but that would be lying. It was part of who we were and how we lived.

Chapter 30

Under the direction of our behavioral consultant John, we tracked, for what seemed endlessly, aggressive and concerning behaviors. It sounds simple, but until you've "walked the walk" you really can't imagine how encumbersome tracking and scrutinizing makes everyday life. Even simple, well-designed track sheets and charts added another unneeded complexity to our home.

And with Hayden, there seemed to be so little rhyme or reason, with few patterns other than the fact that he was extraordinarily emotionally fragile and susceptible to bombardment. That's a mouthful, isn't it? Tracking his sleep patterns did confirm that there was a *definite link* that proved that when I was home a lot and gave him extreme amounts of physical closeness, he often slept well. If I was busy and "in and out," running errands and such, consistently the result would be a horrible night of screaming.

Tracking sheets and charts were strategically placed throughout our home. We were used to seeing them but they must have been really confusing and concerning to school friends, on the few occasions when we did have someone over. They reinforced to these visitors and to us, how different we were from the rest of the world.

It's not to say that in some ways we weren't wonderfully different; but we were definitely and seriously different!

Creating successful behavioral programs for Hayden and Genevieve brought new dimensions of challenges. Despite their "tuning us out", both kids were oddly aware of *everything* that went on in our home. They were dramatically shaken up by changes, or by what Genevieve articulated as "ulterior motives." *She could spot a behavioral strategy a mile away.* It had to be presented strategically, so that she would embrace it or "not notice" that it was, in fact a strategy.

Genevieve's emotions and her difficulty in understanding and dealing with her emotions, complicated almost every potential strategy. For instance, one clever and well-formatted strategy designed by John to address Hayden's aggression caused such a dramatic reaction in Genevieve, that it was quickly discarded. It had involved a chart with a happy and a sad face. It pushed her to the point of despair, because she couldn't stand the thought of there being a "sad" face in our home.

That was a rude awakening for us and for John. For us, there *always* seemed to be a catch. This was one item on our growing list of "catches" that told him and us how complex our family dynamics were. It *was* discouraging.

And, you have to remember that any obvious behavioral strategies for Genevieve, indicated to her, that people considered her to be "like the brother she despised and was fearful of." That was a dangerous and damaging link.

Aggression wasn't the only thing we tracked with Hayden. There were so many behaviors linked to him and his struggle to remain amidst the world around him. Often social situations, for instance, resulted in massive and instant diarrhea. Most times, this translated into green slime that went up his back, to his shoulders. One "memorable evening" it happened within ten minutes of Sydney having a few friends over for a sleepover. There were countless "slimy" incidents, for years, especially hitting when we were out in the community trying to do "typical" family activities.

In response to many activities and outings, Hayden would withdraw into *Nowhereland*. Sometimes it was hard to tell if he was letting himself go there, or if it overtook him. *Was it an art or was it another one of his symptoms, over which he had so very little control?* We never really knew for sure; I'm quite certain it varied. Most times, maybe all, I think he had no control; it was *not* intentional. Often, when driving to preschool, he would be asleep within literally five or ten seconds. When we awoke him, he would be well into an anxiety-ridden state of withdrawal. He had fallen into *Nowhereland*.

Emotionally, Hayden was unbelievably fragile. There was just so much that he didn't understand. This little story will show that:

> Until the age of three and a half, Hayden had never gone out on any real outings, where it was just him and his dad. Then one day, Nolan took him for a long outing in a park. Hayden was thrilled and had a great day. But for the next two nights, he screamed hysterically and wouldn't let *even me* touch him. Each night, he screamed "Mama!" and frantically grabbed my hair. He had to feel it on his face and in his hands. *It was like he couldn't touch me and then he couldn't get close enough to me.*
>
> *It seemed like he loved his new-found relationship with his dad; but he was deeply threatened and overwhelmed by it, like he just couldn't comprehend that he could have both of us.*

Chapter 31

*C*ostumes...we loved costumes! All four of our kids loved to dress up in costumes and act out scenes from their favorite movies, and to create brand-new ones. Our costume room was filled with magical bits and pieces, and fabulous creations. (It continues to evolve today). They all loved to perform for us and Sydney and Kobe *loved* the opportunities to play their roles as big sister and big brother, teaching their special skills. *Instinctively, I think they both knew that that was how they would be best welcomed into their autistic siblings' worlds.* They cherished it and they embraced it.

> I could paint fabulous images here for you to read: each was an adventure of imagination and of loving and of caring! One night, for example, they created "Kobe's Ninja Show" and billed it as having "vilent and exiting Ninja stuff." Kobe and Sydney did flips and dances to music in the basement, the furthest depth of our castle, while the rest of us watched. Both Genevieve and Hayden were absolutely captivated, soaking up the delight of the precious performance.

> *We were an entity unto ourselves, our private, tucked away and often magical world!*

On some occasions, Genevieve and Hayden would join in. Sometimes it worked; but most times it ended up with Hayden going over the edge. He'd become overwhelmed by the noise, the chaos, the physical contact and the *socialness* of the moment. *He would transform, right before our very eyes, from being captivating and cute, to a terror, on a rampage of biting, screaming and pinching.*

We carefully orchestrated special moments, like playing interactive games like charades. They were enormously fun; but almost always ended up with Hayden getting overloaded and reactive. Simple things that typical families would take for granted, scarred us emotionally. *And they scarred us deeply.* A game of Monopoly, held in private between me and Nolan, and Sydney and Kobe, would usually do more damage than good, as Hayden would find us and do his best to seek us out, interrupt and destroy.

> *There was no escaping him. Yes, we lived in a castle-like existence, but it was just us, a family. We didn't have "servants or keepers to assist us or court jesters to entertain" the force that was Hayden. We were just a family.*

Were the precious moments worth the traumas? I think so. How could they not be; they were just so precious and so uniquely us. And we always kept coming back for more. *And every once in awhile, we would be blessed with one that was completely and gloriously trauma-free!* One of the sweetest was Hayden and Sydney's re-enactment of the fabulous Mambo dance sequence from the Jim Carrey movie *The Mask*:

> Dressed in a yellow suit and hat, my creation to match the movie, Hayden danced dramatically with Sydney, much to her absolute delight. But as the end of the song drew near, she laughed but looked fearful, saying: "Oh no…" Sure enough, re-enacting the movie, our charismatic and romantic Hayden ended the song with a big and *very passionate* kiss! We all just howled, even Genevieve!

Chapter 32

The summer when Hayden was about three and a half, was, as Sydney, Kobe and I still refer to it (and not so lovingly) "the summer that took six months of therapy to undo!" The lack of routine was tough for both Hayden and Genevieve. And for Hayden, having everyone home each day increased his aggression and his territorial land-marking of me. He loved and adored his siblings and was at times thrilled to have them home; but he swept from "incredibly sweet and loving," to instantaneously "pinching, biting, kicking and screaming." The aggression was unbearable.

Our dream of having a tightly-knit family was shattered by the reality that we had to do our best to keep the four of them *apart*. As for me, I swept from feeling ridiculously challenged to bored, because I couldn't commit to any home projects or even art projects with the kids. Instead, I had to be ready at a moment's notice, to spring into action to try to control Hayden or undo the damage.

When I wasn't feeling captive and abused, I felt like a spectator. I was stifled and burnt out. I used to take such pride in all of the activities that I could do with my little gang, and the more I did, the more I found energy to do; but this was a ridiculous, non-stop juggling act, with rarely any harmony. Hayden was disruptive and aggressive; and Genevieve had to have things her way or no way at all. And though sign language definitely reduced Hayden's frustration, it wasn't as significant as we'd all hoped, not by a long shot! *Clearly the aggression wasn't just a frustration issue.*

Even during the school year, when it was just Genevieve and Hayden home with me, I wanted to play with them and just be with them. But basically, the only thing that I could do with them both at the same time, was watch a movie. And even then, I was constantly *working*, trying to reach them, to animate them and pull them out from their reclusive worlds.

Our camping trip was a disaster. We lasted only eight days instead of the planned fourteen, though truthfully, had we not been so stupidly stubborn, we probably should have abandoned it after the third. From the moment we arrived at the lovely, sunny and placid campsite, it was Hayden versus Sydney, Kobe and Genevieve. Most of the time, he perceived them as the enemy wanting Mommy's attention.

Hayden was also completely overwhelmed by the outdoor setting and the fact that he had no TV and VCR to mellow him out. He stalked and he screamed, and we exhausted ourselves trying to keep him occupied. Our close friends and their two young kids met us at the campsite, all of us hoping for a two-family camping vacation. In a thoughtful attempt to give me break, the mom offered to take Hayden for a walk around the campsite in his stroller. Her kind offer was met with a terrible "reward," when Hayden grabbed and clawed the face of a small child that they'd stopped to chat with along the way.

This very sweet mom and friend was reluctant to tell me about it and tried to take it in her stride, but she was unnerved by it. Who wouldn't have been? Nolan and I were horrified.

Genevieve managed the trip surprisingly well. She tagged along *after* Sydney and Kobe and their friends, and was sometimes *alongside* of them, joyously in her own little world most of the time. At least she was venturing out. But she also spent hours upon hours in seclusion, drawing in the tent. She too was in a foreign environment. And the placidness of camping also meant that the rest of us constantly walked on egg shells, doing anything to avoid temper tantrums, *from her and Hayden.*

> Our lowest point was the morning I went for a run. Meanwhile, Nolan had set Hayden up in the car with a Disney audio tape and a book, while he washed dishes nearby. By the time I got back, thirty minutes later, Hayden had slipped into withdrawal and subsequently screamed relentlessly for the next hour. He was "stuck" back in *Nowhereland*, that place where he just couldn't seem to get back on his own.

Hayden became hysterical and frantic and pushed away everyone, even me. *And this was all in the outdoor splendor, with our kids and neighboring campers all forced to endure.* It was heart wrenching, frightening and unnerving to have my baby push me away like that, and being under the scrutiny of strangers made it all the more stressful, draining and imperative to "get him back."

When Hayden finally settled down, all I wanted to do was throw up and cry. I don't think Nolan really understood, until that day, that I meant what I had said about my having to give Hayden almost constant attention and supervision; otherwise there was always a multitude of consequences, some of them severe, like *Nowhereland.* Even during the moments when I wasn't working directly with Hayden, I was *always* listening and looking for signs and responding to them....*always.*

The five hour drive to our vacation campsite had been horrendous; the drive home was even worse. In our huge station wagon, we must have been quite the sight from *the outside*, much like "The Griswalds" from Chevy Chase's movie *Family Vacation.* But what went on from *the inside* of our car was much worse and not remotely comical. Hayden had to sit in the front seat, between Nolan and me; otherwise he'd constantly unbuckle his seat belt and thrash the other three kids. In the front seat, he'd kick the tape deck, pinch the driver and put us in constant fear that he would grab the steering wheel.

Even short errands at home were often a nightmare; it was ludicrous to think that we could have survived a long drive. I guess, as always, our desire to do "normal" family outings clouded our judgment.

But the trip was not all bad and there *were* moments of magic. A delightful game of charades for one...somehow we pulled that off and that's what I choose to remember most about that trip. I think our friends and their two kids were in awe. They *never* did things like charades! It took them awhile to shift gears and jump into our world of creativity and self expression; but I think they liked it once they got there.

The magical moments weren't enough, though, to hide the fact that we clearly could not exist without a TV and VCR to allow Hayden to mellow out and *safely* tune out. *He needed it and we needed it, to give us refuge from him.*

....A family vacation: when we finally walked through our front door when we got home, it *was* like hearing a huge door slam shut behind us, trapping us inside, limiting us even more than before. When we got home, we did something we'd never done before: we actually *asked* Nolan's sister and family to take Sydney and Kobe for a few days. It nearly broke my heart because really, we were sending them away. But they needed a break from *both* of their autistic siblings.

To the two of them and to us, those days seemed like forever. They didn't really *want* to go; but they knew they needed to.

It was fascinating to see how differently both Sydney and Kobe responded when they got home. Kobe was full of renewed energy and determination to make things work. His first two days back, he spent dreaming up wonderful games to play with Genevieve and Hayden, and he was sweet and loving towards them. Sydney, on the other hand, was more frustrated than ever. The break from home and the chaos made her see that she'd taken all that she could take.

To end the summer with everything put in pretty tragic perspective, I found a picture Genevieve had drawn that was fascinating but, alarming. She had drawn Hayden, lying down, dead. Surprisingly, she drew herself crying, and yet Sydney and I were not. When I asked her why, she said that we "were okay with still having her". She did have such an intense desire to keep her family safe and happy, that I guess she thought that she could make us all happy again.

Our friends, the Foxx family, also made their way into her picture. She told me that they would use their magic to make Hayden alive again. Maybe she thought that Hayden would be better the second time around.

All of these thoughts and images were captured and translated into the drawings of a six year old autistic mind...are you getting a pretty good idea how complicated life was in our home?

Chapter 33

*N*ow *this* will spin your head just a little bit more: "the summer that took six months of therapy to undo" was also sprinkled with some of our *favorite* summer memories *ever!* The contrasts just never stop. Let me tell you about Twyla:

> Some local funding was generously sent our way that summer to pay for someone to assist me with the kids for a few hours on Saturdays. That someone was lovely, twenty years old and on her way to becoming a speech therapist.... maybe we couldn't do malls anymore; but with Twyla's help, we could once again do forests and trails and ravines....we could climb up mounds of dirt and journey through creeks, sometimes waist-deep in cold water, to see where they would lead us.
>
> We could once again do what we did best: we kept to ourselves in our own little world of adventure! Our favorites always seemed to be the ones where the kids came home giggling, naked in the backseat under a blanket, having stripped off their wet and caked-on muddy clothes and shoes.
>
> What magic! It was fabulous! It was "us", the good side of us!

We adored Twyla and I was elated to have her; but it hurt because I had the motivation, desire and imagination to do so many great things with my kids. But it was like trudging through life with a ball and chain on both feet and my hands tied behind my back, trying to do all the things that other families took so much for granted.

After our camping "holiday," we were all stressed and discouraged. My stomach was in a constant knot. I paced around the house and I rarely ever slept. I simply couldn't take anymore temper tantrums, or the walking on egg shells, or the biting and the pinching. *None of us could.* The impact was really scaring me; it scared all of us.

The lack of harmony was the toughest thing to deal with. I'd always loved "kid chaos" and had long planned for our home to be the one where all the neighborhood kids would hang out, where summers would be one long, continuous sleepover.

But this wasn't survivable chaos. This was beyond ridiculous. And as this tumultuous summer came to an end, even the glimmers of magic and the wonderful adventures like the ones with Twyla, weren't enough to fight the reality that we were moving from a terribly stressful summer, directly into the jaws of a new school year. *That had chaos written all over it.*

Chapter 34

E ven before Hayden had turned four, we'd come to the realization that we could hardly take him *anywhere*. The contrast and his "personality change" when it was just him and me, home alone, was absolutely bewildering! He was sweet and loving, and he loved to putter around the house, staying close by my side. I literally often fought back tears seeing his genuine sweetness and how much I loved being with him.

But when the others were home, it was a different story. His sibling's possessions weren't safe, especially Genevieve's because he knew she was an easy target. Within minutes of her receiving a beautiful, framed picture from *Snow White* for instance, he maliciously smashed it. Another time, he went into her bedroom armed with a water sprayer; he drenched the *Sailor Moon* posters she'd spent countless hours coloring with felts. To this day, she believes the lie that I told her, that the disaster had been caused by the angle of the rain and the window that *I* had supposedly left open. There just was no good that would have come from adding this crisis to Hayden's list of crimes, so I was more than willing to take the blame.

Hayden obsessed about needing specific objects and would scream for weeks if he was unable to get them. Increased aggression *always* resulted. He would fall apart, completely unglued, making life unbearable for the rest of us, until he got it.

Attempts at toileting Hayden were futile. We tried countless strategies but he simply didn't care about the state of his diaper or his training pants. In fact, most of the time, he seemed totally oblivious.

Sensory issues continued to intrigue and baffle us. Hayden "kissed himself better" frequently and obsessively. If he bumped his head (a part of his body that he couldn't reach to kiss), he would kiss his hand and then touch his kissed hand to his head. It was very bizarre; but it did serve as an *emotional barometer*.

In other words, I could often measure the degree of *underlying, brooding stress* in him by noting the frequency of these "self-stimming behaviors." It was clear that he and his body were so wary and threatened by the world around him, that he had to literally soothe it when he came in contact with "the world around him."

On the days when Hayden was, for whatever reason, feeling exceptionally threatened and unable to withstand the force of the world around him, the need to "kiss himself better" increased, often to ridiculous, almost non-stop levels.

> It was just so odd. People don't do that sort of thing. *At least not people who don't have autism.* But if you think about it, really what Hayden was presenting to us was *exactly* what autism is: a mind, a body and a sensory system that is unable to effectively process incoming sensory information. It is then overwhelmed and bombarded by the world around it.

> And what Hayden had created really, was a pretty *logical* coping mechanism: *if something hurts your body, you kiss it and make it get better.* With his own little body and his oddly intelligent mind, really he was telling us exactly what was wrong.

> It was very powerful messaging, to those of us who were insightful enough to be interpreting it. *To me, it spoke volumes!*

Hayden's aggression was showing increased malice. For example, when he came upon Genevieve reading his book, he grabbed a wooden bat and hit her on the head. Thank God he wasn't strong enough to be really forceful, but *he knew* what he was doing. He was also clever and he knew the sensitive spots, particularly the eyes and he instinctively went for them, time and time again.

The animosity between Hayden and Genevieve grew and she literally would not allow us to use both of their names in the same sentence.

Often Genevieve and Hayden engaged in incredible, animated arguments. Nolan, Sydney, Kobe and I would stand by and watch, with our mouths wide open, not knowing whether to laugh or cry. We were powerless to interact. We couldn't understand a single word he said, but the inflection was there and they *both* seemed to understand exactly what the other was screaming about. It was intense and bizarre.

Hayden learned quickly how to ruthlessly put Genevieve in pieces. He'd "go in for the kill," blowing her kisses and saying: "I love you!" You have to understand that at that age, and even still today, Genevieve is unnerved *by anyone*, even me, saying those words of affection or offering her a simple kiss. And to have it coming from Hayden tormented her to the core. *And being that she was autistic, she pulled those feelings and those associations very deeply into her body.* It was a serious issue.

> *Genevieve frequently isolated herself from us, just to escape Hayden. It was a terribly complex relationship between them. He adored her and was utterly fascinated by her. He saw the world much the way that she did, through fantasy and through a "third person," with a wall between him and the world. He wanted so desperately to play with her. But if the only way that he could get attention from her was to hurt her, physically or emotionally, so be it. He wanted her but was shunned by her.*

> *The thing was: he couldn't have handled attention from her anyway. He responded to her as he did to the rest of the world, with bizarre and often aggressive acts.*

Sydney and Kobe expressed great concern for their own safety, as well as that of others. Through a lot of digging, Sydney was finally able to articulate her fear that by the time Hayden was in grade four, "he'd be breaking people's arms."

It was strange and alarming to see how often Sydney and Kobe "taunted" Hayden and egged him on, even though they knew it would bring on even more aggression. Often they seemed compelled. I wrote about it and contemplated it many times. I wondered if it was because they got such mixed signals from him: one minute he'd lash out and hurt them; the next he'd be sweet and loving. Or he might tune them out completely....maybe they taunted him because they would have rather gotten an *aggressive* reaction from him, *than no reaction at all.*

Or maybe it was more empowering to them to have the "upper hand," so that they could "pounce on him" rather than waiting for him to pounce on them. How much of it was just sheer and utter frustration and confusion? *Oh my God, we lived in a home of never-ending mind games and "body games." This was serious. These weren't games. These were complex behaviors and equally complex reactions and responses. And these were only children.*

Chapter 35

till one of Hayden's favorite things to do, was to literally crawl under my sweater (while I was still wearing it), with his stomach pressed against my back and his arms alongside mine, *inside* the sleeves. It was like he just couldn't get close enough to me. It was unbelievably sweet, but very odd. All three of my kids were snuggly, but this was on a whole different level; crawling inside my sweater would never have even occurred to Sydney or Kobe, and certainly not to Genevieve.

That was the curious but lovely side of Hayden. The impact of the "other sides" of Hayden ran rampant in our home and who we had become. On one hand, Sydney and Kobe continued to be inseparable. Yet for weeks at a time, Sydney had major anxiety attacks, was wild and temperamental, and was horrid *specifically* to her best friend Kobe. She'd actually kick him and find ways to irritate him; she'd be completely un-Sydney-like.

She and I did a lot of soul searching together and uncovered that she felt *jealous* of Kobe, because she interpreted him as being better able to handle the stress of both Hayden and Genevieve, than herself. When I explained to her that Kobe was also "falling apart" under the stress, but that he simply reacted and responded *differently* to it than her, she was strangely consoled. Immediately their relationship improved. It was a huge "relief" to her that he had health and behavioral issues that proved that he struggled as much as she did, but in a different way. He kept his emotions in, and his body paid the price.

It was no wonder that our home wasn't the place where the neighborhood kids could hang out, the way I'd always dreamed. Here's a snapshot glimpse of a typical morning in our home:

Every morning before school, I'd start at 6:30am. Genevieve and Hayden seldom cooperated and both needed special treatment in terms of how we communicated and responded to them. We walked on egg shells not to set them off, especially first thing in the morning. Four to five mornings each week, Genevieve refused to get dressed, there was tremendous screaming and agitation as she fought her own demons with the stress of grade one.

Meanwhile, I'd try to prepare breakfast, recess snacks and lunches, in keeping with the various food allergies and sensitivities amongst them. Hayden, of course, still needed breakfast to be spoon fed. Sydney and Kobe were still young and needed assistance to keep them on track with the morning routine as well.

Though our school was only a seven-minute walk, it would have been an impossible task, so I'd load everyone into the car. Hayden, struggling with the transition and the physical closeness of being near his family in the car, would bite, pinch and use toys as weapons. (He had one Wolverine figurine, in particular, that was made of hard plastic. The pointed "ears" of this figurine made it a serious weapon, to the point where we had to throw it away. Kobe also had one that he loved; but we had no choice but to rid ourselves of both of them....to this day, *even the cartoon image of Wolverine on TV* is to me, immediately recognized as a "weapon against my kids," and I shutter).

Many mornings, before we even got out of the driveway, Sydney would run back into the house, locking the front door and refusing to go because she knew that the level of anxiety that she was feeling would be too intense to handle once she got to school. Kobe would then be overloaded by the chaos, and bearing the brunt of Hayden's aggression, would run back into the house with instant diarrhea or to throw up.

Sometimes I could calm them down and get them back on track and off to school; sometimes not. Many of the bite marks and scratches that pretty much continually marred Sydney, Kobe and Genevieve's skin were inflicted by Hayden *during* that morning transition time.

The impact of these mornings would carry on through the day. Sydney missed twenty-one days of school that year; her grades were poor, her attitude was negative, non-motivated and often belligerent, both at home and at school. The previous years, she'd been a model student.

Davina, our psychologist, was concerned that Sydney seemed totally consumed by concern for her family and her own well being. It screamed out at me that her teacher and school staff *had* to be brought up to speed with the seriousness of the situation at home. If nothing else, it just wasn't fair that Sydney be misjudged or reprimanded, as being a lazy kid or worse, an obnoxious kid with a bad attitude. That just wasn't fair and it would have been counter-productive.

Nolan and I viewed all of the staff involved with both Sydney and Kobe the same way we did with Genevieve and Hayden: they were important members of our team. We all needed to work together. I can honestly say that throughout the years, almost *all* staff rose to the challenge and responded with genuine interest, respect, and compassion. They saw what was bizarre and stressful in us; but they also saw what was extraordinary and amazing. *They were an important part of our team and of our lives.*

When you live the way we did, you have to reach out. You can't do this on your own.

Kobe's two teachers felt that he was suffering from depression. He was only in grade two but he got into fights and was often very disruptive in class, like he had a "chip on his shoulder." In the past, he'd been well known for his brightness and his caring, sensitive and happy personality. Teachers I didn't even know had, in the past, stopped me in the hallway many times, to tell me of kindness Kobe had shown to other children in need. It was now quite a contrast.

His behaviors were becoming alarming. At home, he was often hostile and physically aggressive towards both Genevieve and Hayden. I think it was out of sheer frustration, resentment and confusion. Life in our home was so terribly confusing. Genevieve's quirky and disruptive behaviors were enough. And then there was Hayden who was so horrid to them and yet so sweet. Capture this image, for instance:

> One day Sydney was very upset about something and *to her rescue* came Hayden. He put one hand on each of her shoulders and sweetly kissed her forehead. She looked into his blue eyes, at his red hair, the dimples on his cheeks and his cute little cleft chin… she just melted.

No matter what Hayden, or Genevieve, put them through, Sydney and

Kobe always came back for more. *Sydney, a fair maiden, and Kobe, a knight in shining armor? Yes, they most definitely were, and are.*

Chapter 36

We did endure the "typical school-day traumas" for about a year. Looking back, and re-reading what I've written, of course I wonder: "How did we do it?" But also: *"Why?"* I find I have to remind myself, and probably defend us to anyone reading about us, that there simply weren't many choices.

And though each of us was aware of the stress of how we lived, it was our norm; it was who we had become. And don't forget, we were a family of six, living pretty much on one salary. There wasn't much left over to hire help.

Probably more than anything, it was the deep and intense love that we all felt for each other. It superseded our concerns and we just found ways to survive and endure. *There was always room to forgive, to focus on the beautiful and to keep going, to forge on.* But for us, it was like things never changed: life continued to sweep from incredibly wonderful highs, only to be contrasted by incredible lows. Always, it was one step forward and six steps back. *But at least the step forward was always amazingly sweet!*

Genevieve was well liked at school because of her unique and fascinating presence. It was a priority that we tap into that to focus on improving her ability to socialize. We needed to invite school friends over. But that was almost an impossible task, because Hayden needed constant supervision around other children. He struggled enough with his own siblings; the presence of outsiders in our home was totally overwhelming.

And truthfully, Hayden wasn't the only issue. When Genevieve did have friends over, after a short while, she'd isolate herself and I'd be left with the predicament of caring for two autistic kids, two typical siblings and in addition, the school friend. I always felt obligated to "entertain" them, so that they'd want to come back!

Though Genevieve's school friends were probably mystified by the bizarre behaviors of Hayden, and of Genevieve herself, I think we won them over with the wild creativity that also filled our walls. Ours was a house where kids could paint murals on the windows or slip into costumes any day of the year. And then there were our theme parties. No child *ever* missed a chance to come to one of our theme parties!

> Magic *could* exude from our house, our castle. We *could* be vibrant, spectacular and unique. Sometimes it was on a small scale, like the glow of little sparklers. Sometimes it was dramatic like fireworks. It was unique, it was magic, it was from the heart; *but it was also very much a plan.* And all plans take work, determination and a hell of a lot of conviction to pull them off!

> *Stop and take a peek at the cover of this book.* Imagine it like you would the Disneyland castle, the air aglow with the shimmer and sparkle of fireworks bursting from within. *That* was the way our castle *did* sometimes appear and present itself to the world. *It wasn't all grey and murky.* Remember that. That's what *we* remember the most.

One little family, the Foxx family, shone above everyone else. No doubt there were times when we frustrated them and pushed their patience; but they "got" us and they accepted us. And the older two kids were the best friends that Sydney and Kobe could have ever asked for. Creative souls that they were, they *adapted to us.* I'll never forget the time one of them sweetly suggested that Hayden could join their game of playground tag, by making him an alligator, because he liked to bite people!

> Do you know, on that particular playground day, I don't remember there being *any* altercations with Hayden at all? Maybe it was the level of acceptance that he felt, because ironically on *that* day, that crocodile didn't take a single nip!

The kids and I created a little theatre group, called "The Gangsters." We strategically transformed the story of *Peter Pan* into "*Peter Pan and His Brother Dan,*" because both of the Foxx boys had their heart set on playing the lead role of Peter. We spent months re-writing the script, learning lines, making costumes and props, depending more on imagination than the tiny amount of money we could afford to spend.

Hayden was affectionately cast as the crocodile, because he "couldn't talk and liked to bite." I made him *the* coolest crocodile costume because I wanted him to *feel* his role, and to feel that he was important.

During most of our rehearsals, Hayden was horrid. But when the performance came, on a church stage, with families to watch, *he was amazing.* We couldn't believe it! He knew exactly when to appear and what to do. Somehow he managed to withstand the anxiety and excitement of the evening, I think because it just meant so much to him to be a part of the production. And, he was in character. *He wasn't Hayden, he was the devilish Crocodile.* It was all so real to him, just like it was to Genevieve. They both were truly in character on a level that the other kids couldn't be.

We were all so proud of Hayden's performance. Finally, we had a successful family event! And the sweetest icing on the cake was the fact that it had happened *outside* the safety of our castle walls. With Kobe as the dastardly Captain Hook, Sydney as the ever-mature Wendy, and Genevieve as the "dare to be different" John (and Nolan and I as the very darling Mr. and Mrs. Darling), our performance was the first "flawlessly positive" thing the six of us had done together in a *very* long time. It was indescribable! Now, years later, I can still remember exactly where in that church gym I was standing, when that thought ran through my entire body. *That's how important that evening was!*

For the finale of the play, we altered the words of the classic song *"You Can Fly"* to say:

> *"Just use your imagination; that is all that you need.*
> *Even when you're all grown up, never let your childish spirit up;*
> *And you can fly, you can fly, you can fly!"*

We were flying that night. And there was no doubt that for our unique family, *imagination, fantasy* and *theatrics* were the keys to unlocking doors and keeping sanity!

Chapter 37

*A*n evening of magic was something to treasure, but it didn't alter the fact that we were in serious trouble. Every morning I *did* pace around the kitchen, wringing my hands together, asking myself how we'd survive. But somehow, we did. And if I were to give this chapter a name, it would be called *Miracles*, because miracles *are* part of the reason that we did survive. We have had many, and some of them were not so little. *This is one of the big ones:*

At this point, Genevieve and Hayden were still home with me much of the time, their behaviors odd, bizarre, stressful and complex. I was sliding deeper and deeper into their worlds, and becoming more and more reclusive. Some of it was out of pure fascination and need: I *needed* to be entrenched in their worlds to work with them and to co-exist with them. But I was also succumbing because there was so little that I could relate to other people about, especially "typical" parents.

More and more I experienced the world like my autistic kids did, on sensory levels that I hadn't done before. And eye contact…it was bizarre really, now that I look back at it. It was learned behavior *from* Genevieve and Hayden. Trust me, when you consistently have someone shift their gaze away from you every time you speak to them, it becomes a part of how you then respond to others. At least that was how it went for me. I had to remind myself to make eye contact with people and sometimes, I literally had to *force myself* to maintain it, even with people I felt safe and "me" with.

I know this must all be odd and confusing to read. Of course I was *functional* and able to take care of my kids and our home and all of that, but *I was altering.* I was affected. *I was living deep inside their worlds, and the stress was brutal.*

Life seemed an endless battle of double-edged swords. When Genevieve or Hayden would agree to go out for short respite activities, we *always* paid a price when they got home. And we had to move so slowly. One time Genevieve went for a few hours with a caregiver and seemed to enjoy herself. But later, she literally later ran through the house screaming: *"I'm lost, I'm lost!"*

For Hayden, he was at first thrilled at the concept of going out with a respite worker twice a week, but for many weeks it led to whining, screaming and aggressive behavior that was almost unbearable. For many of those nights, he screamed and wouldn't let even me hold him. When he finally did, he would hold on to my shoulders and pound his head into my chest as if in intense pain. *It was too high a price for us to pay.*

Our reality was that basically our home was calmer, and Hayden's aggression was less, when we kept to ourselves and pushed away outside help.

This is the part where you have to brace yourself, just a little bit:

In the afternoons, when Sydney and Kobe were at school, I'd be alone with both Genevieve and Hayden. Often they'd be at each other's throats, screaming, or they'd flop themselves on the floor, tune out and scream. Two afternoons rush to my mind, both of them so graphic that I'll never forget them. One of them, *this* one, *I wish* I could forget. I truly thought I was going to lose my mind. *No, that's wrong; I was loosing my mind.* And I do mean that literally:

….I sat and listened to them scream as I had hundreds of times before….I watched them spin. *The room literally spun around me.* I hated being at home and that was a painful thing for a mom like me to admit. *But I just couldn't take the screaming and the aggression and the bizarre behaviors anymore….I was going over the edge….I don't mean I was stressed…. it was an edge and I was going over it….I was way over it….I don't even know that I should be writing this for you to read….but there has to be honesty…. and there are other parents like me who have been pushed to where I was and they have to have someone who is bold and honest enough to say that this was serious….the room was spinning….my children were spinning in these bizarre "autistic circles"….I was loosing all sense of reality….*

When I first wrote this segment, in the original hand-written draft of this book, I was shaking so hard that I could barely read what I'd written. The dark intensity still hasn't left me. And even at this moment, as I try to decipher that hand-written draft, and type it here onto my computer, tears are streaming down my face. I'm looking down and there are tears on my keyboard. I'm close to hyper-ventilating because I remember this all so clearly: how desperate I was that afternoon, how hopeless I felt and yet how much potential and sparkle I saw in both Genevieve and Hayden, and how much I loved and adored them *and* Sydney and Kobe. They all deserved for us to be successful. *But I just couldn't stand it anymore and the room kept spinning....and they were spinning.....it was like I was just zoning out....*

But miracles do happen. And on *both* of those afternoons, our social worker, a gifted, big-hearted man named Barry Norlan, "just happened to call." He had no specific reason; he had just picked up the phone and called. *What would I have done had he not called? What would have happened?*

I don't know; but I *do* know that I was so far over the edge. But the point is: *he did call.* And somehow, in my terrible state, I did find the presence of mind to pick up the phone. The sound of Barry's warm, deep voice was enough that *I did pull myself together.* The room stopped spinning.

Miracles really do happen.

Barry was a miracle. He was and is an extraordinary gift to us, and who knows how many others. He is worthy of a chapter all of his own. Those two timely phone calls would have been enough to prove what a gift he was. But he also set us in a new direction and he changed the course of our lives.

It was Barry's heart and his intelligence and the faith that he saw in us as parents and as a family, that motivated him. He fell a little bit in love with us; I know he did. We *were* lovable, despite all of our complexities and he was *amazing!* He had a way of just sprinkling warm magic, especially over Sydney and Kobe. It was a time in their lives when they needed someone absolutely exceptional, to remind them how absolutely exceptional *they were.*

And Barry had a way of cutting through government red tape that was life altering for us. He trusted us as parents, and he empowered us and encouraged us to trust our instincts when it came to our family, and the path that *we felt* we needed to forge. He knew we would never have asked for more than we needed and he worked tirelessly and creatively on our behalf. He was absolutely instrumental in altering and obtaining new services for us. He understood us.

I still feel Barry; I know I always will. He and I still keep in touch from time to time, and the sound of his warm, deep and positive voice, is one of the most treasured sounds I've ever known. I do mean that. I know he's not exaggerating when he tells me that of all the families that he's ever worked with, ours touched him the most. We even spurred him on to advance professionally, so that he could have a bigger role in the lives of families like ours. *He was a gift!*

Chapter 38

More change needed to happen, drastically and soon. Nolan and I soul searched and analyzed every possible option. We scrutinized everything from Nolan quitting his job and finding something else, where he'd have fewer evening meetings and weekend work commitments, to the grim prospect of us selling our home and renting, so that we could use the equity to hire a full-time in-home worker to assist me.

But Nolan loved his job as a Parks Board manager and he'd worked so hard for years to climb to that status and level of job security. And we had to think of our futures as well. We knew we'd be living essentially under one salary for years to come, so selling our home meant that we'd probably never be in a position to own a home again. None of these were good options.

Then we scrutinized the complex behaviors of *all four* of our children. Theoretically, we should have been implementing the strategies devised by our psychologist and behavior consultant; but few were practiced regularly because it just wasn't possible with our family dynamics. There weren't even enough hands to do it. And clearly, respite services, that *"magic-wand strategy"* that's supposed to make everything right because your child is taken out for a few hours every week, *for us, usually did more damage than good.*

What was the answer? I focused my thoughts on the look on our behavior consultant John's face, the day he had happened to be in our home at 3:15, watching as Sydney and Kobe emerged on the scene, after their day at school. Prior to that moment, John had *heard* for months, my vivid descriptions about the bizarre and serious "personality and body change" that their daily home arrival always caused in Hayden, *but he'd never seen it.*

During those months, I knew John had had genuine concern, but he really wasn't *getting it.* It was one thing for him to *hear* about it; it was quite another for him to *see* it and be *amidst* it. I literally saw his jaw drop. It was unnerving to see his reaction; but it reinforced to me how serious the issues were and that it wasn't just my perception.

On that day, John and I looked back at each other, both understanding that his role was simply redundant under those circumstances. How do you design changes when there is no possible way of implementing them? How do you ever become more than a swirling mess of chaos and trauma?

The answer was: our family needed to be in *this* home, with me at the helm orchestrating and working from within. Nolan needed to be working in *his established capacity* to maintain that level of present and future security and structure. *And we needed in-home, full-time assistance and support. And we needed it now.* There was no time to lose.

Extraordinary times take extraordinary measures. *We were extraordinary and yet we were not going to survive.* It was time for us to swallow pride and stop trying to do this so much on our own. Both Nolan and I were independent, hard working and resourceful. We had *no desire* and took *no pleasure* in devising a plan that gave us no option but to plead absolute hardship to the Ministry that dealt with Children and Families. *But there was no other possible choice.*

Barry and John were our allies. They saw the damage but *more* than that, they saw our potential; and they saw our dedication and conviction. And Nolan, an incredible provider, was on a mission. He was determined to push through any and all levels of government red tape to get what we needed to survive.

There was no joy in this process. It was *not* an easy thing to do: to bare our souls and put our family's history on paper for strangers to read and discuss. It was humbling; it was painful and it was foreign to our independent natures.

But the four of us worked as a team. We were realistic and creative and we presented it in terms that made sense to the Ministry. In their eyes, how much of it came down simply to dollars and cents? If they "paid now" things would improve and ultimately, in the big picture, they would save money. In other words, down the road, Hayden and Genevieve's skill level and ability to function would increase, and Sydney and Kobe would not grow up, completely messed up teens and adults.

An incredible amount of energy went into carefully designing every aspect of our plan, *and* exactly how to present it. *I don't believe we would have had even a chance for success without Barry and John.* We submitted our proposal a couple of days before Christmas and Nolan and I barely dared to breathe over the holidays. *I'm not exaggerating. The prospect of help being around the corner glowed like a star atop a Christmas tree. But there were no assurances. This sort of proposal just wasn't done back then, nor is it today.*

What if it wasn't approved? How would we survive? How *could* Nolan or I dare to let our breath out that entire holiday season?

Though we desperately needed help, as parents we weren't without talent or insight. Nolan and I learned fast and we got good. We knew, for instance, that Genevieve and Hayden simply couldn't do line-ups, so rather than fight it, we worked *with* it. Out of that came one of our favorite Christmas memories *ever*, our trip to see Santa:

> As we had carefully planned, Nolan arrived before the mall even opened, chair and newspaper in hand. He waited outside Santa's castle for two hours; we weren't willing to risk there being a single person in line before us. It was an amazing feat, perfectly timed, for me and the kids to then arrive at the mall and journey down to the castle *the very moment* Santa arrived...
>
> We were an incredible sight of childish excitement and wonder, as the five of us dashed through the mall, all dressed in burgundy and white, with "visions of Santa Claus" running through our heads!
>
> And what a reward! All four kids were calm and happy. This was Christmas, as it was meant to be! And it didn't end there. This Santa, his real name Percy, *was* truly a magical man. He had a real beard and a sparkle in his eye, and a presence that would make the most non-believing adult wonder if he really was real. I whispered to Santa that

Hayden used sign language. Santa turned his head toward me and winked. Then to Hayden, he signed: "I love you!"

Our little boy melted and snuggled his head into Santa's velvety chest. Santa spoke his language!

It was magic! It was hard work, but it was pure, family magic! Those are the moments that have made us most of who we are today.

Chapter 39

That January did bring us a New Year, and new hope. Our proposal was accepted. We were approved for enough funding to hire an assistant for thirty-six hours a week. It wasn't just handed to us though. We had to revamp and lessen some of our behavioral therapy and respite support services, and we did need to follow through with our end of the bargain: we did something Nolan and I swore we would never do, we took out a second mortgage on our home. Our commitment was to physically re-structure our home, to give each child their own bedroom and personal safe place. That was critical.

As grateful and relieved as Nolan and I were, we did feel guilt at receiving as much as we did. We would have rather been able to do it on our own. But people like Barry and John and countless others in the years to come, were quick to point out that they saw children get put into foster care or into residential care all the time, some of them no where near as challenging as Hayden. He was a severe and complex case. *Look at what we were providing him.* How many families would have even tried to make it work, they way that we did? How many have that capacity?

You would honestly be shocked to know how many people in this field have expressed surprise and amazement that we did not give Hayden up. I still hear it today.

By the time Hayden was four years old, it was like that was what everyone seemed to think we should do: give him up. But those words just *were not in my* vocabulary. Hayden's impact *was* pervasive but he was our child! And it just always seemed to me that emotionally, each of us would have paid an even higher price if we'd given up on him. *We loved him and he was a part of us.*

If you bring this back to dollars and cents, the terms and the words that the Ministry talks and understands, this *was* a winning situation for them. The monthly amount that they allotted to us for assistance was *a fraction* of what it would have cost them, if we had given up, or had gotten so burnt out and damaged that we had no choice but to give Hayden up. If we had dropped him on their doorstep, it would have cost them thousands of dollars more, every single month, forever more.

> *And Hayden wouldn't have become who he is today. We could give him things that no one else could, no matter how much money was spent. We could give him us. We could give him a home, his home.*

And there's another reality that you have to remember: we're talking about an autistic child. Even living in a home amongst a family who loved him and did everything they could to adapt to him, Hayden ran the daily risk of sliding into withdrawal, into *Nowhereland.* What would have happened to him if we had given him up? He would have been heart broken and I suspect he would have withdrawn deeply, perhaps profoundly, *perhaps forever.*

> Those fears loomed over me. *But regardless, the possibility of total withdrawal or not, this was my child and I don't give up on my children. He needed to be with us.*

The search was on, funding was there and all we had left to do was to find the perfect person. There wasn't enough funding to pay her well, but well enough. In our minds, Sydney and Kobe needed the most support, so that I could focus on the other two. That meant choosing someone who was young and "hip" enough to be more like a big sister than a nanny or a therapist. We wanted some level of skill, but not so highly skilled that they'd be caught up in the rapture of "being a therapist." She would have to fit in with us because our vision meant that we still wanted our home to *feel* like a home.

After weeks of newspaper ads and interviews, we found her. Her name was

Delilah, a tiny but captivating young woman in her early twenties with a lovely presence, and brown eyes that could stop traffic.

Delilah was more than a breath of fresh air; she was sunshine and rainbows! We all fell in love with her, especially Sydney and Kobe. Not only was she our salvation, she brought little bits of the outside world into our home. She helped us to manage inside our world, and she helped to enable us to escape and venture outside of it. And, she brought refreshing "early twenties" perspectives, new music and cool dance moves!

She had a challenging role: it's one thing to care for children when the parents are away; it's another to do it when they're in the house with you, working alongside of you. And she was dealing with children with complex behaviors. But she did it well. The morning and after-school routines went better the days she was there. The dreaded after-school transition improved dramatically, because I could leave Hayden at home with her and focus on Genevieve. And five evenings each week, she stayed until bedtime, helping and giving me more time and energy to focus back on my kids.

Immediately we saw improvements in Kobe and even more noticeably in Sydney. That was exciting and a huge relief, because it really had felt like we had literally lost a *two year chunk* of Sydney's life. Many times I had written in my journal: "Who *is* this? This is not our Sydney!" But with our new home environment, gradually the old Sydney was coming back: the sweet, mature, calm and loving Sydney.

It's an odd thing to describe about Sydney and her re-emergence. It was like she had taken a big step forward in time, almost like she had been away on a long trip and came back, suddenly a little older and more mature. But she was back, lively, talkative and animated. Counseling had helped; but what she had needed the most, were changes from *within* our home. And that was what Delilah helped to bring!

Sydney became a natural at setting up behavioral programs, and she was *only* nine. One of her strategies was a sleeping program for Genevieve. In truth, she was motivated out of desperation because when Nolan had finished building the addition, Genevieve had a tough time adjusting to no longer sharing a room with Sydney. Each night Genevieve followed Sydney down to her new room. When Sydney exclaimed: "She can't sleep here forever!" Genevieve responded innocently with: "Sure I can!"

Of her own design, Sydney devised a clever chart and program that worked! She did another program for Hayden, skillfully teaching him to tap our shoulder when he wanted something or needed attention, instead of screaming for it. It was one of those "Duh, why didn't we think of that?" moments, but the rest of us were too exasperated with him to "see the obvious." Somehow, coming from her, her strategy worked, not always of course, but it had a huge impact.

What glorious examples of "Ministry money" being well spent!

Kobe, our intense athlete and hip hop dancer, instantaneously connected with Delilah. The stress level seen in his behaviors and in his body was immediately altered. With our Delilah's assistance, we were all more relaxed and there were *most definitely* more glimmers of wonderfulness, and of harmony! It was amazing what an extra set of hands and another lap to sit in, could do. And her eyes and her spirit...she was beautiful!

Chapter 40

I wish I could say that Delilah's role and presence had a magical, Mary Poppins' "snap-of-the-fingers" effect...but if you take a quick peek at the number of chapters still to come, you'll probably guess that it *was* a big step in the right direction; but it didn't mean an overnight success. In fact, it brought on some new challenges. *This is us, after all!*

Hayden was *not* accepting of Delilah's presence in our home. It wasn't surprising really, given his history. He was a little calmer; he tuned out a little less and he even spent new bits of time on the couch, looking at books, instead of just sitting with me and his bottle. Maybe because *we were more relaxed*, he was a little more relaxed and receptive.

Delilah, like the rest of the world, was quite mesmerized by Genevieve and they cautiously carved out a casual relationship together. With Hayden, it was different. On one hand, he invited Delilah's attention. He loved, for instance, to re-enact home events and she was a new member of his captive audience. He loved her delight in seeing him act out the time he sat playfully on Genevieve's face and knocked out her very-loose tooth. He acted it out over and over with Sydney playing the role of Genevieve.

But though Hayden had his moments with Delilah, often her presence caused him more anxiety and aggression than if she was not there at all. And I think she was afraid of him. We could hardly blame her; most of the time he was so horrid to her. Maybe he picked up on her fear; maybe it worked against her. He knew easy targets when he saw them and she was so tiny and sweet.

Hayden *was* very overwhelmed and threatened by Delilah's presence in his home. He wasn't able to understand that her being there actually allowed me to focus *more* on him. He saw her as an enemy. In his world, a third "big sister" was more of a threat than someone to welcome in.

More double-edged swords....with Delilah's help, we could do more activities that were fun, creative and social; we could venture out more. *But it was bitterly frustrating to me to see that often her presence could dramatically lighten my load, yet often be the catalyst for behaviors that were worse than if she wasn't there at all.*

And our family was doing better, but I was still so burnt out. And the emotional scars were deep, even just from the early years of Genevieve, long before we'd ever received any kind of "respite". And the constant knowledge that I couldn't manage my own children on my own, haunted and tormented me. It gripped my heart.

Maybe little traumas like "The Sand Timer" incident were meant to remind me that it wasn't that I was inadequate. It was that we really had a lot to deal with:

> *The Sand Timer.*.... another one of those turning point evenings, one of those "contradictions" that Sydney, Kobe and I had come to know so well. How do I put that in words? *It was like trauma and amazing all at the same time.*...it was just a little incident but at the same time, not little at all....it was a Friday evening, one of the magical ones where it was just me and all four kids, me on my own, no care giver/foreigner....just me and my kids. It was one of those beautiful, unplanned moments in the living room that we loved....playing games, laughing, it all working.... beautiful....until Hayden picked up a small glass sand timer from a game we were playing.
>
> Instantly, he popped it into his mouth, too quick for any of us to intersect....as he chewed on the glass and sand, we all watched in horror, imagining what those tiny bits of glass were going to do to his mouth and his throat, his intestines......
>
> Miraculously, there were only tiny cuts in his mouth; but in those moments when we all gasped, and stood frozen and powerless to

respond, it was a painful reminder to each of us that even in the safety of our home, I / Mom couldn't manage on my own.

Hayden needed almost constant supervision. He did things in the blink of an eye that wouldn't have even occurred to other four year olds, even toddlers. And it went deeper than impulse. What prompted him to put the sand timer in his mouth in the first place? This is important: *it was because it was a joyful, fun and social moment amongst the five of us, and he and his body couldn't handle it. His natural response was to lash out and sabotage the moment.*

At that instant realization, the reality that this was a safety issue *as well as* a complex behavioral issue, I just lost it. I fell into a mass of tears, right there on the living room floor. Then Sydney broke down, then Kobe; then even Genevieve. *It was a poignant, turning point, a sad realization, a graphic confirmation.*

Then magically, Genevieve piped up, with the voice of an angel saying: "We need our hankies!" Kobe burst into laughter, remarking lovingly and perceptively: "How does she do that?" Then we all laughed. We laughed until we cried; but those *weren't* sad tears.

Kobe was right: Genevieve always came to her family's rescue. *She had so much difficulty understanding the world and the people who lived in it; and yet, there she was, on her constant mission to keep us safe and happy.* She was extraordinaire! It was her sparkle, her innocence and her oddly-mature wisdom.

Really, it *was* funny....this room a flurry with kids and a mom crying. So what do you do with tears? You get your hankies and then the tears go away. She was brilliant.

We *were* such an amazing, remarkable, living and breathing contradiction.... *traumas yet amazing*....that was us. We survived that little trauma; we learned from it. There would be more....but no matter what, we would still keep moving forward.

We just had to keep holding onto each other and loving each other. We couldn't manage on our own. That was painful. That was a reality displayed by the sand timer. But we had our castle and we could bring people in. We were different from the rest of the world around us; but if we stuck together, magic *could* happen.

Chapter 41

*L*ife continued, pretty much *me and Hayden against the world*. He followed me like a shadow and navigated through each day with one hand, while the other clung to me. There remained the omnipresent and dangerous fine line between over stimulating and under stimulating him.

Power Ranger figurines marked an exciting turning point because Hayden would spend hours sitting on the couch, flicking the switch that made their heads alternate between normal head and ranger head. He was mesmerized and *he was occupied!* It got even better. Gradually he learned to actually play with them. Though he couldn't maintain that level of sustained play without our constant input, it helped! *It was a reprieve and it meant we were moving forward.*

Playing Power Rangers with Hayden was exhausting, but important. And it was something that Nolan knew more about because *he* was the one who stepped in and dedicated the most Power Ranger time. I don't know how he did it. I was done: I didn't have much super-hero play left in me.

Hayden and Genevieve's obsessions were driving us to the point of distraction! It was tough enough during the day, but when it continued into the night, exhaustion complicated the issue even more. One evening near bedtime, for example, Hayden had it in his head that he wanted to watch his new *Batman* video. For some reason, I dug my heels in and said it was time to look at books instead. He screamed, and after awhile, he fell asleep.

Three hours later, he woke up and resumed the screaming, right where he left off. By then, it was the middle of the night and he was *hysterical.* There was no choice but for me and him to watch *Batman* right then, at 3:00am. If we

104

hadn't, there would have been no possibility for peace in our home for three days. Our history made that clear.

You have to understand: it wasn't that we didn't try behavioral strategizing. We did; but nothing seemed to work, at least not with Hayden. His level of anxiety and his lack of reasoning ability diffused even the best laid plans and strategies. Often we agonized about "giving in to him," but it was like his mind and body were always going so berserk that logic, explanations, strategies and consequences often couldn't touch where he was.

> With both Hayden and Genevieve and their "obsessions," it's important to distinguish that it wasn't just that they wanted to accumulate objects or toys. It was *why* they needed to accumulate them. Like everything with autism, it all revolved around feeling safe, and feeling some level of control. *That is night and day different from manipulating or being spoiled.* You have to remember, to these children, our world is an overwhelming place on levels that you and I can barely begin to understand, much less relate to.

> I believe, at least as far as my two autistic children go, that they instinctively learned from a very young age, that focusing on an item, (what *we* would call obsessing), *was actually a very brilliant coping mechanism. It was an economical navigating tool.* To be honest, I think it is a sign of a brilliant, complex mind, *not* a manipulating mind. One of my favorite parts of *Effervescence* is the description and the interpretation of how absolutely brilliantly Genevieve used these tools, and the absolute proof that came in her later teens, *that these were in fact, part of a masterful plan. It was a plan devised intuitively by her, certainly by the very young age of four.*

The trouble with "obsessions" is that they can get out of hand. They have to be handled strategically and *as* a strategy. *That can be a fine line.* But many, many times we were able to handle the stress of "socialness" and actually have some level of normality, when Genevieve and Hayden had an obsessive "fix' to get them through. We're talking simple things like Archie comics or toy figurines; that are pretty economical and age appropriate.

But there were often loopholes, like what if we couldn't find the item we'd planned on; then the fall-out and the trauma would be even greater.

105

Chapter 42

*S*imultaneously, we lost the support of both our psychologist Davina and our social worker, Barry. That was a profound loss. With heavy hearts and no effort to disguise the loss that *they* felt, they both moved on in different capacities. *That* was tough and it brought to light a new complexity in our complex lives: *needing* to open up and accept the help of others, and then having our hearts break when they'd eventually have to leave.

But even for "complex us," new doors always opened!

And through this door stepped Kiera Barton. Whether it was a coincidence or an act of God, I don't know; but it was a beautiful story how we found her and who she was. But *we did* find her and I can't think of a *single* person (outside of the five of us) who has ultimately played a more important role in the life of Hayden Brenneman.

Kiera's role was to be a Sunday respite worker. I remember the moment she sat down at the dining room table for an interview. I knew something really important had just happened. I could feel it. The match couldn't have been more perfect for Hayden, or for us. It wasn't just that she had a good level of training (and she definitely did have training in special ed); it was as much her personality, her resilience and her skill level. And, as fate would have it, she had another bonus, a big one: her parents lived across the street and two doors down. That was instrumental.

What a godsend....the perfect person *and* the perfect "logistics." The plan was low-key and *realistic*. Hayden could literally stand inside Kiera's family home and see and feel the comfort of his own home, just doors away. It was magic and inch by treacherous inch, Hayden branched out. And Kiera's family, became *his* family. *Can you imagine what that was like for us, to see this sparkling twenty-four year old woman, and all of her family, and her friends, fall in love with our little boy?* And that was despite his aggression and his odd behaviors and bizarre complexities!

Can you even begin to imagine the pride and the relief that Sydney and Kobe must have felt?

Don't get me wrong, this didn't come easy. It *was* a treacherous path. And it was literally inch by treacherous inch! There were many ups and downs, and many times when Hayden lashed out for whatever reason, and refused to make the journey across the street. But Kiera persevered. Many times she and her identical twin sister could be seen, dragging him over to the Barton house, Kiera gripping his hands and Shanna gripping his ankles, like a wild, captured beast. They were quite a sight!

But once Hayden got there, within minutes, he found his spot and his composure, usually centre stage, showered with love and lots of attention. *He evolved and he grew.* Kiera helped change the direction of his life. Her whole family did. Sometimes he could even handle sleepovers. He'd have to *overdose* on my skin and my hair for days afterwards, but he grew; he evolved.

One of my favorite photos ever, is the one of tiny Hayden, snuggled up on the couch with "Pa" (Kiera's dad), reading the newspaper together. This big, burly Australian with a booming voice that could be heard a block away, has been known to shed many a tear, as he watched our Hayden, *his* Hayden, and the countless milestones along the way!

⸺⧽⧼⸻

Kiera was an answer to our prayers. And to me, she was more than family; she was my partner. She worked to know Hayden on a level that was just a few notches below me. She really "got him." And she gave invaluable support over the complex years, when we struggled to unravel the mystery of Hayden.

I don't think Kiera could articulate Hayden the way that I could, but she saw and felt Hayden's many sides, as we did at home. That was critical. *I don't know how we would have ever survived the years that were to follow, when we would have to challenge the school system and support staff, to open their eyes to Hayden's uniqueness and complexity, without her input.* She gave us credibility. And she worked in the school district, so she wasn't viewed as I sometimes was, as a ranting and raving mom!

Kiera got Hayden; she got us. She even got Genevieve. Try as Genevieve did, to keep herself separate from anything having to do with Hayden, even she couldn't help but be drawn to Kiera. Slowly and cautiously, Genevieve's walls lowered and she would often hover around Kiera at a distance.... and ever closer....the connection grew:

> One of the most amazing images of Genevieve in my memory, is a
> Sunday afternoon, when Kiera and I sat on the front steps, chatting

107

about her afternoon with Hayden. I noticed Genevieve had stealthily *slid* herself in between Kiera and me.

Genevieve's leg was extended, her foot nuzzling Kiera's lap, as she listened in on our conversation. Uncharacteristically, she added some of her own comments. I was secretly *amazed.*....I wanted to shout it out to the world. *This was a big deal!* Forcing myself to remain nonchalant, I wondered if Kiera had any idea how monumental that "simple" gesture with Genevieve's leg and foot was. *Genevieve was letting Kiera in on a level that was unexpected and profound.* This *was* a big deal, on a whole bunch of levels!

A couple of weeks later, when Kiera and I finally had a private moment to speak, she described how that afternoon she had been almost an hour late for an engagement, but she'd been so moved and so thrilled by Genevieve's actions with her foot and her leg, and her bits of conversation, that she couldn't make herself move. *She did get it.* She knew that Genevieve was letting her in on a level that was monumental, and almost unheard of, beyond her immediate family. *Kiera got us! And she felt completely at home with us!*

It just got even better! Kiera's husband Garrett was equally pulled in, to Hayden, to Genevieve and to all of us. Sydney and Kobe instantaneously connected with both of them. For Kobe, year after year, the ultimate goal was to beat Garrett at basketball. Now towering over Garrett at six foot five, Kobe has long since left him gasping for air and for height.

With Kiera and Garrett, we could throw open our castle doors. We could just be us. There were so few people who were allowed in on that level, few people that we could trust. Kiera and Garrett were always welcomed in because we knew that they loved us and respected us. They were drawn to us and they were fascinated by us, despite all of the chaos and madness that they saw and that they were often strewn amongst.

Our castle was a richer place because they were at peace with us, and when they entered, they were a part of us. And they kept us a little more connected to the outside world, through them and their amazing, far-reaching extended family. But do you know, as many sentences as I could write in her praise, Kiera would be the first to turn this all around and say that as much as she gave to Hayden, he, and we, gave her more. Even her twin sister, Shanna, the one who would be on the other end of Hayden's writhing body, being dragged across the street, was once asked to write a paper about the person who'd made the most impact on her life....she wrote about Hayden.

For eight years, until Hayden was twelve, Kiera stayed with us, every Sunday at minimum, dedicated to him. What a gift! Only the three arrivals of her little girls were enough to break her remarkable commitment. But bonds like that don't ever break. The six of us and the five of them, are entwined forever more. It's just spread out a little more differently now.

Chapter 43

he good, the bad and the definitely ugly....so if you lose one psychologist, you just find another, right? Not quite; they are *not* all created equal, especially back then when few had specific training in autism. Davina was a dream: insightful, and a joy to work with. Then there was Rachel.

After spending hours and hours, month after month "counseling" Sydney, Kobe and myself to address the stress, the strain and our guilt that we weren't doing enough, Rachel flatly revealed to us the problem: *it was that our expectations as a family, were unrealistic.* Granted, she was insightful enough to see that Kobe was struggling to accept the reality that the brother he'd prayed for, was never going to be the buddy and partner in crime that he'd anticipated. She could see that essentially Kobe was mourning the loss. And she could see that he was intent on building whatever kind of meaningful relationship he could with this love of his life, his little brother. She was insightful to see that it was the single most important goal in Kobe's life....

....Then Rachel told Kobe, who was then only eight, that there was *no reason for him to be consumed with grief and loss because: "he and Hayden were three and a half years apart and so they wouldn't have had a close relationship anyway!"* Can you imagine?

You should have heard the comments Rachel made to me, in response to my never-ending quest to hold my family together. Apparently I was very unrealistic as well. It didn't surprise me to learn that this woman was a single mom with only one child. She really didn't understand how it works with large families, in her life or in her training. Though I hope to never cross paths with this non-insightful "professional" again, I would give almost anything for her to see Kobe and Hayden, and the amazing bond that they have today.

The day this woman made her comments to Kobe, was the day we left. She did all of us more harm than good. I did my best to undo her damage, but the reality loomed that without professional support, I was left in the position of acting like a twenty-four-hour psychologist for all of my kids, and myself. *I was insightful and knew our situation better than anyone; but I didn't have training. All I could do was watch and document and scrutinize and ponder and document more.*

But was I doing it right? Were my instincts and insights right? The demands on me increased and I pretty much resigned myself to have faith in my abilities and to have faith in God, that He would direct me if I fell too far astray.

But we needed somebody, and somebody who knew what they were doing! And even if we did find someone really skilled, the thought of how much effort it would take to bring them up to speed in our world, was overwhelming. It would have taken more time than I was even able to give. It *was* an overwhelming predicament.

Amongst the murk, *as always*, lay glimmers of delight! One night at bedtime, I took a chance at getting emotionally close to Genevieve by telling her that she was very precious; then I asked her what she thought was precious. Uncharacteristically, she answered the question. This was her answer, in her sweet, angel voice: *"Loving you!"*

Chapter 44

Verbal communication was definitely lacking in our home. Genevieve went through a phase where she literally made signs to show her emotions, like "Don't bother me!" Hayden, of course, communicated through sign language; but very slowly, words were emerging. One of his first sets of words was: "I wuv you Mom." I'd waited a long time to hear that!

In our kingdom, where we lived, *everything* was a milestone. Simple, everyday accomplishments that most parents would take for granted, *were* milestones, and often turning points. That's another one of the lovely things, but also one of the toughest. It's because you can't really share or celebrate those moments with outsiders, the way that you can with the "traditional milestones" that kids make. It's because most people really don't know how to respond. Look at this magical moment:

> One morning, before Hayden had speech or even sign language, I was absolutely "over the moon" thrilled because he had been able to *understand* that his throat was sore *and* he was able to indicate that to me! Later that morning, still wrapped in the glow of that remarkable milestone, I listened while a close friend mentioned something cute that her little son had accomplished that morning. I couldn't resist telling her of Hayden's accomplishment.

> But the look on her face destroyed the moment. She was a wonderful, compassionate woman and a very close friend, but there was that horrid, awkward moment when she was at a loss for words. Even though she was "into kids" and had a houseful of young kids, as I did, I could see that *her world and mine* were barely even connected. *There was no joy in sharing that moment with her. It only made me feel odd and, kind of pathetic.*

I learned that the "little milestones" that were to us incredible turning points, were better kept to ourselves or shared with trained professionals, who would recognize the wonder and see *only* the pure joy and excitement. *I know that sounds harsh*, but when you live this kind of life, these are big issues. You need to fill yourself up with the good and the joyous, and get your fix *every* chance that you get. You can't risk anyone not feeling the joy or understanding the significance. *You can't risk it. You need it because it might be awhile until the next one; and you will deal with a hell of a lot of abuse and stress in getting to the next one!*

And these moments are just so pure and joyful. They deserve their perfect moment in time!

My experience is that most people *genuinely* do want to be supportive and be a part of you and your family's emergence; but most people need help in knowing *how to do it*. It isn't so much that they're inadequate; it's that these *are* extraordinary conditions and few people have any kind of reference point to draw from.

Recently, in promoting *Effervescence*, I was invited to speak on a popular radio talk show in Montreal. One of the listeners had a fabulous question, and I was so grateful to have the opportunity to answer. He noted that his nephew had recently been diagnosed with autism, and he wanted to know what *he* could do to offer support to his sister. From my perspective, the answer to him and to anyone is:

> Let yourself be fascinated by the child, and show that child, and his/her family, in small but *genuine* ways, that you find that child *lovable*.

> Let yourself be *amazed and impressed* at the amount of work that *every single day* is for that child and for the family, but know that there is *always* growth.

> And last, *never, ever* make it sound like you "know exactly what they're feeling or what they're dealing with"....because you don't. *Instead, just marvel and be proud of them.*

Here's a little example why of I've written and said that:

> Most of the time, Nolan and I would try to take our challenges in our stride; but every once in awhile, I thought maybe I should give outsiders a glimpse, a little snapshot of what life was like "in the trenches". It wasn't because I was complaining, but more because I knew people were interested and caring and *wanted* to be supportive. One day I let a friend in:

> > We happened to get on the topic of diapers, specifically poopy diapers. I let my guard down and revealed my calculation that having had four kids, one who was in diapers until the age of four, and one until almost

112

the age of ten (that's how long it went for Hayden), I estimated that I had dealt with a staggering *seven thousand poopy diapers!* I said it light-heartedly, mostly in sheer amazement; but it *was* definitely a reality check!

Unfortunately, this woman was quick to laugh it off, saying: *"Oh, me too!"*

The reality was: *she hadn't. No mom* with typical kids has. And not only that, there is a huge difference between changing diapers for an infant or a toddler, than changing diapers for a ten year old. (And if you're at *that* point, you're in fear that you'll still be doing it when you're eighty). The result was that rather than feeling supported, I felt angry, frustrated and *weird.* I thought: "Why do I even bother? I should just keep it to myself!"

Again, this was a lovely woman who wouldn't have hurt my feelings for the world; but her response was so typical. Why do outsiders think the best thing to do is to *downplay* our issues and challenges? Why do they think they need to make them seem like they're no big deal, or that they're *not* bizarre or serious, or out of the ordinary? The reality is: *they are all of those things!*

But it's no secret to us or to anyone else. We know it and have basically come to terms with it…it's who we are. It's not like we hadn't noticed!

What would have been more supportive and helpful in this case, would have been for this woman to have simply said something like: "Oh Simone…that can't be easy? But you guys have come so far; one of these days that's got to come too!" Then I would have felt validated. I wouldn't have felt like I was complaining, and I would have agreed and said: "Yeah, I know; we just have to keep working on this!"

Sometimes, especially back then, it would just be such a gift, to be able to be open and laugh with friends, and shake our heads at the oddity of it all, and say: "Ah what the hell!" rather than having them pretend it wasn't all just so odd!

Chapter 45

*B*ack to Delilah, our assistant. If we brought her along, sometimes we could venture out as a complete family, knowing that she could remove Hayden and take him home when he'd had enough. Our bold decision for a family afternoon at a major amusement park became a glorious work of art: maneuvering Hayden, and then Delilah *removing* Hayden when he needed to leave. Nolan and I watched as Sydney, Kobe and Genevieve held hands, literally skipping through the fair grounds, free from the stress and shadow of Hayden. They were absolute angels! The next morning, they were so renewed and happy to see him, that they made him breakfast.

We were then inspired to put the horrors of the previous summer's camping trip behind us and plan another; this time with *all* angles covered. We brought both cars, to keep Genevieve and Hayden separate, and to use in case Hayden and I needed to come back early; *and* we brought Delilah.

But, driving with Hayden had worsened since last year's vacation. Just two days before leaving for our trip, he had, in a fit of anger and frustration, for the first time *grabbed the steering wheel* while I was driving. It didn't set the tone for a happy holiday drive to peace, serenity and wilderness! How we survived the treacherous, five hour drive was another work of art. It was largely a masterpiece created by Kobe's antics and him graciously offering up his head of hair, for Hayden to fondle and then pull out, one strand at a time, towards the end of the drive.

We'd brought Delilah with shining hopes for success; but Hayden would have nothing to do with her. He lashed out at her even more than he did at home. *If she wasn't afraid of him before that trip, she had every reason to be by the time we got home.* At one point, he purposely burned the palm of her hand with a sizzling marshmallow roaster.

At first, the passive campsite setting had a calming effect on Hayden; but he was quickly overloaded. I remember him shaking the tent pole relentlessly. Despite our attempts to explain to him why he should stop, *he just couldn't.* It was how he and his body responded to the outdoor environment and from being away from home.

Hayden needed to be home; there was no denying that. On one hand, it was so hard to leave Nolan and the others there; but on the other, it was such an incredible relief to know that once he and I got home, it would be just the magic of the two of us, and life would be calm and reasonable.

Delilah stayed with us for nine months and then left when stressful issues in her personal life, combined with the stress in our home, were just too much. She didn't want to leave; she loved us, especially Sydney and Kobe. And we loved and adored her; we've never stopped loving her. I think I pretty much had to fire her, so that she could take that step; she *needed* to leave.

Beautiful, lovely, fun Delilah! She brought so much of herself into our lives and our castle; she brought so much "normal" yet in a way that still let us celebrate being *"unique us,"* not *"disabled us."* In Sydney and especially in Kobe's eyes, she was also our savior. It broke all of our hearts to watch her leave, especially his. He had many tearful nights, and many days too distraught to go to school. She was in his heart and he worried how or even if, we would survive without her. We all did.

Chapter 46

Delilah's departure meant a new search. There were more newspaper ads and more interviews to throw into the daily juggle and chaos. And it would mean letting another person into our lives and into our hearts. More than that, it would mean another person who would jeopardize Hayden's stability, or at least what little stability he had. And it took months.

During those months, the pressure of meeting each day without assistance mounded seriously; yet it was glorious to be "just us" again. It was so welcomed, especially by me. The stress was intense but my self esteem rose. It was a bizarre juxtaposition, really. More bizarreness to our lives!

Bizarre, intense....but we were getting "cozy" with at least being "just us," though we were paying the price and sliding downward. Maybe this little trauma *needed* to happen, to get our feet back on the ground and continue our search:

> One wonderful family evening, we were watching slides (photographs) on our projector. It was just us, in our castle, where we did our best, where each of us was most at peace. It was *perfect* until out of nowhere, Hayden bit Genevieve's arm, very hard.
>
> I could see it coming but he was so quick and so intense, that I just couldn't react in time. Poor Genevieve; she was so undeserving. It hit us all hard. As sweet as Hayden could be, this was a poignant reminder that no one could relax when he was in the house.
>
> *It was no wonder that Genevieve retreated so often to her bedroom haven, with her drawings and her safe world. It wasn't just because she was autistic and struggled with "socialness." She needed to escape Hayden.*

We did find another assistant. We had her for about six months. Then there was another, another and another, over the course of the next few years. It was a good plan. Each of them brought new personalities into our home that we benefited from. In a perfect world, an in-home assistant would have been the perfect solution. *But ours was definitely not a perfect world.*

Each assistant, to some degree, fell in love with us. And each had their own issues, and living amongst us wasn't easy either. And me being me, I was a magnet for each of them to feel connected to. Inevitably, I not only had my four kids and all of their issues to deal with, but then each of our in-home workers naturally gravitated towards me and their issues and life stories became a part of mine. I loved and respected each of them and that just seemed the natural consequence.

And when each one would leave, for whatever reason, it ripped our hearts open.

> If you are a therapist or a working in this field, or even if you are a friend or family member wanting to help and support a complex family like ours, *I've included this segment, to remind you that there are no*

easy answers. For families like us, you just keep chipping away. The best well-laid plan *will* help bring success and growth; but never walk away thinking: "Whoa, we got that one figured out." *It's all evolution....steps forward, steps back....always complex....but always there is hope....you just keep chipping away....and you do whatever it takes to focus on the positive.* But there are, *definitely*, no easy quick fixes or easy answers!

Chapter 47

"*I* love Mickey Mouse. He's not a mouse, he's a Mickey Mouse and she has a wife. Her name is Minnie. But they're not married yet!" These sentences were choppy and tough to understand, but finally Hayden was talking! He began kindergarten at our cherished Amity Elementary using sign language and a few words; but within months, he was speaking. He moved literally from almost no speech, to phrases and sentences. *And with his words, came more bits of his adorable personality and new glimmers of the little boy we'd waited so long to discover!*

The Amity staff embraced Hayden and all of his challenges, as they had with Genevieve. The transition from his tiny preschool to elementary had its challenges, but it was approachable. He needed lots of support and we had lots of tricks. By now, we *had* learned a lot! At circle time, we gave him a furry rabbit's foot on a Velcro bracelet to stroke; otherwise, he'd compulsively reach for the long hair of any of the little girls around him. They were *not* okay with that, no matter how cute he was!

Hayden had a special little chair that sat right on the ground and wrapped partway around him, to guard him against the edgy feeling of close proximity to the other children. Picture symbols helped to prepare him for class activities and transitions.

But, like Genevieve, these "tricks and tools" were a drop in the bucket.

School assemblies were ridiculously overwhelming, and like his sister, Hayden would respond by spinning in circles, tuning out the chaos. The afternoon transition was tough, even after only two hours of kindergarten. In grade one, he was initially very proud when he worked his way up to a full

9:00 to 3:00 day; but it was too much for him. *The aftershock was brutal.* The same pattern followed that we'd seen with Genevieve and her teachers: it was mystifying to them that often Hayden could *appear* to manage at school. Why then would he fall apart after school, and even worse, once he got home? They didn't understand it or recognize it.

The days when I had our assistant with me, sadly, were even worse than the days when I picked Hayden up on my own. He was so stressed from holding himself together all day, that one look at her and he would fragment into a million pieces.

Here's an image for you to hold in your mind (but please do know that there will be better images to come):

> At 3:00 on most school days, I'd find myself juggling all four of my kids, set amidst the halls and the after-school chaos of hundreds of kids heading for home. Both Genevieve and Hayden would be completely unglued, after holding themselves together all day at school. They would literally be at each other's throats, scratching and kicking, as swarms of children shuffled around them.

> If I directed the four of them to an empty multi-purpose room while the school emptied, the transition was a little more subtle, but not much.

> We'd hang out in the room for twenty, sometimes forty minutes, playing and trying to catch up, at least with Sydney and Kobe, on the day's events. Then there was the walk home. What should have taken seven minutes, took *forever*. Often Hayden would have several meltdowns along the way. Physically I'm not that big of a person and carrying him, with his six year old body twisting and contorting, wasn't easy.

> Sometimes, we took the car, but it wasn't that much better; and with me behind the steering wheel, I wasn't able to *protect* the other three from the wrath of Hayden.

One day we brought the video camera. It was quite the footage. We added to it, "typical moments" at home and in the car, showing life with Hayden. Wow! I look at it now and think: "How *did* we do it?" I'm glad we took all of that footage. A video is not as graphic as actually being there; but it helped open doors because it helped people to understand what we called "the mystery of Hayden."

This video was pretty clear documentation and proof of what happened to Hayden when he was pushed too far, and in the wrong direction. And it showed the prices his family paid.

Chapter 48

hemistry, bio-chemistry, drugs, Ritalin....what parent doesn't agonize before filling their child's body with chemicals? We did. Finally, there was just no choice. Something had to change, if only Hayden's ridiculously short attention span. Honestly, I've never seen anything like it.

Nolan and I didn't even think Ritalin would work. We didn't expect it to make any difference at all. It just seemed too easy. But the thing about Ritalin is, it enters the body quickly. It's not one of those drugs that needs to accumulate for weeks and weeks. You find out pretty fast if it's going to make a difference! By chance, the day we were scheduled to give Hayden his first dose, was the morning we'd planned to set up our Christmas tree...what *should* have been a trademark family *disaster*, riddled with sensory and social bombardment (and hence a time to forget), was a *lovely adventure*, a memory *to keep* forever!

Nolan and I were dumbfounded. We thought: "No way. It has to be a coincidence, just an exceptionally good morning." But it continued on. Later the same day, we visited friends and even that went better than it *should* have!

Why had we waited so long? Ritalin certainly didn't solve everything; but it helped! This complex boy's body needed chemical alterations. There was no denying that. And this family needed those alterations! At least it took some of the edge off and made room for more growth, as he faced the daily challenge of grade one.

Despite the tracking and documenting, even despite medication, Hayden remained a mystery. Often, he still pinched, bit, scratched, threw toys and objects at people and used them as weapons. Frequently, he was relentless, sometimes full of malice and intent. *It didn't happen all of the time, but it happened too much of the time.*

Sign language, gesturing and his improved speech all helped Hayden to get his point across, *but this wasn't just about communication.* The aggression issue seemed insurmountable, largely because so often, there just seemed no rhyme or reason, *even for someone diagnosed with autism.* A beautiful moment could inexplicably transform into a bizarre trauma. I'll never forget taking Hayden to the recreation centre swimming pool:

> It was a weekday and the pool was almost empty. The water was warm and smooth and Hayden was on my back, his arms wrapped around my neck. It was a lovely, calm time and I was so joyously grateful to have that time with him. I was happy that I'd had the idea to take him there that day. It was just me and my little boy and the smooth, warm water, his warm little body against mine....
>
> And then out of nowhere, he bit my shoulder, hard. *It really hurt.* I just didn't see it or feel it coming; there seemed no reason....

Hayden's siblings had dealt with his aggression for so long, that they were edgy and nervous in their own home. They constantly braced themselves against further attacks. *They were emotionally and physically abused.* Sometimes Sydney and Kobe lashed out at him, adding fuel to the fire. Some-times they pounced on him before he could pounce on them. But they loved him so deeply that they continually sought his attention and his affection. It was a testament to Hayden. There was something so sweet, so personable and captivating that no matter what, he kept us coming back for more. Kobe in particular, was often inseparable from Hayden, snuggling up with him to watch TV or in the bathtub to play and connive. I have no idea how I would have survived without Kobe to entertain Hayden almost everyday after school.

Hayden was an important part of our lives but the reality was sinking in that his autism, his ADHD and his mental disability and behaviors, were not something he was going to snap out of or outgrow. Not even medication could do that. And most behavior modification programs were not working.

Over-stimulating and the fine line between that, which was under-stimulating *and* the potential of sliding into *Nowhereland*, continued; that was life. And as always, there was wonderfulness contrasted by horrid. This was one of the worst:

> Hayden was seven and had his heart set on a book from the grocery store we were in. It was more expensive than I was prepared to spend; but the cost I would end up paying was more than money.

> He *shrieked* incredibly loudly, for what seemed like forever. Finally, there in the middle of the dairy section, I couldn't stand the shrieking any longer, nor could the other shoppers. He was too big to carry and the shopping cart was loaded with groceries, so there, right in the open dairy section, I lowered him and me onto the floor and held him as tightly as I possibly could.

> I talked to Hayden softly, though he was shrieking so loudly I doubt that he could have heard me. Finally, he fell asleep. It was one of the worst experiences of my life and it was indescribably exhausting. All I wanted to do was collapse and cry.

> This was a store that we went to often; so did many of our friends and acquaintances. It was exasperating and embarrassing. *But the bottom line was: how could I not have compassion for Hayden? It wasn't his fault.* He hadn't done it because he was a selfish person who wanted to make life horrid for me or anyone else. *The book that he'd wanted to buy wasn't the issue. It was the reason why he needed to cling to the book* that was the issue. It was because of *overload and aftershock.*

> Hayden was struggling....struggling to be in that grocery store, struggling to handle the people and the sensory overload within the store....he was struggling to deal with the stressful issues in his life like having to hold himself together at school each day....

> Hayden was struggling because of *our* unrealistic expectations on him.

Some days he could handle it, it being *Life*; most days he could not.

Looking back at that day in the grocery store, I can't even remember: did I abandon my shopping cart filled with groceries and go home? Did I wake Hayden up and then magically find that everything was okay? Did I carry that large, sleeping child in my arms, while I checked out and paid for my groceries? *I have absolutely no recollection, like it is erased from my mind, a trauma.* It haunts me because I remember so much of our history in detail. But this one is blocked.

But I do remember being absolutely drained. There was just nothing left. And I do remember vowing that I *would not and could not*, ever take him into any store unless I was prepared to buy him exactly what he wanted, if he needed me to. That wouldn't be smart behavioral strategizing, but I couldn't put myself in that position again.

It was a frightening turning point, because Hayden was clearly no longer a toddler that I could toss into a stroller or shopping cart, or carry if he was distraught. At least in this trauma, in this store, the bright side was that he had "only" been shrieking; at least he hadn't been biting or pinching, kicking or clawing at me. *But this was enough.* I couldn't ever allow him to shriek in public like that again.

Clearly, behavior strategies were not enough. Few worked for him. What he needed were changes in his life. He needed us to be more respectful of what it was that he could handle. That's what his shrieking was really telling us.

I was listening; that day I was forced to listen. I had to find ways to make the world around him understand and see that. Changes had to be made.

For days after this "incident", I agonized: *Why couldn't I get in Hayden's head deeply enough to anticipate his behaviors?* I could with Genevieve; but with him there was just so little rhyme or reason. I couldn't get in. Our behavior therapist couldn't get in. And these behaviors were far beyond what could have been expected from school staff. What was holding us back?

What was holding me back?

We needed another psychologist but, oh, the last one had been such a disaster. But I got on the phone anyway and I researched. I spoke to some personally and was shocked to learn how few had any direct experience in dealing with autism.

Even the seasoned psychologist who'd diagnosed Genevieve admitted, when I finally tracked him down, that she had been *the first* autistic child that he'd ever diagnosed. He warmly and kindly offered his services, saying that he wasn't well versed but was "willing to learn," at a hundred dollars an hour.

I felt so alone. We had a behavior therapist but he too was pretty much scrambling with our complexities. And his level of training and experience just wasn't high enough. *He* needed direction. I knew I had a huge aptitude for connecting with my kids and for understanding how they worked; but we needed expertise. And I needed someone who I could bounce ideas off of, who wasn't in the trenches twenty-four/seven as I was. *And we needed someone with an open mind. I craved for someone who could work at the complex level that I was working at, not a basic level, and most definitely not at a level where I would be teaching them.*

The search seemed hopeless and for a year, we managed without.

Chapter 49

"*I* love you." What is it about those three little words that make parents want to say them to their child, and to hear them spoken back? A couple of times, literally twice, ever, Genevieve let it slip. I guess she had her guard down and responded, and I got to bask in the glory. Most times if I pushed, I paid a price and was shut down, so I learned very early on that those words were just not in her and my vocabulary. When she was six, I forgot myself and let those three words slip as I was leaving her room. She stopped me and said: "I'd like you better if you just said: I like you."

Her words stung, like a slap on the face. *But it's all perspective.* I don't ever think of saying those words to her now; I haven't since that time when she was six. I don't have any expectations of hearing them back, ever. But her body language tells the words that I hear. When her feet are nuzzled up with mine or snuggled in my lap, tossing and turning or welcoming me to rub them; or when she turns to me to be the one to help her solve the mysteries of the world around her, *that's* when I hear the words "I love you." Or at least I hear the words: "I get you and I feel safe with you." *It's more than enough!*

Life with Genevieve shared many common threads with our experiences with Hayden, but it was also a curiously different and fascinating *contrast*. They both struggled with accepting people into their lives but she didn't have the overt physical aggression that he had. But like him, her life was a constant battle between *wanting* to let people (a chosen few) in /*not wanting* them in / *not knowing how* to let them in and then being *overwhelmed* by it all.

> One remarkable night, when she was five or six, Genevieve called out for me, terrified by a nightmare. It sounded incredibly foreign to hear her actually call my name. That rarely happened. My heart throbbed for whatever it was that had frightened her so deeply; but at the same time, I reveled in the fact that her nightmare made me feel that she actually needed me. And there, in the middle of the night, she allowed me to crawl in, under her blankets and snuggle for the rest of the night.

> The next day, hoping we'd nudged our way to a new and deeper level, I suggested that perhaps her nightmare had been triggered by one of her allergy foods that she'd eaten before going to sleep....she responded, in her most authentic Judy Jetson voice: "Mom, please stop ruining my life!"....back up went the wall and she had slipped into her world of talking through characters, and keeping me at arm's length away.

The contrasts between Genevieve and Hayden were draining to deal with, but at the same time, her uniqueness constantly forced me to shift gears from the non-stop trauma that was Hayden. *She was often such a welcome reprieve.* Often my journal entries were: "Genevieve is so amazing; it's like her feet never quite touch the ground!"

Chapter 50

astle walls are strong and solid; they can keep the world out and they can contain what's inside. The "moat" that encircles can offer warning time to arm and mentally prepare that visitors are approaching. I *physically* stepped out of our castle regularly; we all did. We had school and commitments, errands to run and sometimes we had people to see. *But for me, I stayed in that frame of mind, every minute.* I knew what my role at home was doing to me and that I had to break out of it; but my hands always felt like they were tied behind my back. And I'd just become too different from everyone else.

I saw and lived through the eyes and the bodies of autism. *Every setting that I entered, I surveyed in a glimpse, the sights, the sounds, the people and the activity, to protect my kids and myself.* I often thought of police officers who could arrive on a scene and in the blink of their trained eyes, they could take in more than typical eyes could ever see. That was how I lived and there *was* much about it that I loved, because it was full of wonder and insight, and it was me. I had evolved and it was who I had become.

But I was reclusive; we all were. For me it wasn't in ways that people would automatically interpret as odd, because I was *extremely* skilled at covering it up when I had to. If I were with people who were conducive to our creative ways, I could let my guard down and slip out; but I was very guarded and lived a very different life from the "typical outsiders" around us. I saw bits of the same thing in Sydney, Kobe and Nolan; but they had enough outside connections, that pulled them out. *Mine pulled me in and it was a complex place to be.*

Sometimes now, people ask me how I did it. Most times, I think people are probably afraid to ask. But really, it was through art, through costumes and our wonderful world of creativity and make-believe that saved me and saved us. And that was how we could best let people in, especially children. And part of my salvation was my dance classes. They were my connection to the real world and how I maintained little bits of myself. Often that was the only time that I could really transcend my world of total focus and orchestration. But it was tough; often the transition from home to class was difficult. Before class, I turned to the kind of visualization and sensory-based techniques that I used with my autistic kids.

Honestly, for me, more than dance classes or counseling or anything else, I credit the rock group, *The Moody Blues*. For me, they held the key. I really do mean that. That's why this book and *Effervescence* before it, is dedicated to them. Through all of the tumultuous years, and even today, they get the ultimate credit for this family's success. I do literally mean that because I do not believe I would have survived the stress, or the number of times that I succumbed to depression *because* of the stress, without them. *I really do mean that.*

Moody Blues music, their words, their positive and insightful philosophies played in my head, in my car and in my home; they saved my life and gave me my sense of direction. All of their lyrics are about hope and potential, about life being a journey. Their tunes are melodic with layers of fabulous harmonies, rich and potent, that even after hearing a hundred times, I could still find something new. *Always* there have been songs that I gravitated towards, each with words of strength and direction that fit whatever it was that I was struggling with. And there's more:

> During the early years, when my autistic kids screamed, both of them spinning in circles on the floor or crowing and tuning me and the world out, *Moody Blues* music and philosophies filled my head. *I used them and drew everything I could from them.* During Genevieve and Hayden's countless temper tantrums, when I needed to be with them but there was *nothing more* that I could do besides wait it out, I would close my eyes so tightly, blocking out everything but the music that played in my head. I'd focus so deeply, not only on the music, but the actual concerts, the times I'd seen my singer/songwriters onstage, live. *I'd literally relive that magical moment when they would first walk onstage, the first note, the songs that they played, the stage, the surroundings....*it filled me with such an amazing peace; it was like a drug. *That was how I could survive the screaming and the chaos without completely loosing my mind.*
>
> *You've read already, that there were two incidents so extreme, when not even the power of the Moody Blues prevailed...those were extreme. But for most every other incident, they did hold the key.* And each time, after I had filled myself up with my Moodies fix, I could then step back into the autism world and respond to Genevieve and Hayden, the way they needed me to respond, with compassion and intelligence.

It was a fabulous irony, really: I learned the art of surviving autism *from* my autistic children. *Who could be more brilliant at blocking out stress and re-directing in order to survive, than someone with autism?* They have so much to teach us all. Yes, it was unfortunate that I had such an extreme *need* to learn these coping methods; but if you were to ask me if it was worth it, of course I'd say "Yes, absolutely!"

Sometimes I look at friends struggling with their day-to-day stresses and often think how they could benefit from the tricks and the techniques, that my family and I have learned along the way. *I think we have been quite brilliant, actually!*

A few years ago, when I had plummeted into a state of depression, I happened to catch *The Moody Blues* in concert on TV. As I watched, I was mesmerized, seeing how despite their ages and their long career together, they had such sheer pleasure being with each other and with their audience, spreading their magic. I focused on that image for months. It inspired me to lift myself out of the fog that I was in. *They were magic;* and if they were able to maintain their inspiration after all these years, I vowed that I could too.

And that's what I did, right then and there! I pulled myself out of that horrid state of depression and moved onward and upward.

Chapter 51

As speech emerged in Hayden, a new little boy really was emerging as well. He knew what it meant to be proud of himself. He had the most amazing facial expressions that proved the depth of emotion that he was capable of feeling and articulating. He used his hands and his face to be adorably emphatic and dramatic. That was pretty amazing for a little guy who'd had to be taught how to understand and label emotions!

Speech helped, but still Hayden's unpredictable war with the world raged on:

There was one warm, sunny day when I was desperate to get out of the house. The other three kids were busy doing something with Nolan, so it was just Hayden and myself. Thank God they weren't a part of this "adventure gone wrong."

Hayden and I went to a local water park, one we'd been to many times before. I knew it would be the usual challenge for him, but he did enjoy water parks and I thought that since it was just the two of us, I could keep a really close eye.

I stood within arm's reach *every* second and he seemed to be doing well, tolerating the other kids and their presences. Up on top of a little boat, about four feet off the ground, Hayden played, seemingly happy. Then in the blink of an eye, he purposely and for no apparent reason, pushed another little boy off the boat. *This child landed directly on the top of his head, onto the concrete below.*

I was horrified. I was desperately concerned for the little boy and I will forever feel terrible guilt, for not rushing first to attend to him. But other parents were there who could help him....I was so scared that others had seen what Hayden had done and that they would turn against him....I had the instant vision of a "lynch mob"....

I had to get him out of there. I knew I was not emotionally strong enough to deal with comments anyone might make. I felt sick; it was a nightmare. All I could do was pick him up and run, to get him out, to get *myself* out before I went completely to pieces.

With Hayden in my arms, I ran to the safety of our car were I cried and cried and cried. I cried for the innocent little boy, I cried for Hayden, I cried for the sorry state of my life; but what I cried *most for* was the fact that it wasn't Hayden's fault. It wasn't his fault; he didn't wake up that morning saying to himself: "Today's the day I'm going to push some kid off a boat." It was something going on in his body. He just couldn't deal with all of the stimuli of settings like that. *That was his reality.*

If it was anyone's fault, *it was mine* for not honoring who he really was and what he could handle. All of us: teachers, family and therapists, we were all asking more than he and his body could handle, in that moment and in *all aspects* of his life.

Chapter 52

At home, Hayden victimized us, yet he took care of us. One morning Genevieve was sleeping in Sydney's bed, because she was rattled by the absence of Sydney who was at a sleepover. Outside some neighbors were making a tremendous amount of noise; Hayden ran to the sundeck, and shouted: "Quiet! Genevieve is sleeping!" He ran back into the house, then ran back to the sundeck, adding: "…in Sydney's bed!" That boy had a way of redeeming himself! It helped.

When our third in-home assistant left us, it was September, our toughest month of the year. She knew that. How could she have done that to us? We were left to confront a new school year, unassisted, with Sydney and Kobe once again traumatized by the loss, and the increased fear of letting themselves get close to yet another. For me, once again, October meant another birthday where I found myself in deep contemplation and angst about our situation. But *this* birthday was beautiful, because it was just the six of us again, and we did what we did best, we lapped up the "creative us" factor:

> The evening of *this* birthday, I walked through the front door, to find all four kids scurrying around the house, putting together the final touches on a surprise magic show. Kobe was in a cape, Sydney and Genevieve were in costumes and Hayden was in the audience with Nolan and me, constantly ready to put up his hand, whenever they asked for a volunteer. There could have been no better birthday gift! *It was magic, literally, castle magic!*

And so it went….more ads, more interviews and finally another in-home assistant, Lesley. She would end up being the most stable and stayed close to a year. But we were unraveling. Hayden, in grade two, was a mess. He was completely overloaded by his long days at school. That translated into him needing to be literally on top of me, physically, or to be completely wrapped around Sydney or Kobe, or to be relentlessly pinching Genevieve. He literally walked in circles much of the time.

At the end of each school day, he'd be happy to see me; but the moment he saw Lesley there, he would flip out in the hallway, screaming, biting and pinching her. There was *no value* in her trying to do anything for him; that only made things worse.

Worsening the picture, Sydney and Kobe, and even Genevieve made it clear that they didn't want Lesley to be their "big sister." How much was a personality clash? How much was the reality that they were *done?* They were done welcoming people in and done watching them leave. They were scared of letting themselves get attached to another, knowing that at some point, she too would leave as the others had before her.

To my kids' credit, there was something "off" about her; I think it was an innate comfort level that she did *not* have with us. She tried to cover up; but they felt it. And for each of us, Lesley was *a constant reminder of how different and disabled we were.* We had to find a way to increase our independence.

It was a daunting predicament. *We needed assistance, but assistance was causing as many issues as not having assistance.*

The sea of chaos grew deeper and stormier. We all suffered from the ravages of stress, probably Kobe most of all. He suffered from migraines, stress-related food and health issues, and dips with depression. He had terrible nightmares. For months, he and I spent Thursdays together, allocating each as a "mental health day." He needed to spend that time at home, alone with me, creatively and peacefully. He wasn't putting it on or just trying to get out of going to school. It was lovely time spent together, until3:00, when we went to pick up the others from school. Then it was like flicking a switch and instantly he became sad and miserable. It was written all over his face and all through his body.

Kobe's dedication to his family has never wavered, especially his dedication to "the brotherhood." That he took to his heart. Now a grown-up man of twenty-three, he's an accomplished university baseball player, and a *brilliant* writer and complex philosopher. He could write a book all of his own, that would have you *captivated.* He already has given to the world, bits of his experiences and insights through the rap songs, poetry and prose that he's already written and produced. *He too, is a remarkable and gifted hero.*

Sydney, "old soul Sydney," craved as much as I did, *family independence.* Her insight and worldliness about our complex lives, marveled me back then as it still does today. Her experiences paved the way for the incredible "people person" and "natural negotiator" that she is now. She studies people; she watches them and she thinks. *She has concrete but magical abilities to figure people and situations out.* We saw that then and we see it more finely tuned today. *She too, is extraordinaire, especially for someone so young.*

There was a lot that was good about what we lived through and what we experienced!

But at this particular moment, at the top of each of our lists, was getting rid of our in-home assistant.

Chapter 53

Hayden was seven, Genevieve was nine, Kobe was ten and Sydney was twelve: swirling amongst the bizarre and the amazing, life *was* very much a sea of chaos. We dipped and bobbed in and out of it. It had been that way for years. For me at that time, it was the feeling of drowning, like I could never really stay above water for very long. Finally another gift, an amazing gift and what we had been waiting so long for, swept into our lives: Dr. Benjamin Bryson. At last the search was over and I immediately saw why "he was the guy" everyone said we needed to see!

As a child psychologist, Dr. Bryson had rare perceptiveness, sensitivity and experience, *particularly* in the field of autism. Finally! Even rarer was his ability to actually listen and learn from parents and then greet it with his own expertise and experience. *That* was a powerful and dynamic combination. He shared my fascination and passion for autism. At long last, I had someone who spoke the rare language that I had become so fluent in!

I learned incredibly from him. Right from the very beginning, there was a deep connection between us. Though my style and strategizing techniques with my autistic kids were sometimes out of the ordinary, Dr. Bryson, Benjamin, saw the level of insight and he quickly understood our complexities. I think he was mesmerized by them and by our sheer tenacity. *And he truly was, and is, extraordinarily gifted.*

As a strategist, Dr. Bryson was brilliant. When designing programs and strategies, he always took the process one step further than other therapists that I'd worked with, because, *before* initiating any strategy, he would take the time to stand back and say: "Now where have we screwed up? Where is the one little loophole that will stop this from being a real success?" It was that attention to detail that could make all the difference in the world. I learned to be meticulous about all aspects of any given strategy.

And, Dr. Bryson was one of the few who seemed to understand the need to make strategies jump out and draw the child in. *Again, finally!* Like me, he felt that they needed to be child-specific and as he put it, "marketable." That became one of my specialties: getting inside my kids' heads and designing vibrant, meaningful and fun themes and programs that did just that: *drew them in.* Really, I had already been well on my way in that direction all on my own; I had been for years. But now it was re-iterated and taught *directly* to me by a specialist in the field. *Magic!*

And as important as any strategy or concept, Dr. Bryson recognized my abilities and encouraged me to continue to trust my instincts. He was always quick to remind me that there were few roadmaps to follow for *any* autism family, and even fewer for duo-autism families. My instincts and insights had taken us far. He empowered me to take them even further.

If you've read *Effervescence,* you'll recognize Dr. Bryson's words:

"Ms. Brenneman uses her gifts of sensitivity and creativity to enter deeply into the unique worlds of her autistic children, to truly understand them and to see the world through their eyes. Genevieve and Hayden have both thrived with their mother's ability to enter their worlds well enough to feel understood and valued. She has guided them forward not by pushing and pulling but, like a fairy, skipping down the path ahead of them, weaving stories and images so well that her children often followed.

She has been able to translate our "mysterious" world to her children and, when necessary, translate her mysterious children to the world."

Benjamin and I were, and still are, a magical partnership. And I know that he'd openly finish this thought by adding that *he* also has learned enormously *from us.* I and my family sometimes forced and enticed him to take his science and step even farther beyond, to be creative and open. *I pushed him, just as he pushed me, to expand and to dig deeper, and to be relentlessly resourceful and inventive.* "I'm sure there were times over the years when he questioned our path, probably more than he let on. Many times I did challenge him to look outside of his comfort zone, but *equally* there were times when he had to skillfully and carefully find ways to harness and guide me. Always he saw the results and he recognized and celebrated them" (from *Effervescence*).

Dr. Bryson brought about a dramatic turning point and he was a huge part of the reason for many of the improvements that we recognized and celebrated!

Chapter 54

At home, we were thriving but in a totally abnormal way. There was no denying the pattern: if I gave total focus and responded quickly to behaviors and was constantly pro-active, and always *one step ahead*, everyone improved. We saw it most in Kobe.

What was most curious was that when times were good, *you probably could not have found a typical, " non-autism home" that was calmer than ours.* When we were on, we were on. But it was so orchestrated! And it was so much work. I spent incredible amounts of time documenting, strategizing, organizing and orchestrating. *That* was hardly typical! And the moment I let up, things would slide and we would snowball into disaster.

In our castle, the six of us were very self-contained. At this particular time, when Genevieve and Hayden were nine and seven, we pushed away the outside world, more than ever. We rarely took either of them anywhere, outside of school. *School was enough for each of them to handle.* If we honored that, at least they were calmer and more secure, and they could learn and further emerge.

Within those realms and those restrictions, we flourished. The reward was many, many wonderful "six of us" times! We accepted who we were and we had fabulous times together.

When Kobe was ten, he saw a news segment about Secretin, a "wonder drug" at that time, supposedly a cure for autism. A few weeks later, he said to me: "Mom, I don't think you should ever give Hayden and Genevieve Secretin." I asked him why, intrigued by his pensive interest, but pretty certain of what his answer would be. He explained simply that: "It would be like putting them in a garbage can! It wouldn't be them anymore!"

In our home, in our castle, there was absolute acceptance. There was insight and there was deep, unconditional love.

At home, the "in-home assistant" concept *had* run its course. Sydney and Kobe both readily agreed that they would gladly "step up to the plate" if it meant we could have our independence back. And God knows I needed it even more, because my self esteem had faltered so seriously with the presence of a "helper" in my home. With Dr. Bryson's input and with changes that he and I devised, Sydney and Kobe were now stronger emotionally, and both Genevieve and Hayden were a little more manageable, and so we set our plan into motion: we would lay off our in-home assistant.

The new plan was to hire a more casual "babysitter," more like a typical family would have, one who would come when we needed her and then leave. And we would pay for a "buddy" to spend time with Hayden and with Genevieve, but she would not be actively *a part* of our home.

It was an exciting evening as the three of us, Sydney, Kobe and me, plotted out the details of our strategy. Afterwards, Sydney scurried down to her cedar "hope chest" in the basement, returning with her packed-away wine glasses. The three of us made a toast to our independence!

Looking back to that night, years ago, I know our timing and our instincts were right. *It was a move we needed to make and we've never looked back.*

Chapter 55

hree months into Hayden's second grade, it was obvious we needed to make changes, and fast. He was still mainstreamed with the support of an assistant; but as Dr. Bryson quickly observed when watching him, *he was lost*. In response he'd tune out, get overloaded and be disruptive and aggressive. At home, he often screamed and refused to go to school. He complained to me that other children were making fun of him, his repetitive and obsessive behaviors and his difficulty speaking clearly. His teacher was in disbelief (until months later when she happened to watch some videos of her class; she felt sick to see that what Hayden had complained about, was in fact, happening. She just hadn't seen it at the time).

Dr. Bryson and I carefully analyzed the possibility of using Hayden's passion for superheroes to *empower* him. *Our plan was for Hayden to be taught to look to his own inner strength when he was feeling threatened or overwhelmed.* Nolan found an old school desk which I painted blue, (Hayden's comfort color) and we equipped it with a Gameboy:

> The concept was for the desk to be kept in a quiet, spare room near Hayden's classroom, giving him a place, a lair or head-quarters, to "recharge his superpowers," when he needed to. *It was a multi-layered concept, designed to also form the basis for further strategies.* Though it didn't follow the typical approach to autism, it was the kind of approach we'd always used with Genevieve. It was the powerful concept of *embracing* her strengths and uniqueness, rather than trying to mold her into something she was not.

> And it was the same philosophy we had *always* followed with her, of

135

honoring the reality that she needed time out from the noise and socialness of
the school around her, to process and recover.

Benjamin and I were excited at the prospect and felt confident that it would be a catalyst for positive change. We were *convinced* that Hayden's tolerance for the school environment would increase. School staff was intrigued and receptive, *except* for the District Mainstream Liaison teacher, Mrs. Perry. In fact, when I presented our concept, she literally stared back blankly and said: "Ah, right....now here's what we're going to do...." She then proposed a very flat, traditional plan, void of any creativity, insight or "Hayden-specific strategies." Her underlying concept was: "If we just treat him like he's normal, he'll be more normal." She wanted to overtly *manage* behaviors, with *no insight or acknowledgement* of looking *behind* the behaviors, at what was *really going on* and what needed to be altered or taken into consideration. She even objected to using the term "recharge."

> *In my eyes and in my experience, I see this kind of attitude as being disrespectful to anyone who has autism. I felt that back then and I sure as hell feel it even more today, as I've accompanied my children and others, through their amazing journeys.*

This woman would not open her eyes to see how complex Hayden's behaviors were *or* the impact on his family. She seemed to have little compassion for the magnitude of our situation. What was most frustrating and alarming was that despite her apparent training, *she had no understanding of how important superhero characters were as tools.* She wanted to normalize Hayden just as she had tried to do with Genevieve. What little bits of behavior strategizing she was willing to incorporate were seriously lukewarm and sadly generic. They absolutely did not reflect the complexity of a child like Hayden.

That same year, we had struggled with this educator's attitude and lack of insightfulness with Genevieve and saw the disastrous results. They had set poor Genevieve back dramatically. This woman seemed *unable and unwilling* to comprehend that using superheroes and the "Mommy and Baby theme" for Hayden, was what using the Spice Girls, art and cartoons had been to Genevieve. Essentially, they had been like magical keys that opened doors!

We were beyond exasperated by this woman and her impact! *I shouldn't have had to defend strategies devised by Dr. Bryson and myself, not at our level of insight.* The other staff members present the day the plan was unfolded, were focused and receptive to our concept; but the moment I was challenged by their superior,

Mrs. Perry, they sided with her. To some extent, I didn't blame them, as frankly, our concept *was* far from typical. But Benjamin and I were "in the zone", and *in Hayden's head* when we designed the concept; *we knew him better than anyone and we shouldn't have been challenged.* It was bad enough fighting her tooth and nail about Genevieve; but to now be fighting the same battle with Hayden was all too much; it was ridiculous!

It basically became a big, ugly mess. The bottom line became that life at Amity School for Hayden, just *wasn't* going to work. We loved this school; we loved the staff. We had always worked so closely as a team. And Sydney, Kobe and Genevieve were all still there. But there seemed no choice but to leave.

Chapter 56

To our surprise and relief, the "perfect new school" was just minutes away. We didn't even know it existed. It was just a public school like Amity, but it offered a "high-functioning resource room" type of classroom. Amazingly, Hayden embraced the transition and initially his self esteem rose. Mrs. Thorpe, his teacher, welcomed him to bring toys to school for security and to set them on a shelf so they could "watch him" while he worked. *She* was receptive to our "Superhero Re-charge" strategy. Hayden quickly became skilled at recognizing when he needed to remove himself to his "lair" and recharge with his Gameboy. *He never took advantage or used to it excessively.*

But Mrs. Thorpe never really understood specifically *why* Hayden needed toys, strategically placed in the classroom to "watch him." Nor did she see how intense and deep-rooted the need was: the world was still such an overwhelming place for him. He felt proud of himself for making the change to a new school but before long, the academic pressures weighed on him, though they really were not high. And for all of his difficulty in understanding people and emotions, he could sense that even his class mates had difficulty understanding his speech *and* his behaviors.

Hayden was seven and a half, still in diapers and unlike anyone in his school, *and he knew it.* Often he had little control with bowel movements and the teaching assistants expected him to clean himself up with only verbal assistance from them. He began holding bowel movements in, sometimes for as long as two weeks. The staff's lack of perceptiveness and support resulted in a deep rooted issue that would take us *years* of strategizing to turn around. That was one of many issues in this school.

The physical presence of hundreds of children within the school itself, affected Hayden dramatically. All of it quickly became too much, again proving sadly how affected by the world our little boy was. Within months, after-school transitions worsened and Hayden refused to go to school, responding with desperation and panic. At home, aggression and temper tantrums were rampant. In less than a year we were once again, heading into a tail spin!

Again, school staff was mystified. From their perspective, Hayden often *appeared* to manage. For God's sake, how long had we dealt with that illusion, with both Hayden and Genevieve? It was one of the mysteries of autism, how they can sometimes hold themselves together, until they get home. But this was also a matter of staff not reading Hayden's body language and the signs of stress the way that we could (or the way *I had tried* to teach them). *And* it was also, them closing their eyes and *not listening* to our descriptions of the dangerous aftershock.

❧

Spring Break....always a stressful and challenging time for us....there's the mid-year change of routine and the *lack* of routine. But being bold and desperate, we tried something new: a short trip. We had three days, a lovely ferry boat ride to an island, a small but vibrant city...hard work but *fabulous!*

Sydney fell in love with the charm and romance of the little city; Kobe mostly loved being together as a family. Genevieve loved walking through the historic parliament buildings and the unique tourist attractions. She was *seriously* rattled by being close to Hayden for three days, and by the "too-real" wax museum; but she managed. To compensate, she spent most of our trip wearing my huge, down-filled parka....it dragged on the ground and she looked like an orphan, but she was able to "wrap herself up in security" and ventured out with us. *Fabulous!*

Nolan and I knew the tricks, like packing the Playstation and lots of movies for Hayden. Who cared if we spent a lot of the trip in our hotel suite, all of the kids huddled and captivated by Kobe's video game expertise? *At least we were away from home and we were together!* And we had a brand new strategy...this one was one of mine:

> It was devised from getting *inside* Hayden's mind and body, from watching and documenting and thinking, but most of all *feeling* him....I witnessed, and then relived in my mind, the way that he would sometimes react in places like malls: he would literally crumble and unravel, physically and emotionally *sinking into* himself; *you could actually see it in his posture.* It seemed so obvious to me that *he needed to feel contained and protected....*
>
> A wheelchair: *that* was my vision. As fate would have it, I stumbled across an old one at the very time that my plan came to my mind. It was old but it fit the description. It was worth a try *because I knew it would help. I could feel it!* To personalize it and to add tactile security, I covered the armrests with fake fur.

The wheelchair worked wonders and the timing was perfect for our trip. It was tough for Sydney, Kobe and in particular Nolan, to accept the concept: after all, Hayden wasn't *physically* disabled. But there was no denying the success! Tourist attractions that *should* have been a disaster worked, not every minute, but most. *Our trip was a different trip because of this godsend technique.*

For a long time afterwards, the wheelchair became a part of all of our outings with Hayden. It literally did help to finally open up a few doors. Sometimes we could even venture out to malls. The thing was, *Hayden himself could feel that he was different when he had the security of his wheelchair.* He would actually ask us to bring it. It wasn't remotely because he was lazy and wanted to get out of walking. *He was learning more and more about his body, his limitations and how to respond and work around them.*

A year later, we took on an even bolder adventure: a family trip to Disneyland! It took years to pay off, because we spared little expense: we were well equipped. We *needed* for this trip to work. We didn't even tell the kids that we were going, not even Sydney or Kobe. How could we risk Genevieve and Hayden finding out? The anticipation would have put them in a tailspin.

Instead, we simply picked each of them up from school, telling them we were going back to that little island city for another short adventure, but that *this* time, we were flying. Their bags were in the car, packed and ready to go.

At the airport, Sydney and Kobe *finally* started cluing into the plan. In the moment of truth, when we revealed our long-kept secret, they both literally jumped up and down off the ground; Genevieve sang "Celebrate good times, come on...." *Meanwhile, Hayden's face just dropped and he was filled with disappointment and angst.* He said he couldn't go, because we had always told him we would go when he was nine....at that moment, he was only seven and a half! We had to do some fast talking to convince him that just this once, it would be okay "to break a rule." You gotta love rule-based behavior!

In Disneyland, we used the same travel tricks, *especially* a wheelchair. Sydney and Kobe worried that onlookers and staff would think we were pulling a scan....and Hayden didn't help as he would frequently jump out of his wheelchair and prove that he wasn't physically disabled. But once they figured out that the wheelchair helped us by-pass lots of line-ups, and that Hayden was overall *amazingly calm because of it*, they got over it!

Five days in Disneyland, the travel days and flights there and back, and the months of secret planning were exhausting, but absolutely magical! Nolan and I worried that maybe Sydney and Kobe regretted that they missed out on all of the fun of planning and anticipating, that because of their brother and sisters disabilities, they didn't have the option. But to this day, they both say that *that* was the very best part....that we pulled it off without them suspecting a thing.

I think Nolan and I were pretty damn amazing!

Chapter 57

It was a godsend to have the glow of our Disneyland trip; we needed it the following Christmas, the one Kobe described as the "worst Christmas ever." *As always there were glistening moments*, but both Genevieve and Hayden were so stressed by their school situations *and* the chaos and lack of routine over Christmas, that the six of us barely left the house. We didn't even get to make the trip to see Santa.

Genevieve was in worse shape than Hayden. She was stressed and argumentative. She was so unglued that she even took offence to the clothes that *we* wore; simple things like having candles on the table had her screaming, saying it was all "too perfect." *It was completely indicative of the bland and conventional atmosphere that Mrs. Perry had been intent on instilling at school. It was that concept of trying to squelch Genevieve into being like everyone else, instead of embracing who she was and what she could offer.*

We survived Christmas, but things got even worse. I'd been working (since the previous year), in a high school as a special ed assistant for a class of dependant-handicapped teens. I loved my work there and it *should* have been the perfect setting: just three hours a day, under a teacher who specialized in autism, and who welcomed me to bring Genevieve with me to work, the days when she was too stressed to go to school.

But Genevieve was more than crumbling. This *was* a breakdown. *This was serious.* And Hayden was falling apart at the seams. All of us were crumbling. *This was serious.*

I hated to leave this classroom. I loved the students and the classroom staff was a dream and I felt so valued being there. But this *was* serious. It was at least a relief to know that if I left, I could focus *solely* on my own kids. *But I was scared, really scared. We were a murky mess at home; yet again. How bad would it be? Would I have the strength to get us through? This was serious.*

The staff was caring, so supportive. They saw my apprehension but they had no idea of the magnitude, of what *I knew* I was about to walk back into. They "worked in this world" *but they didn't live it.* And my family was so extreme. It had been years since we'd been in such a serious state.

I remember "painting a picture" for my favorite co-worker, Liza, because she was so keen and wanted to *really know* where my thoughts and concerns were. But she was a "typical mom with two typical kids" and the look in her eyes told me that she was trying, but she really couldn't comprehend what I was saying. She had no idea what it meant to *submerge yourself* into a different world, and a different way of existing. *That's where I would be after my last day of work,* when I would then be able to give absolute focus to Genevieve's breakdown, Hayden's near breakdown and the rest of the mess at home.

I remember the words and images I gave Liza well:

> It was like standing on the edge of a big, black hole.... one that I'd worked so hard to get out of, one that had almost drowned and defeated me years before. In many ways, I *wanted* to jump back in because it was fascinating and it would allow me to *feel* my autistic kids on a level that I hadn't needed to do for quite awhile. But it also meant that I

141

would have to leave a certain amount of Sydney and Kobe up there, on the edge, looking down at me, submerged there with Hayden and Genevieve.

The submersion meant that I would be, once again, *thinking and breathing* in a way that was *not* typical, because I wasn't typical, *nor was I autistic. I'd be somewhere in between, again.*

In some ways, I knew it would be *the most amazing place to be*: it was a gifted place, and a blessed place. In some ways it would be an oddly *simple* place because it would just be me and the kids and I'd be "given permission" to shut out the mediocre things in life, like newspapers, politics, and (extended) family squabbles. Nolan would have to deal with all of that.

But it would also be a very complicated place, where I needed to live, once again, with animal-like instincts and senses, always watching, listening, contemplating, tracking, getting into other heads, whether it be my autistic kids or my typical kids'. Even their teachers and the people around them...it meant observing and questioning how they were responding to my kids, and to us as a family, and to me as the "orchestrator."

Maybe this doesn't make much sense to you, but *The Black Hole* was a real place, just like our castle was a real place. Some of you reading this, maybe just a handful, will know exactly what I'm talking about.

But the prospect of delving into *The Black Hole* wasn't *as black* this time. I had Benjamin Bryson and we spoke the same language; I'd gained more insight and experience. *And* I'd had a reprieve. *I wanted* to be deeply in the minds of *all four of my kids* again. That was where my heart was. *I saw us as kites, each individual, with our own shape, size, color and texture, our own unique tail that danced in the breeze. Each of us bobbed around in the sky, sometimes on our own, sometimes crashing into each other in turmoil or in complete and playful unison! It was us and it was beautiful.*

The Black Hole meant trusting instincts; it meant being explicitly intuitive. It meant *being me.* Maybe the prospect of *this* Black Hole wasn't as scary because so much of the "old stuff" was behind us and there was *so much that I could gain by returning there!* But I worried. *Would I be strong enough to embrace it?*

In some ways, the prospect of submerging made me feel very alone, like I'd be a giant amongst fairies. But when I closed my eyes, and breathed it all in, I knew *I'd become* one of those fairies; *but I'd be the one blessed with the knowledge that this would all be something special. It would be worth whatever I'd be giving up, back there in the "normal world".*

Maybe what I was seeing, if I looked more closely, was that the color of *this* hole wasn't really black at all...it was that deep shade of purple that is so dark and so rich, that at first glance, it only *appears* to be black.

And purple had always been my color for power and inspiration...

Chapter 58

*E*ffervescence and *The Castle We Called Home* would both have completely different endings if we'd never met Benjamin Bryson. A huge part of that was because of his insight and his heart. But it was also because our bi-weekly sessions were often the only time I could really stop to breathe. So often he and I would both shake our heads at how much could change or happen with my kids, in that short two week period of time. We'd just get the ball rolling with one issue, only to be stopped mid-air while another issue of *equal or greater* urgency would slide in.

But Benjamin and I had a process. Step by step, we made sense of the mysteries and the impact. When we worked directly on a focused Genevieve or Hayden issue, it was almost like being in a state of hypnosis. He would walk me through the different components, while I would *think, see and feel Genevieve or Hayden on a deep level.* Then the concepts, the strategies and the path to follow usually just popped out in front of us. Then he and I would tweak and adjust, and make sure there were no "loopholes" that might sabotage our plan.

I was always amazed at how completely drained, physically and mentally

I'd be; usually I'd have to sneak in a nap as soon as I got home. It didn't take long before I got good enough that we could get our concept down together, leaving the fine details for me to peruse and work out on my own. And I *loved* the details. That was where my real magic came in.

Benjamin and I joined forces with our new behavioral therapist, Rheanna. Hayden's aggression was at the top of our list; he was still just seven. It was exasperating that after years of documenting and scrutinizing behaviors, there still seemed so little rhyme or reason to explain why he did the horrid things that he did. *And why didn't he respond to behavioral strategies the way he should have?* Robyn was talented and Benjamin was one of the best in the field; but even he was mystified and at times expressed: "This should have worked."

The dilemma tormented me. I could get so deeply into Genevieve's head and into her world. Why couldn't I get as deeply into Hayden's head?

The question consumed me. Desperate for an answer, I finally put myself into a deep, meditative place. I realized that the stumbling block was that *I wouldn't let myself* get deeply inside his head and into his world. It was because of the aggression, the lashing out, the tuning out and the withdrawal.

Each of those things was so foreign to who I was. And as Hayden's mom, it was a traumatic reality to let myself "visit that world" on a deep, cerebral level. I knew it was what was holding me back, that it was the missing piece of the puzzle that we desperately needed to solve. But I had to let myself go there. I had to let myself see and feel Hayden on a level I never had before. I had to be able to see through his eyes, feel through his body, all that I'd seen and documented for years before. I had to make myself Hayden.

It was like I had to let myself forget everything I'd ever learned about autism. I had to forget about *everything* really, and only *feel and see and be Hayden.*

I had to be Hayden walking through our house. I had to be Hayden walking through a mall or sitting in a classroom. I had to be Hayden standing next to

another person. I had to be Hayden in a room or a building swarming with
people and socialness.

Then I had to bring myself back and then decipher all that my body
and mind had experienced. I had to decipher my little boy Hayden, his
mind and his body. I had to let it trickle in, bit by bit, so that I could
make sense of it.

The images were so clear. They were alarming. The world that I saw
and experienced, where Hayden lived and where he would retreat to, was so
different from the world that I could feel and describe as Genevieve's.

Even on Genevieve's roughest of days, there always seemed *a beauty* to her
worlds: *our* world that she lived in, and *her* world that she retreated to. In my
observations and deep conversations with her, and in "feeling her," there was,
to me, *always the images of softness and pinks and fluffiness, a sense of openness and
fluttery, beautiful things, and of humor and wit. There was pervading sweetness. There
was always the image, the sensation of pink, fluffy clouds.* Yes, she had fears, and
the images of clouds could act as a barrier between her and the real world;
sometimes they caused her to feel loneliness. But more often, they soothed her
and inspired her.

But Hayden's world was different. It was aggressive and leering, so unlike
my world and my existence. No wonder I had instinctively fought letting myself
enter it. Of course the images that came to *my mind* in my epiphany (and this
was such an incredibly deep, life-altering state of mind, that it *was* an epiphany),
were not necessarily the images that Hayden literally saw himself. *But they were
my way of describing what I felt, when I inched my way deeply into his head and into
his body.*

I can only assume that my words and my images did have some level of
accuracy, because once I experienced them, I acted on them. It drove me
to *spearhead* changes in Hayden's life and to insist that anyone involved with
Hayden, needed to acknowledge how truly difficult a place the world really
was for him.

That is what led to the real emergence of Hayden Brenneman. *It was a matter
of honoring and respecting who he was.*

What I saw and felt when I was *inside Hayden's body and his mind,* was this:

*It was a castle, laden with beauty but also armor. I was his queen, and he was
the prince. There were dragons and knights lashing out at him (just look at the*

145

toys he was drawn to). I could feel when he put his armor on, and when he took it off. I could feel why he needed to wear it.

I could feel how some of the dragons were real and some were ones that he perceived as being real. All of them he was threatened by. I could feel the scents and the colors, the sounds, the feeling of being surrounded by "socialness" and not knowing how to respond because of the sensory and emotional overload, the limitations of his body and its chemistry, his inability to process things the way the people around him could.

Then I could feel how easily he could go the other way, into withdrawal. It wasn't a safe place to be. It wasn't a joyful retreat. Maybe it was for a few moments, but then it would turn into a place he had trouble getting back out of. Sometimes he would cling desperately to his "queen", who was me. I could feel him clinging to me, as if for life. Sometimes it was all so overwhelming that he was clouded by a nowhere place. There he would lash out at everything, sometimes even his queen, whom he loved and exonerated.

The walls around him felt dark and cold. I could feel them, how barren and void of décor they were. When he was not feeling threatened, they were enough. He didn't mind the starkness because that was his home and he felt love there, and a sense of being. But when those forces, for whatever reason, pervaded his sense of security, they were cold walls.

But there wasn't coldness in his heart. That's not what I felt from his heart at all. It might have been faint, but there was beating. . .beating with warmth, with room for happiness. But I felt within him so much confusion and so much fear, and so much possibility for void, for a place of nowhere and nothingness.

I know that some of you reading this will think I'm crazy. All I can say is: "I knew my kids. And I knew their worlds. I'd lived deeply in their worlds for a long time." Not *everything* in life is clear, flat and simple. But then that's one of the amazing things *about* life!

At last, I *was* in Hayden's head. I knew that nothing would ever be quite the same, not because of the cold and dark things that I discovered, but because of the level of respect and sensitivity it gave me. *His warm, pulsating heart inspired me and drove me, from that intense moment on, to find ways to replace cold, dark walls with ones that were radiant and safe.*

I knew I could do it. I knew I *would* do it, but that I couldn't do it on my own. I would do it with the help of others. I was good at chipping away, piece by piece; it was what I did everyday. *At least now I knew what the walls looked like.* And I knew that others needed to know.... even if I was seen as overprotective and overbearing, or just plain flakey, maybe even crazy. I was *not going to lose sight* of just how complex this little, precious boy's world was.... no matter how many "Mrs. Perrys" stared back blankly at me, questioning and challenging my logic!

That was what would bring about changes.

Chapter 59

Hayden responded to overwhelming social situations, by being aggressive and out of control, or by withdrawing. Sometimes he did both, all within the same couple of days. His aggression towards his siblings, and his difficulty in getting close to them without lashing out, showed that they were, to him, still very much the enemy. And yet he loved them and was mesmerized by them. Add to that, the omnipresent pressure of school and the stress in his life soared.

At home, we paid the prices. One day, Hayden snuck into Genevieve's bedroom and maliciously pulled the head off of one of her beloved Spice Girl dolls... the mere thought of him being in her room in itself, would have been unnerving and scarring to her. Often his behavior was terribly defiant. One day he deeply scratched my hand. Often he would go into his own room and thrash it, pulling down posters and destroying toys. One afternoon, he sought out Kobe's room and ripped down all of his posters. That act resulted in locks on each of the bedroom doors.

A Saturday outing to a department store ended in disaster for Kobe and Nolan. It was one of our most intense tantrums to date. When Nolan tried to contain him, Hayden deeply scratched and punched Nolan's face, then kicked him in the shins and screamed intensely. It was a sad eye opener for us all, especially for Nolan. He was a big man of almost 6"4; yet he could do little to defend himself against his son, who was only eight.

On the drive home, Hayden irrationally opened the car door and Kobe almost fell out, saved only by the seat belt. Understandably, both Nolan and Kobe were *very* shaken up; we all were. But when I scrutinized and analyzed the incident in detail, it wasn't all that surprising. Nolan had not, for instance, used any of the proven strategies, such as Hayden's wheelchair. He didn't feel comfortable using it and I think, until that moment, being a big man in size and stature, he really hadn't experienced what it was to be physically challenged by Hayden's outbursts. I think he got it then. Imagine what it was like for the rest of us, who were much smaller.

By bizarre contrast, the day after this trauma, Hayden was calm, happy, loving and delightful to be with!

With Dr. Bryson's help, we became extremely skilled at removing the antecedent, rather than trying to rely on only modifying the behavior. At school, we'd reduced his schedule to three days each week, and two of those mornings were home with me. My morning dance classes came to a halt: how could I take my son to the babysitting room? He would have gone on a rampage against my students' little ones.

Maybe having to quit my morning classes for *that* reason was a mixed blessing. The morning stress was so intense at home, that often in class I'd draw complete blanks. Genevieve needed so much of my focus each morning that I'd have to get up early enough, to let myself *see and feel* her state of mind, so that I could hopefully get her to school. Then having to shift my focus to my class and choreography, was just too much of a transition. Downloading "from her world to mine" in a journal before class helped; but there was rarely enough time to do that.

As for Sydney and Kobe: more mind games and their hearts being twisted by the mixed signals from their siblings; and all of the stress and bizarre behaviors! At school, Kobe was the relentless class clown, who had too much energy and too much stress. Again, Dr. Bryson shone light and helped Kobe with the complexities. But it *was* complex!

Often, when Kobe got home at six in the evening, after a full day of school and then baseball, the *first thing* he would say when he walked through the door, was: "Where's Hayden? I haven't seen him all day!" And often, after a particularly aggressive outburst from Hayden, the next night Kobe would ask to sleep with him....we'd hear them both giggling as they'd doze off to sleep. Kobe could make Hayden laugh so hard that he would gasp for air. Kobe had an amazing capacity to forgive and forget.

The higher the stress level, the higher the need for creativity....that's the way it works in my world! And so was born, our new children's theatre group, called "The Dream Players." Now *this* was a strategy, and one of my best. And it was also a labor of absolute love.

This group was bigger than our original group The Gangsters. It was made up of about half of Genevieve's class at school, plus Sydney and Kobe....and to Genevieve's regret, Hayden. I didn't have much choice. It would have broken his heart *not* to have been a part. And he was so thrilled, thrilled beyond words. He was entranced by the script but most of all, by the cast. He saw them as real life actors and he was *captivated*.

Every Friday, month after month, the actors arrived at our door, full of life and energy, eager to create. And to them, *we* were a world of wonders. This was a place where kids could be kids....and kids could be artists and actors and script-writers! It wasn't just that we had costumes; our castle had a costume *room* for God's sake, and that was over and above what we created for each of our plays.

These children learned scripts; they designed and made props, backdrops and costumes. *They got to experience being in a home that was unique, not because of the kids with the curious behaviors, but a home that exuded creativity and imagination.* These plays were a work of art. I'm laughing as I write this because our theatre group was so much fun and it was so perfect! I was in my glory, and in my element, surrounded by kids and chaos, by fabrics and paints and scripts and words.

Each play was a ridiculous amount of work and an even more ridiculous juggle, for months on end, but we made magic and we brought magic into our home and beyond! The Dream Player concept was incredibly powerful *as therapy for both Genevieve and Hayden*, on many, many levels. And, it offered us, a distraction from the stressful chaos. It was a reprieve that we desperately needed. And for Genevieve….can you imagine a better way to help her to feel natural amongst her peers, than bringing them *into her world* and seeing her shine?

This *was* magic! But make no mistake: this *was* therapy, well thought out and formulated to work on a multitude of levels. *I had a plan*. And wow, did it work!

Over the course of a few years, we managed to pull off three plays, each one a little longer and more complex than the one before it. With each, we took a classic story like *The Wizard of Oz* and re-molded it. Each was perfect! We (primarily Genevieve and myself), could rewrite the script, adding our own unique twists and turns. We could alter characters to meet the personalities and strengths of each of her "actor friends." Most importantly, we could design tailor-made roles that would highlight Genevieve and even Hayden's skills and comfort levels. It *was* perfect!

That's not to say everything went smoothly! You've read almost sixty chapters….you can't possibly be anticipating that. *Every* rehearsal was a challenge, especially for me, the director. A house full of energetic kids in costumes would have been a walk in the park for me; even supporting and directing Genevieve through the chaos, would have been a breeze. The challenge was, of course, Hayden.

At times Hayden participated calmly and sweetly; other times, he was *unglued!* He loved the other actors and all of the artwork and the rehearsing, but naturally he was completely overwhelmed by it all. He constantly got under their skin, wanting to touch them and interact with them. Sometimes they thought he was adorable; other times they must have been horrified. At one rehearsal, one of the boys had his leg in a cast….we all watched, stunned, as Hayden walked over to him and kicked his cast! Try explaining that one to a bunch of elementary school kids, who you want to have coming back to your house for months of rehearsals.

No matter how well each rehearsal did or didn't go, there was *always* aftershock and hours of screaming from Hayden. And Genevieve would need to retreat to her bedroom haven, to recover from the social and sensory overload, of having her home being infiltrated by kids and chaos.

But every cloud does have a silver lining, and the lining of this one was life altering! Our theatre group was the perfect vehicle to teach Hayden about the way his body responded to overt social settings.

I was able to teach Hayden to recognize that as much as he loved being around the other actors, *something happened* to his body in the process. He learned to *see it* and *feel it* and *to recognize the transformation as it began to happen*. During calm times, he and I could talk about how, during play practices, he needed to listen to his body, to take a break and to remove himself *before* he got to that strung-out place.

This was life altering! It was a turning point.

It was a slow process, and there were lots of tears as Hayden was guided into taking breaks and leaving the other actors during each rehearsal. But gradually, he was able to see that his body did better *and* he felt better *about himself* if he retreated to his own space with a movie or video game, to recover and recharge. *This was the beginning of a new awareness that genuinely changed the course of his life.*

In our first play, our rendition of *The Little Rascals,* Hayden played a character called "Uh-Huh," who, according to the original movie script, only ever said: "Uh-Huh!" It was perfect for him because this was back when he still didn't have much speech, and he was pretty tough to understand. But at the very end of *our* play, we slipped in our own line that Hayden recited perfectly. With his slurred and choppy speech, he said: "Actually, I'm very fluent in many different languages!"

It was adorable! Hayden really did have a language all of his own, but he was truly becoming more fluent in the language of life!

Chapter 60

Outside of our carefully-orchestrated theatre group, Hayden simply was not a child who could be involved in social activities. Team sports and clubs were out of the question. Even Summer Fun programs designed for special needs children *always* ended dismally. There just was *nothing to be gained* that could possibly have been worth the price he, and we paid.

At school, Hayden literally carried his teddy bear almost constantly, desperate for security. He was eight at that point so it didn't exactly go unnoticed. It was alarming to see how our attempt to increase his school day by even *ten minutes*, threw his sense of security. He spoke of not fitting in and of other children making fun of him, even some of the other special needs kids in his classroom.

> The staff assured us that recess and lunch times were well supervised and that he interacted with the other children....maybe they were referring to the odd good day, but that wasn't what we were sensing from him, *and* his body and behaviors. When I secretly observed him one lunch hour, it broke my heart to see him sitting alone on a bench. When the bell rang, he got up to go but was visibly overwhelmed by all the kids whizzing around him. *Good God, were the staff blind or were they hiding the fact that Hayden wasn't supervised and he certainly was not supported during lunch and recess.* He was left to fend for himself, in a ridiculously overwhelming social environment.

Staff did remark that often Hayden felt openly threatened by the classmates around him and lashed out aggressively, even in class. Once he choked a child who was sitting in his chair.

At home, we were mortified seeing the increase in aggressive and irrational behavior. Places like Costco were now absolutely banned from the small list of places we were willing to take him. The memory of the last visit was too deep, when Hayden had absolutely flipped out, screaming and so distraught....people stopping to stare....me just leaving my shopping cart filled with groceries and dragging him out, back to the car and privacy.

The increase in self-stimming behavior at home was equally alarming.

Kissing himself better had risen to ridiculous levels. If I asked him, for instance, to help me press the bank machine buttons, even *that momentary contact* required him to "kiss his finger better," in between pressing each number. *It was like the world was closing in on him, and physically hurting him.*

He would repetitively open and close cupboards and doors, by the hour, especially the spring-loaded TV cabinet as he watched TV. His sensory fixation with hair increased and he would literally try to cram his hair *into* his ear. Of course we'd seen these behaviors before, but *never* to this degree!

For months, Hayden became tormented by nightmares. He'd wake up and panic about school. He sobbed, and described to me his nightmare about "a boy being lost". There was another one about him being kidnapped by four witches, who surrounded him and killed him. He was extremely distressed and eluded to these nightmares often. They were real and *the intensity* was disconcerting. This was not a child trying to get out of going to school!

I couldn't help but wonder if the four witches in his nightmare represented the four female staff in his classroom.

At night, Hayden would often climb in bed with us, his arms wrapped tightly around me, incessantly pulling my hair, hour after hour, while I tried to sleep. It hurt! I tried to transfer his hands *away* from my hair a number of unsuccessful ways: I sacrificed a thick strand of my hair and stitched it to a ribbon. But even in the middle of the night, he figured it out and thought it was too creepy.

My next attempt, I attached fake hair to his teddy bear; but it wasn't *my* hair, and he had no interest. I even tried sleeping in a toque (I was desperate); but that didn't work.

The final attempt will sound cruel, but it shows how *desperate* I was: one night, I was ready for him....as he reached for my hair, I slipped him a realistic wig from our costume room, certain that it would work. But even in the dark, I could *feel* his horrified look, like he was holding my scalp in his hands! He screamed and threw it on the floor, and I felt sick thinking what a horrible thing I'd done, that I'd probably scarred him for life. I don't mean that in a joking way.

The point was: these behaviors were happening for a reason. *Hayden was talking to us. His body was talking to us.* We were being told that he could *not* go on in this way. There were so many issues at hand: yes he had always struggled "with the world" in general; but it was also so clear to us that the environment of school was exacerbating everything, to dangerous levels.

And there was that age-old mystery at hand, baffling school staff, who *did not* understand autism, and certainly not Hayden, the way that we did. Often he *appeared* to handle being at school, at least when they were watching, or should I say, watching with their mildly-trained eyes. Really, it was "weird." On one hand, staff would acknowledge and report that he was "choking a class mate" and yet on the other hand, they'd tell us everything was fine and he was handling things well. *I'm shaking my head as I write this!*

Driving with Hayden was becoming more dangerous, forcing us to go into yet more debt, to purchase a van. On the bright side, we told the kids that at least we no longer looked like "The Griswalds" in our old, huge station wagon. And the van gave us more space to protect them from Hayden, with the added bonus of tinted windows. At least the world outside wouldn't witness the mayhem that went on *inside*.

That July, another turning point....not a good one, in fact, one of the roughest:

One Sunday morning, Nolan and I left Hayden and Genevieve in Sydney's care, as we sat glued to Kobe's baseball game, just a minute or two's drive from our house. Sydney was fourteen, and she was exceptionally responsible and well versed in Hayden, and we were very nearby. It should have been okay. It was such a rare pleasure to be able to focus on Kobe's pitching, with no distractions.

Part way through the game, my cell phone rang. It was Sydney. Even her controlled, crisis-mode voice couldn't hold back her concern. She described how Hayden, dressed in our Captain Hook costume as he often did, had essentially attacked Genevieve. She had been down in the basement on her own, playing on the Playstation. Hayden took the plastic stick he'd deemed a pirate's sword, and hit her many times. There were bruises and welts all over her arms and back.

Genevieve was horrified. Sydney was horrified, though she handled it more calmly and compassionately than most adults could have. (But what did it do to her subconsciously?) Nolan and I dashed home, the guilt almost unbearable. *We both knew that despite all the aggressive acts Hayden had inflicted upon us over the years, this was different. This was on a whole new level.*

This could never happen again. Genevieve had done nothing. She was so undeserving.

Obviously, the "Hook attack" *was* a turning point. We all felt it. For me, I was completely overwhelmed by it, and for weeks, I could barely stay awake during the day. I'd literally fall asleep, mid-sentence, when I was talking with the kids. It wasn't like earlier times when I fought exhaustion, during speech therapy. *This was different.* It was like my brain would just shut down. I'd probably say that it was frightening, except that I was so out of it, that I didn't really have the presence of mind to recognize it as frightening. I just wanted to succumb to the intense desire to sleep, all the time. It made me think of a funny episode on *Frasier* when Niles kept falling asleep; but this wasn't at all comical.

I went on a rampage. I searched through our house for any toy, any book, any video that had *anything* to do with aggression or fighting. I even threw out Hayden's "Search and Find Batman" book. What few things I didn't have the heart to throw out, I hid. All I could think of was Genevieve and how completely undeserving of that attack she'd been.

Thinking back, as I tore through my house searching for objects to rid our home of, I was looking for an easy answer. Who hasn't read the literature supporting links between aggressive toys and movies and aggressive behavior? But the reality was: that wasn't *the cause* of Hayden's attack, or *any* of his aggression, really. It was so much deeper and more complex than that. Kobe was equally enthralled by Ninja Turtle and Power Ranger kicks and moves, but *he* didn't attack his sisters. He didn't even get carried away in playfulness with those moves, to harm anyone. In my state of remorse, guilt and regret, I was temporarily using them as our scapegoat.

And in the specific case of Hayden's attack on Genevieve, he wasn't even portraying himself as a Ninja Turtle, or a Power Ranger or any malevolent Marvel superhero. *He was dressed as Captain Hook, a sinister but lovable character from a playful Disney movie.* Nothing about the music or the characters or the storyline of *Peter Pan*, was overtly violent or aggressive. This was Disney; this was our favorite movie that reminded us that we would never really have to grow up! TV and movies: they *weren't* the cause.

Gradually, the Power Ranger figures returned to our home, along with many other toys. The point was, Hayden got so much pleasure from them and he did learn a lot about life *through* them. *They* weren't the problem.

Maybe when Hayden was little, he sometimes imitated aggression that he saw, but that wasn't *the cause* of the behaviors, even back then. I think I can prove that right now, by flicking forward to the present time:

For years now, Hayden's coordination and skill level have enabled him to become extremely adept at video games. Often he plays games and watches movies that have lots of blood and gore in them. He also has a massive passion for the *WWE* (World Wrestling Entertainment). And yet despite all of those things, including the *WWE* fighting and flailing limbs, and all of the blood and sweat and testosterone-driven aggression, it *doesn't result in aggression from Hayden. We honestly don't see it reflected in how Hayden responds to things.* He understands that what he sees on the screen is on screen. That's their job and their passion, like an art form in his mind.

Likewise in movies and on video games: I personally get grossed out and unnerved by violence and "blood and gore" onscreen, because I associate what I see with reality. But Hayden constantly shakes his head at me and says: "Mom, it's not real." In his mind, complex as it is, he separates what he sees.

Hayden's aggression at the time of the attack on Genevieve, and further aggression when it did happen in later years, came down to three things: 1) Hayden feeling overwhelmed and unsafe; 2) Hayden feeling threatened by the world around him; and 3) the limitations of whatever unexplainable misfiring that goes off in his body, because of his genetic make-up.

None of that rationale or any rationale, *excused* the horrid "Hook" attack. No matter what, it *was* alarming and it hit us all deeply. It did force us to re-evaluate, over and above Hayden's emotional state, his "biochemical state": our strategies weren't working well enough. And maybe Ritalin wasn't enough.

What other answers were there? All we knew was that we couldn't let this happen ever again.

Chapter 61

In addition to Ritalin, Risperdal was the logical choice, because of its reputation for helping to take the edge off of anxiety, for some children with autism. Within weeks, we noticed huge improvements in Hayden. He was often calmer and more able to do activities like grocery shopping and appointments. This year our family trip to "Playland" lasted seven full hours! Typically, after two hours, Hayden would have been wasted. *This year, as we watched the four of them navigate through the park, I held back tears saying to myself: "This is why I wanted to have four kids!"*

But Risperdal had side effects: a huge weight gain of more than thirty pounds in a matter of months. And the dosage had to be kept to the lowest possible level, or Hayden's speech became so slurred that even I could barely understand a word he said. Also, there was an increase in rocking and pacing. But once the dosage was under control, Nolan and I knew we'd made the right decision.

With updated medication, we could now revisit some of our most forbidden places, like Costco. Not only could Hayden handle it, he was calm and outgoing. One day I stood and literally cried, right there in the middle of Costco, *not* because his behaviors were so horrific; but because, all on his own (with me watching from a distance and holding my breath), he ordered and bought for himself a slice of pizza. He even went back for napkins. What a conquest!

Ritalin, Risperdal, strategies and getting inside Genevieve and Hayden's heads:

157

all of those things were bringing us to a more livable place, everywhere but socially.

Nolan, Sydney, Kobe and I *longed* to open up our doors a little and the timing felt right. The prospect of letting in *carefully-chosen bits of normal socializing* held so much appeal, like an irresistible force. Despite our family's challenges, we were popular amongst all of the families whose lives were intertwined with ours, through sports and school. *We craved to expand on to that.* In little bits and pieces we *did* become more outgoing and social.

The lure drew us in a little too deeply and we stepped a little too far.... what was supposed to be an evening at home with friends, intended to mark our emergence as a reasonably-social family, ended up being a door that slammed in our faces:

> Christmas vacation....two other families, both lovely and ever-supportive with our challenges....a bunch of kids, all connected to Sydney and Kobe for years through sports....

> It should have been a perfect match, with a good chance for success.

> After dinner, Nolan and I had a wonderful time, upstairs conversing and laughing with the adults. *It felt so good; it had been so long!* But downstairs in the basement, there was major ungluing in the works. Genevieve and Hayden were intrigued but unnerved by the presence of foreigners; *but they were doing okay.* It was more *Sydney and Kobe's reaction* to the situation that brought the evening down, and made us swear that *that* was the last time.

> For Sydney and Kobe, the evening meant just too many levels of complications for them to deal with. They were probably *scared to death* that their siblings would revert to their usual social-overload behaviors....consequently, both Sydney and Kobe became unnerved, less patient and less in-tuned than usual....both Hayden and Genevieve picked up on that, and *their* comfort level *decreased*....then both Sydney and Kobe lashed out at them, out of frustration.

> Their friends picked up on their apparent discomfort, which in turn, rattled Sydney and Kobe even more. It was like a self-fulfilling prophecy that ultimately led to both Sydney and Kobe being caught in

the middle, between loyalty to their siblings and discomfort with their friends....*so they turned on their friends.*

It turned into an ugly night. Obviously, the price of trying to be normal, of trying to let people in to our carefully-structured and protected environment *was still* unrealistic.

Hours later, after I'd settled all of them down, and soul searched with both Sydney and Kobe, she insightfully surmised: *"It's not that we want Genevieve and Hayden to change; we don't. But we need to be in environments where we all feel relaxed and ourselves, and enjoy being who we are, as individuals and as a family."*

Those were really profound words, and Sydney was only fourteen at the time.

She was right; deep down, I think I knew it too. But somehow, I guess we had to prove it to ourselves. Whatever we gained that night, we lost. We learned that for us, what little socializing we did was best done at school or at sports events. We just couldn't submerge others into our world and expect that we, and they, would respond naturally. We were still just too complex and too foreign.

On a personal level, within the realm of autism and the impact on my family, my world was incredibly complex. Yet at the same time, it was *extraordinarily uncomplicated.* That's because I had to simplify my life, to always be positioned to spring into action, to address issues and their impact at a moment's notice.

Any outside activity that was remotely complicated, had to be on my own terms. It had to be creative and meaningful so that if it meant my taking away focus from my family, I would at least be gaining positive energy to recharge and pour back *into* my family. There definitely was a fine balance.

Most commitments had to be done late at night. Midnight was my favorite time, when the house was finally quiet and I had my brain all to myself. Most activities revolved around writing or sewing or creating or dance and movement. I couldn't commit to very much during the day; but by night, *I could make my impact.* For Sydney's high school play, for example, I designed and created intricate and spectacular mermaid costumes, so that at least I could feel that I was *a part* of her play. More importantly, *she* could feel that I was a part of it.

I dressed up as "Willowmina the Witch" at school for Halloween, or taught dance to the whole school. For my own dance classes, I'd dig deep and come up with captivating ideas for theme classes or just bits of fun. The tiny details often came to me in the middle of the night, reminding me that *I still did have a place in the real world. I still could create and make a positive impact.* I grabbed whatever little bits of magic, or ways that I could *give* magic, any chance I got. They were like drugs. They *were* powerful drugs, as long as I "took them" when it fit in with what kept the six of us on track.

> It was all quite the juggle! Being highly organized barely describes it. But when things were good, and we stayed in our rhythm, life *could* be good for each of us, though certainly not typical. Autistic kids need *a high level of organization*; they thrive on it. In our home, we all needed it or we didn't thrive. *I* needed that organization and the "safety net of organization," because I knew that *at any given moment, our family could go over the edge and it could take weeks, sometimes months, to pull us back up again.*

Organization also meant that everything, like unique materials for behavioral strategies, needed to be at my fingertips, 24/7, *if and when* we needed them. I was always on the lookout for interesting items that I could store away, knowing that at some point, I would transform them into some kind of a behavioral strategy.

And *always*, I had a journal and a pen. Without keeping all of my safety nets intact, I would have plummeted into the throws of chaos, *unarmed,* within the blink of an eye! I knew that.

That summer, we dared to take another camping trip, just the six of us, with no assistance. Amazingly, Hayden was calm for the six hour drive. By now we were smarter and we had new strategies: *two separate tents which we set up the moment we arrived.* It gave a certain structure that each of us responded to. The moment that was done, we dashed off to check out the breath-taking lake.

By the time we made the fabulous hike up cliffs and over massive rocks to the lake and back, we were hit by a monsoon rain. We all scrambled into our designated tents, and into our sleeping bags. We stripped down to the skin to warm up and dry off, because our clothes had been drenched in a matter of minutes. In my tent, Hayden and Kobe laughed and giggled, like it was a deliciously naughty but comical adventure to be captured by a rainstorm, stark naked inside sleeping bags. We still giggle about it today!

Not all of our trip was as glorious as that; but it was glorious enough. It was us!

Chapter 62

The new school year, as Hayden turned nine, started out promisingly. But even with the addition of Risperdal, it was discouraging to see how he struggled. On his home mornings, he and I did a casual home school program and he was surprisingly receptive to doing simple worksheets. Often he'd say: "Come on Mom, let's study something."

It wasn't really studying, but at least Hayden was receptive. At that point, he could print a few words at a time, but it was faint and barely legible. Reading was slowly emerging, and he was slowly learning how letters and sounds fit together, but most were simply sight words.

It was disturbing and disappointing that Hayden's teacher was threatened by the concept of "partial home school," even though we carefully presented it as a reflection of Hayden's limitations, *not her inadequacies as a teacher*. To her credit, it *was* terribly confusing, because she saw a different side of Hayden. Often he *did* enjoy class discussions and events. But often, he didn't. He showed the signs of stress and withdrawal, but she either closed her eyes or wasn't open enough to the language of Hayden, to recognize them.

School aftershock once again made life unlivable. Hayden put up heart-wrenching fights to stop me from making him go to school. The nightmares and his rants about not fitting in were returning. His teacher and I had countless conversations about it, but she just wasn't hearing it or seeing it. She couldn't comprehend "the other side of Hayden," despite my graphic descriptions of him at home, or when I'd try to get him to go to school. Even when she watched the graphic video we'd taken a few years before, she just couldn't relate to it.

She basically presented her belief that *I was the issue*, that if *I would just open my eyes and see how much fun he was having at school, and if I would just keep him there every day, all day, for the full six hours, all would be right in Hayden's world.*

How could she ignore the fact that Hayden just wouldn't and couldn't go to school? Day after day, I was having horrid experiences trying to convince him, even forcefully dragging him into the school and quickly leaving. But he'd come running back in sheer panic, faster than I could get away. *That's not normal, not even for someone like Hayden.* He wasn't just trying to get out of going to school. He was telling us he *couldn't* do it.

It was all a part of a complex picture. One of the tricky issues was Hayden's awareness. *He knew he was different.* He knew that his behaviors and his limitations were different, *even from all of the other special needs kids in his school.* He knew his mind and his body were "tormented" in ways the other special needs kids weren't. He was so child-like and yet so incredibly perceptive and mature. That was almost like his downfall.

To Hayden, in addition to dealing with the social and sensory overload of his classroom, each day at school was like holding up a mirror. In its reflection, he saw the image of a boy who was very different from the others. *It made him feel bad about himself.*

I thought it was humbling to see such self honestly and knowledge of self. And it was heart gripping.

At this point, Hayden had difficulty actually *articulating* these complex thoughts, but bits and pieces came out. *And it was written all over his actions and his responses.* Behavior *is* communication.

To prove her point, the teacher made a video of Hayden at school. We were, of course, delighted to see snippets of Hayden on a field trip and of Hayden in the classroom. He appeared happy and engaged. But we saw things that she wouldn't allow herself to see, or didn't have the capability to see: bits of mannerisms and jargon that were *his signs* of the stress that smoldered within him.

And interestingly, she only filmed the good moments. Maybe she should have had the video camera ready on the days when I had to forcefully drag him into the school, or the day he tried to choke a class mate for sitting in his chair. And of course, there was no footage of him struggling and feeling lost and overwhelmed during the chaos of recess and lunch. Maybe there should have been some footage of him in the school bathroom, the many times when school angst caused him to have explosive diarrhea when he, this mentally disabled child, was expected to clean himself up, with only the voice of his special ed assistant prompting him from outside the door.

As parents, Nolan and I agonized. Were the good moments at school worth the prices we were all paying? *We couldn't let our family plummet into darkness again!* I agonized on a different level, because I'd been through it so many times before and *I just didn't know if I had it in me to go through the darkness again.*

But the writing was on the wall and we needed to read it; and so we pulled Hayden from this school. It was a painful but familiar course of action to us by now.

"With no suitable school" was a frightening place to be. We'd just weathered the intense stress of Genevieve's grade five breakdown and the presentation we'd had to make to the school district, to get her back on track. Then there was the serious decline in Hayden's behaviors and the futile attempts to pull his teacher into recognition of his complexities. Now we had no school at all. That was the last straw.

We all felt the strain. I slid into a state where my head felt like it was literally filled with cotton. For months, the only time I could lift my head out of that terrible fog was when I went class, or worked with Dr. Bryson to sift through the rubble, or when one of my kids would do or say something that was just so *shining* that it cut through the fog.

One of those critical little glimmers came from Genevieve's lips. As much *work* as she could be, she had a way of making me stop and think. *She made me shift my perspective and take odd delight and insight from things I would have otherwise missed.* It was her unique perspective and her absolute effervescence. This gem was on Kobe's thirteenth birthday:

> Kobe had broken his collarbone snowboarding. He had to spend his birthday party completely immobilized, so the best we could do was invite his buddies over, to watch a movie. I mentioned to Genevieve how he and his friends had "lit up like candles" when they found out

that in sympathy for poor Kobe, we were going to let them watch a scary movie they'd all been hoping to see (but knew they were a little too young).

The moment I said those words, I knew *exactly* what she was *thinking, feeling and seeing*; I could see it in her eyes and the way her body glowed. It made *me* think it and feel it and see it too, because of all that she had taught me over the course of her amazing, little life:

We both saw Kobe and his buddies, each one of them a colorful candle with dangling arms and legs, their faces set within their flame-shaped heads, smiling and flickering with delight!

I'm giggling as I write this, because it was just so beautiful; and it was funny! *Because Genevieve had autism she had a fabulously vibrant and literal way of looking at life.* Yes, sometimes it stood in her way and overwhelmed her. But just as often, it brought delight to her and to the world around her, at least those of us who could experience it that way through her.

If you still don't know why it is that I write books about autism and why I seize every opportunity to speak about *embracing* autism, *this* is one of the reasons why!

At that moment, when she and I shared that beautiful but comical image*, it was the perfect gift!* It helped to remind me how blessed I was and how gifted I had become *because* of my two extraordinary blessings, my two challenged kids.

The other thing that dramatically helped to pull myself out of that terrible fog, was to pick up a pen and my stack of journals, and start writing this book.

Chapter 63

Many of Hayden's self-stimming behaviors decreased *almost the moment* we pulled him from Hammond Elementary. Many stopped completely! And the serious bowel movement issue improved noticeably. For six weeks, Hayden was enrolled in no school. It was time to accept some really harsh realities about his limitations. He struggled cognitively. But more severe than that was the fact that he was a nine year old boy, who walked around talking to himself and to imaginary characters, to make himself feel safer. Often he'd tune out the world around him. Sometimes he'd make us act out scenarios, like all five of the Backstreet Boys having dinner with us. We actually had to set out places at the table for them, and ask them questions. It was fun, but very bizarre. *It was an indicator of how unsafe he felt in the world and how hard he tried to regulate it. It wasn't just that he had a very wonderful and vibrant imagination; it was that there was a genuine need.*

Emotionally Hayden was extraordinarily fragile and yet under the right circumstances, he had such promise, as long as it was in the realm of what he was capable of. *That was the key*: what *was* he capable of? What *could* he handle? During those six weeks, he and I stayed home together, and I let myself enter his body and his head, deeply, *over and over again.*

The concept and its justification simply emerged. I *knew* what we needed and what would work. I saw it and I felt it. *But did it exist?*

> Though Hayden was, on the outside, very bright and perceptive, he was so easily bombarded. Even with medication, his attention span was painfully short. He struggled and agonized about not fitting in. What he needed was to be with children who had toileting issues and speech challenges, so that they wouldn't be put off or questioning his lack of articulation.

> He needed to be in a place where his need to bring security toys to school or to repetitively kiss himself better, would not stand out. He needed to *not be* expected to endure socially-bombarding situations like recess, lunch and worst of all, assemblies.

> With respect to the academics, it needed to be done *carefully and*

creatively, somehow finding ways to *entice* him to learn, so that *the glaze of withdrawal* didn't creep up and overtake him. This program would have to be presented to him in a *totally calm, non-threatening environment with no distractions*. That environment needed to be an extension of home, where home school and school could be embraced and not seen as a threat or criticism of anyone's abilities.

Again I asked myself: *did this exist?*

Not only did this class exist, it was located right back at Amity Elementary, Hayden's original school. The School District Director of Special Ed's face *dropped* when I presented my plan. He was shocked and mystified that I'd suggest enrolling Hayden in a classroom with children *far less* able than him. *Like everyone else, he saw it as a huge step backward and in the wrong direction.* But with all of my "evidence" and reasoning to support me, including the seal of approval from Dr. Bryson (though he too was shocked at first), we made the move.

I can hardly say how scared I was. *I had absolute faith that this was the way to go; but no one could ever be certain about anything regarding Hayden.* If this *didn't* work, there really were no alternatives left. And would there be prices to pay *if I was wrong* and this "controversial environment" was *not* the right one for him? I have to be honest: in some ways it was heart wrenching to put Hayden in a class with children who were academically less able than him; but it was such a relief to finally stop barking up the wrong tree!

We brought Hayden in on the plan and he was receptive and intrigued. As the starting date drew near, he was nervous and obsessed frantically about needing a white Power Ranger costume. The urgency in his body language told me to trust *his* plan, and so he and I took a trip to the fabric store. Together we carefully chose the perfect fabric. Then he helped me draw a model and he "kept me company" while I cut it out and sewed it. That was *unheard of* from him and his short attention span. *But it was like he knew that he had to be a part of the entire process.*

For two days solid, Hayden wore his costume *everywhere*. It was quite a sight because it was May; at least if it had been near Halloween it might have looked a little less odd!

I thought his plan was utterly fascinating! I was so proud of him. *He was behaviour strategizing!* I envisioned the "castle imagery" I'd seen and felt that time of my epiphany, when I'd finally got deeply inside his head and his body"; I thought about the forces *I'd seen and felt* lashing out at him.

Now, here he was, that same child facing an important turning point in his life, brilliantly choosing to find a way *to empower himself.* I was in awe.

⌐━ᵗᶠᵖᶠᶠᶫ━◡

At this moment, you might be asking yourself: "If Hayden had the desire and insight to find ways to empower himself, why didn't he do it at his *last* school?" The answer to me is obvious: in that environment, the forces that leered out at him were simply too great. In his new school environment, *he stood a chance* of protecting himself and thriving. I think he knew that and he embraced that! Bless his soul, *he wanted this to work!* I was so very proud of him.

Chapter 64

The complete school and home school concept was *carefully* devised; we wanted no dangerous loopholes. Hayden's attendance at Amity would be realistic: simply 12:15-2:30 each afternoon. There would be no recess, lunch or assemblies. Classroom time would be used for casual life skills and a social time for him to connect with peers in his room. I worked carefully with Mrs. Vine, his new teacher, to bring her up to speed with the kind of activities that he could likely handle. *Anything* academic would be handled at home.

With respect to home school: *that would be my baby!* I'd only dabbled with it during the Hammond time; but now I was ready to be productive. *The concepts burst out of me.* I'd seen the glaze, the wall that went up when Hayden was pushed the wrong way academically. I was determined to *"go in the back door,"* to make him feel safe yet swept up, animated and at one with learning.

I turned to what always worked best with Hayden: Fantasy. I called it *Personified Learning*. To promote reading and printing, I created an entourage of characters, like "King ing", "Captain er," "Mr. Moon" and "Lightyear ight." I was a terrible artist, but he didn't care. He *bought into* my drawings and characters. I made hundreds of worksheets, some basic, some more challenging, often amazing myself with little tricks that popped into my head. *Every single sheet or activity* was designed to make him feel like he was *a part of the page!*

It was exhausting to create worksheets and concepts because it meant I had to "submerge myself into Hayden's head." But I was on a mission and I was completely wrapped up in it. *And I saw results, quickly.* More than anything, I could see that Hayden *wanted to learn and he was excited about it!* I can't say I was able to summon up enough magic to entrance and engage him for the entire morning; but considering his pervasive limitations, he and I had a fairly well-rounded program. All in all, our morning home program consisted of about forty minutes of academic work, complemented with grooming and walking our dogs, and then brief errands in our community. It was a pretty impressive use of mornings!

> Hayden's appetite for learning increased. My efforts felt well rewarded. And it was *very* precious time that we shared together. One Sunday morning, when he had snuggled into bed with me, he lay beside me deep in thought. You'd think he would have been pondering what video game he was going to play that day or maybe what he was going to have for breakfast. To my surprise and absolute delight, he remarked: "Hey Mom, our dog's got "Captain er" in her name and Mom has a short O!"

Wow! Hayden was definitely learning, now that it was safe and on his terms; now that we were *meeting him halfway.*

At school, Mrs. Vine was mystified, as to why Hayden had been put in her classroom, because outwardly he was much higher functioning than the others. But she quickly noted the range between Hayden's abilities *and* his limitations. Immediately she saw that he was very bright and sharp, that he could figure out complex movie plots and understand the humor in life. But she also recognized that if he was pushed or threatened, he crumbled or he lashed out. He could seek revenge in devious, well-planned ways, against anyone who bothered him.

This teacher saw that Hayden was smarter, more mature and more verbal than anyone else in the class. He looked like a clever and mature giant in contrast to the others; yet at the same time, he was child-like and loved preschool shows and activities like *Blues Clues*. He was articulate in putting his thoughts together, yet he was like a little boy in a big boy's body. That was all a part of the mystery that was Hayden!

The new school/home school concept worked. Basically, what we had begun to do was to *transform* this remarkably complex, volatile and unpredictable child. *We did it not so much by behavioral modification but by finally accepting how disabled he really was and then honoring his need to feel safe and to be accepted for exactly who he was.*

You'd think Hayden's self esteem would have dropped, being placed in a classroom with children "more" disabled than him. But the exact opposite happened, as I'd seen in my vision. It was as like a huge weight was lifted off his shoulders. He was now with kids who didn't make him stand out. All of them had difficulty speaking. And this classroom had a bathroom attached because *all* of the students had toileting issues. Though he was often perturbed by the behavioral outbursts of the other children, *he felt connected to them*. He knew that he too suffered from uncontrollable outbursts, just as they did.

Within his classroom, a new role also emerged for him: *being a role model, a teacher and sometimes a protector of the other children*. He recognized that there were times when *he* was able to assist *them*, because he was bright and knowledgeable about many of life's intricacies. *And he did have a good and genuine heart*: there was one girl in his class, bless her sweet soul, who was very physically disabled and also had a face that was quite deformed, and not that easy to look at, to be honest. But Hayden immediately *saw beyond that* and was very protective and respectful of her.

Hayden was feeling better about himself. As his family, we saw an inner peace emerging in him, that we had never seen before.

Fate or just good luck continued to shine down on us! It just so happened that this classroom also came with one more *unexpected* bonus: Kiera, Hayden's beloved Sunday respite caregiver. She worked there as an assistant. What a gift! Along with her love and dedication to Hayden, she brought a burning desire to *not let* staff fall into the trap the past staff had fallen prey to: Kiera *constantly* reminded them to not simply see *the Hayden that they saw in front of them.* She tirelessly did all that she could to broaden their horizons, to see the *many* complex and confusing sides to Hayden, and the impact that everyday activities had on him, and ultimately, on his whole family.

Hayden, our beautiful, adorable and complex Hayden….at home, he was now calmer and happier. He still suffocated me, but it was *sweeter* suffocation. One evening as I was leaving to teach my class, he looked at me with a furrowed brow and said: "Oh, I already missed you once today. I don't want to miss you again!" Beautiful Hayden.

Chapter 65

With the world no longer ravaging so wildly around Hayden, *and* with him feeling better about himself, there was finally more room for behavioral strategizing. For Dr. Bryson and me, our goal was to help Hayden understand that the people around him *needed* for him to be calm and compliant, and that he would feel better about himself when he did. Certainly attempts had been made in the past, but he was always such a mess that it was futile. But *now* the time was right. And now was *my* time to shine with new strategies.

One of the coolest things about Benjamin is that he "gets" the magical power of *using* themes and items of interest. *You use them to the hilt*, to draw autistic kids *into* behavioral programs. Trust me, not everyone in this field recognizes that. Some therapists think you're pampering the child or giving in, or I just don't know. I don't understand it. In my mind these tools are gold. Often they hold the key! For one, the program may actually succeed in pulling the child in, and two, to design a program that is absolutely child-specific, *you have to be in that child's head and in that child's body to feel it and to design it. How can that not spell success?*

And the presentation*: how and when* you present a program can be *critical* to its success.

Many, probably most, autistic children are extremely visual. Their programs need *to be* visual. And in my mind, they *must be* child specific. One of the reasons that I ended up being the primary program designer for both Hayden and Genevieve was because I understood them and their world better than anyone else; but also, it was because I felt I had *little* choice. Many of the programs and strategies designed for them were generic and bland.

One turning point for me was a mediocre social story designed by a consultant for Hayden (social stories are a brilliant method of using cartoon-like drawings and captions to visually aid autistic children in understanding social interactions, events, schedules and things). But this one was so lukewarm. Other than the fact that she gave the primary cartoon character red hair (actually she used orange, not even red like Hayden's) to symbolize Hayden, it was generic and could have been used for almost any other autistic child. It just rubbed me the wrong way. There was nothing to draw Hayden in and so we ran the risk of it being ineffectual.

To me it just seemed like such a missed opportunity for greatness. Had it been captivating and Hayden specific, we would have likely had more success. And there could have been more depth as well.

I know not everyone will agree with me, but I personally find generic and bland programs to be, more than anything, disrespectful to the child. Beyond that, they're a waste of hidden opportunity.

Many of the smaller strategies I had designed were, in Dr. Bryson's terms "marketable," meaning that they had the visual appeal to draw my kids in. Then there was one, a big one,that was definitely marketable: *"The Co-operation Contest."*

When I designed it, I was in Hayden's head but more than that, I was *inspired by his emergence!* Benjamin and I could see in Hayden's mind and in his body that he was at a place where he could *finally* start to understand that he could learn to take better control of his body and his actions. More than that, I wanted to *entice him* to take control. That's an important distinction:

171

I watched the way Hayden's mind worked when he watched TV shows like *Yugioh* and *Digimon* and their depictions of good and evil. Typically, a behavioral strategy would have focused more on simply rewarding a child like Hayden each time he had positive, co-operative actions. But I knew how intricately his mind worked and how *oddly able* he was to think in abstract terms. I wanted him to feel that if he had a visual of two characters, one good and one evil, it would symbolize *his own mind and hence, his own ability to make the right decision.* That was the twist that made this program really successful. It enticed him and it drew him in.

And so was born *a visual race*: The "Co-operation Contest," two actual Digimon characters on a board, each *competing* to win a race. Whenever Hayden exhibited co-operative behavior, the "good" character got a checkmark; likewise if Hayden exhibited negative behavior and did not co-operate, the "evil" character got a checkmark. If the "good" character won and got checkmarks to the top first, Hayden got a *great* reward. If the "evil" character won, there was *no* reward and a dismal face was attached to the top of that column.

What made this program unique, was that I would watch Hayden, *really* closely. *Anytime* I saw his behavior start to slide, I would physically bring in the chart and say: "Hayden, do you *really* want the evil character to win this race?" You have to remember, his life was very black and white, good and evil based. Honor and dignity were important to him, in his world of kingdoms and superheroes. The visual representation through his Digimon characters made the concept clear in his mind *and* it gave him the competitive edge of him *not wanting to see the evil villain win.* That was critical and it was the little *brainstorm twist* that made this program successful.

Very quickly Hayden was able to make the connection that if he could stop and think about his action, *before* committing it, he could sometimes weigh out in his mind, some level of control and planning as to the way he *wanted the outcome to be.*

This was a powerful program. It didn't work everyday, every time; as always there were days when he was just so stressed or agitated that he lost all sense of reason. But it *was* a dramatic turning point in Hayden's life.

Chapter 66

en months into Hayden's new school/home school program, we assembled our complete team together to scrutinize our accomplishments and fine tune. It was a shining moment for me to present to them the staggering fact that during the previous *seven months* at Hayden's last school, he had missed *sixty-five days*, and on each of those sixty-five days he was absolutely strung out and incapacitated. But in the *ten months* in his *new* classroom, blended with my morning home school program, he had not missed a *single* day! Sure he'd had a few ups and downs, but there was no denying that this was a success!

Hayden's *acceptance* of his new school had been our primary goal: we would have all been happy if that was *the only thing* we'd accomplished! But his increased reading, writing and printing skills *and* his willingness to learn were just as much to celebrate. We all marveled at Hayden's success and the success of the program. I think we were all equally relieved.

Who would have ever guessed this setting would have worked out so well for him?

Well, I didn't have to guess. *I knew it. I could feel it and I saw it.* I did that by getting *inside* Hayden's head and his body. But in that meeting, as I looked around at the level of expertise (and we were blessed with some very gifted people on our team) something nagged at me and tugged at my heart. As I looked around the room at our behavior consultant, our psychologist, the school district special education director, the principal and Hayden's teacher, and all of the impressive salaries each of these people was pulling down, I couldn't help but think: "Who is the *one* person in this room not paid a cent for any of their time or their insight, their expertise or direct experience with Hayden? *And who is the person who soul searched and studied Hayden, came up with the concept, and then had the courage and conviction to push and convince those who were skeptical (which was all of them initially), to make it happen?*"

Those thoughts had barely finished filling my mind when the district director wrapped up the meeting, saying: "Well I guess we have Mrs. Vine to thank!" I think my heart stopped beating for a moment. I felt like someone had knocked the wind out of me, as I heard each person in the room agree. True, Mrs. Vine was a good teacher, but essentially, she followed the program *that I had designed, that I had had to sell to each of them.* Yet there was not a single word of recognition from any of them about my role.

I tried to tell myself that at that point in the meeting, everyone was exhausted and it was an oversight; but it hurt.

> I went home and went to pieces, in part from sheer exhaustion, in part from the lack of validation. I knew I had to look at the bigger picture, that my reward was greater than any salary or any level of recognition. *It really didn't matter who did what or how we got there; all that mattered was that we had got there.* But it hurt. I was absolutely stunned.

I've thought about that moment many times over the years. I guess, really, for that recognition to have been given to me, would have meant that the school district would have been acknowledging *their* negligence in providing the insight that *they* should have been giving this student. *Weird.*

Chapter 67

As sensitive to Hayden's needs and limitations as his teacher was, there still loomed that underlying feeling that in *her* eyes, the ultimate goal was that shining "9:00 to 3:00 daily attendance," like it would be the *real* measure of success. But to Dr. Bryson and myself, it was never part of the plan because it was unrealistic. *Anytime* we moved away from our carefully-designed schedule, Hayden's behaviors nose-dived.

Finally, against my better judgment, we succumbed, *a little*. That was all it took. Mrs. Vine just kept pushing and emphasizing how important field trips were and how they would broaden Hayden's horizons....we altered his schedule, a few full days here and there for field trips, and we paid the price. *We were back to highs and lows, terrible aggression, biting and kicking at home and restless and disturbed sleep patterns at night. Hayden obsessed about acquiring new toys and went to pieces, if he didn't get a new toy or computer game to focus on, and to divert his attention from the anxiety that was overtaking him.*

Again, it was the familiar pattern of Hayden scrambling to gain control, not only over his altered environment, but over his body.

Repetitive, self-stimming behaviors like "kissing himself better" worsened. He missed days at school. On the walk to school, he was genuinely panicky; he would freeze and refuse to go. One day, largely because I felt I needed to appease the staff, I *physically forced* him into the school. He was screaming and kicking, and both he and Kiera got physically hurt in the process of trying to force him into the classroom. *I swore I would never, ever do that to him again. Why would I? He wasn't "wimping out" or just trying to get his way. The limitations of his mind and body were, once again, overtaking him. He and his body were talking to us.*

Again, he was retreating and it was *me and Hayden against the world: a prince and his queen, and our strong castle walls.*

Alarmingly, the witch nightmares resurfaced, as well as new ones of monsters lashing out at him. In one of them, he hysterically described himself as being in a forest with a witch who killed him with her magic. The *intensity* and *finality* of these dreams was heart-wrenching and disturbing.

I documented and scrutinized and found patterns that reinforced my suspicion that nightmares were triggered, *whenever* Hayden was required to alter his schedule, or when his teacher insisted that he participate in gym class. He knew it was too much for him and his body and his nightmares confirmed that.

Some days were better than others; but most days, Hayden was once again, out of control. He then had no ability to reason. For us at home, it was like stepping back in time to when he was four or five. But he was no longer the size of a four or five year old. He was almost as tall as I was. One ugly, ugly confrontation between Hayden and me was in a local mall, where Hayden stood with both hands on my shoulders so that I couldn't move. He wanted to force me into a store to buy something he was obsessing about. I felt exasperated, helpless and quite honestly, scared. I couldn't reason with him; I certainly couldn't pick him up. *What was I supposed to do?*

It happened again, at the same mall, on another day. Somehow I worked our way from the mall to the parking lot, where things got even uglier. How I eventually got him into the van, I have no recollection; but I remember it was an intensely stressful, ugly and frightening situation.

There were other terrible episodes, some that unfortunately involved Sydney, Kobe and Genevieve. The worst one was leaving a department store, where we'd casually gone to pick up a few school supplies. Hayden was so strung out and aggressive that people stopped and stared at us. Getting *into* the van was an unbelievable ordeal. *Inside* the van was even worse, as there was no reprieve from the stress or the danger: Hayden scratched Kobe deeply, squeezed Kobe's privates relentlessly and screamed hysterically.

I hated and regretted the fact that the other three kids had to endure these terrible traumas. But the truly amazing thing was that in *each* instance, Hayden *did* calm down when we got home. Miraculously, *each time* we ended up having a lovely, enjoyable, closely-knit evening together. After one of the traumas, even Genevieve was drawn to eat dinner with us, which she almost never did. I think she needed to *give* her support and *feel* our support.

In the safety of our castle, *it was magic.* But it was also sheer and utter madness. It was as confusing as all hell, that we could have our hearts thrown and strewn and stomped on by Hayden, only to have him captivate and love us and make us love him *because of his heart, and how much he loved us and how much we loved him.*

Can you even begin to imagine how complex it was living with Hayden Brenneman?

No matter how horrible the situation was in the outside world, once we got home, almost always, we could "pull up the drawbridge" and wrap ourselves up in the security of our castle. Magic would happen! It's not to say that traumas didn't happen *within* those walls, but at least there they were softened and less acute. And we didn't have the peering eyes of the outside world around us. They weren't there to judge us or remind us how different we were from the rest of the world.

And the presence of the outside world was, as we all painfully knew, much of the problem. *One third* of our family struggled, and often could not deal with being in the presence of the outside world.

Once again, we were in crisis. All of us at home were fried, not only by the resurgence of current behaviors but the hidden memories and past scars that were ripped open. You have to understand: when you deal, for so many years, with horrendous behaviors from someone that you love deeply, it *does* play so deeply with your head and your heart. Even when that person's behaviors improve dramatically, *the scars are still there.*

The instinct to protect yourself, emotionally and physically remains acute. Small outbursts that really should not have been a big deal, were. It may be only for a split second, but *you do* relive every single past horrid experience, if only on a subconscious level. Sydney and Kobe have articulated that very same thing. New outbursts affect you so deeply because the scars of the past are so deep. *Imagine what it was like to now be dealing with behaviors that were not small outbursts.*

The good times, the magical moments help to heal; but a bad one rips scars open again, each and every one. Sometimes I wonder if Hayden hadn't been so incredibly loveable and intensely sweet during the good times, that maybe it would have been oddly less scarring. Who knows? With time, and with counseling, the scars have lessened; but we were a long way from that, *back then.*

School and Hayden's life had been going so well, and then we were *unexpectedly* thrust into what felt like a terrible time warp, a place where his behaviors had returned to where they had been years before. Sydney, Kobe, Nolan and I, the "typical" members of our family felt it. I could hardly imagine what it must have been like for Genevieve, who was autistic and struggled with people and their confusing emotions and behaviors, at the best of times.

It took us months to pull things back together and sadly during those months, *there were few* of our "trademark glimmering moments." Things got worse before they got better:

> One evening, Hayden was miserable, arguing with Kobe about something trivial like donuts. Kobe hauled off and punched him in the stomach, hard. At that time, Kobe was six feet tall, an intense, fit athlete with a lot of strength and pent up anger and frustration; he had punched Hayden really hard.
>
> *The look of sheer anguish on Kobe's face when he instantly realized what he had done, to the person he loved more than anyone else in the world, was horrible.*
>
> Instantly, Kobe put on his gear and went for a run. By the time he came back, he was purple and almost hyperventilating; he had run so hard trying to deal with the intensity of the crisis and the rush of emotions that had overtaken him.
>
> I was shocked and angry at Kobe for lashing out and my heart went out to Hayden; but I understood. *He just couldn't take it anymore.* I felt immeasurable guilt, because I realized that just a few minutes before the incident, Kobe had likely overheard me telling a close friend over the phone, about Hayden's recent decline in behavior. I think it triggered emotions in Kobe that rushed so close to the surface that he reacted the heart wrenching way that he did.

Kobe deserved more than this. He didn't deserve to be pushed to this extreme.

That terrible night, I vowed to myself to do whatever it took to ensure that our home never reached that level of intensity again, that Kobe, or any of us should ever be pushed that far again.

> ....On Hayden's June report card, his teacher made the comment: "Even though change of routine is hard on him, he should be encouraged to continue field trips."
>
> That concept was laughable: *not a chance; not at the prices we were paying!*

Chapter 68

That September, we began the school year making it clear that the afternoon schedule was *not* to be changed for *any* reason. Dr. Bryson and I devised a few vibrant *Yugioh* and *Digimon* strategies to enhance regular attendance and get Hayden back on track. *Once again, Hayden astonished us with his genuine sincerity to understand his limitations and to welcome the concepts we designed.*

When he was getting dressed for the first day of school, he calmly and matter-of-factly asked me: "Do you think the *Digimon* thing will work?" He was keen and mature; he *wanted* it to work. As he and I walked to school that afternoon, he said to me sweetly: "Sorry about last term, Mom." Here he was, apologizing for things that really were beyond his control.

> How many more ways can I say that this precious soul didn't *want* to have meltdowns or struggle to handle things like school? He *wanted* to do the things that were expected of him, or that should have come to him the way they did for other kids.

> He was willing to do what he could to embrace his challenges and limitations, and to work *with us* to overcome them. Our elaborate school/home school program and all of our vibrant, Hayden-specific strategies were his way, and *our way* of "meeting halfway."

That had been our key for success with his sister and it was our key to success with him.

One time I overheard Hayden in the bathtub, practicing all on his own, a relaxation and calming process he'd been taught by our consultant and myself. How could you not have anything but boundless compassion for someone who had such a desire to practice a process, *because he knew he needed to, because of his body's limitations?*

Hayden's progress with my home school program was quite overwhelming to me. It wasn't just that I'd devised a process of keeping him occupied at home, when he should have otherwise been in school with his peers; *he was learning.* Within the next year or so, he could read at about a grade three level and complete basic, functional math. He was thrilled at being able to read signs in the community, and even more thrilled to excel on his video games with his ability to read and follow along.

Even today, I don't think I'll ever lose the thrill of seeing Hayden pick up a pen and print. It's still messy, but honestly, it's not much worse than Kobe's.

What was most important was the fact that Hayden wanted to learn and he was so proud. During our home school time, when it was just the two of us at his desk in his bedroom, we had the most amazing conversations. He'd tell me his theories on everything from superheroes to hibernation, metamorphosis and how he was certain that teenagers liked to "chit chat about video games and school projects."

Hayden contemplated things deeply and even though he spent a good part of his day playing video and computer games, he learned enormously from them. And he could articulate how he fit that knowledge into his everyday life.

The structure and routine of Hayden's weekdays did wonders to add stability to his life. We were then able to focus on the other wars that raged on in his life.

Life in our castle merged on with our trademark "wonderful, breath-taking highs and often devastating lows;" but at least we were at a point where, *when Hayden was calm, we could talk to him about his behaviors and his moods.* One day, after he had thrashed his room (where he had been sent for a time out), he destroyed even his beloved (and expensive) *Beetle Borgs* playhouse. When I asked him why he'd done it, he answered: "I had to because I was angry."

Slowly, Hayden *himself* was piecing together more and more about how his mind and his body worked. One day he was relentless in wanting to put up all of our Halloween decorations. He became obsessed about it, and was close to going over the edge. As it was only May, I didn't want to drag out our massive collection of decorations so finally, exasperated, I asked him: "Hayden, I don't know where you got this idea from!" Impatiently and emphatically, as if dumbfounded by my ignorance, he replied: "From my head!"

When Hayden was calm and *could* reason, we focused on his relationship with Genevieve. We tried to impress upon him the need for him to back off and stop harassing her. One day he answered: "I know;" then with a pensive sigh he added: "But I just can't control myself." We could see how it weighed on him and that she was often in his thoughts, and that *he did feel* regret and remorse. A couple of weeks later, she happened to dash into the room to watch her favorite part of a Disney video....with bright, hopeful eyes, he piped up: "Do you like me now?"

He was so disappointed when he realized that *he* wasn't the reason she'd come running into the room.

Genevieve, of course, experienced Hayden, and the abuse from Hayden, differently than the rest of us. One rare evening, I was able to get her in a headspace where she could talk openly, on a level she never had before, about her feelings towards Hayden. She even tried to speculate on where she saw life with Hayden in the future. Her body language was alarming and very descriptive: she flinched and squirmed as we spoke.

At the end of our conversation, she looked like she literally wanted to crawl out of the skin that she had worn, the day we had discussed the demon Hayden.

Chapter 69

Inside our castle, we *could be* amazing! We couldn't have our house constantly oozing with neighborhood kids the way I'd planned; but if it was carefully orchestrated, with weeks of planning *and* recovery time afterward, we could sometimes pull off the coolest things!

For Hayden's birthday, Sydney and Kobe hosted a spectacular Magic Show for a small group of classmates. They had their audience in awe. Kobe even lay on a real bed of nails that he and I had painstakingly devised.

One of our very best parties came from Genevieve's design: "The Jammy Awards." It was brilliant! Each of her classmates received an invitation and a blank cassette. They were invited to create a song, dance or short performance of any type, individually, as couples or even as trios. They'd have the opportunity to perform "live" at our party.

We served "Hors d'oeuvres and Cocktails" and *every single child* amazed us with their creations, their costumes and their performances. Many had written original material and rehearsed for days beforehand. We gave out Jammy award statuettes for categories like "Best Comical Song", "Best Duo", "Best Live Performance" and more. *It was priceless and unique. No one had parties like us!*

I sometimes wonder if I would have been as drawn and compelled to pouring as much time and creativity into our events, had I not had the duo purpose of *using them as therapy*. The answer is: "Probably not;" but it was fabulous and it was who we had become, like our trademark. *It was one of the many good things we had become!*

And we latched on to the energy and beauty of each outsider child who was lured into our castle. That gave us the safety of our world mixed with the life and "normalness" of the outside world. . . .very powerful, on a bunch of levels!

> Why were these events so powerful in helping Genevieve and Hayden emerge? *That's easy:* both kids could assume roles and feel safe in those roles. They could tolerate and then enjoy peers who would otherwise have been an intrusion. They could let their guard down, but still have *an invisible wall up*, provided by their costume or even just the character they were assuming.

> They then had the joy of being around peers, while learning *about them* and learning *how to be* around them.

> In the case of "The Jammy Awards," the wall was Genevieve's role as both a performer and the creator of the show. We gave her flowers at the end of "The Jammies" and her acceptance speech and mannerisms were drawn *completely* from award shows she'd seen on TV. *She had memorized and scripted them, in her mind and in her body.* Her peers were probably too young to see that; they just saw her as fascinating and a true performer.

That was my plan. It always worked, and we always nudged a few steps forward! (And Genevieve, conscious or not, recognized that plan and embraced it. She is so brilliant and masterful).

One of the *best* things to come out of Hayden's final year of elementary school, was a boy who could at times, reason. One of the most *quizzical* things to see, was that frequently, he would move full force into an intense tantrum or outburst, and then quite literally, like someone had flicked a switch, divert himself and be calm. It was almost as if nothing had happened. Often we were absolutely dumbfounded; but we were always incredibly grateful.

As Hayden improved, slowly and carefully, we were opening up our castle doors. Both Sydney and Kobe lowered their own personal walls between their outside lives and our home life, and brought selected friends in. *I can hardly describe what that was like.* If you close your eyes and think of *your* childhood: all the sleepovers....your best friend often at the dinner table....that wasn't the way it had been for Sydney and Kobe. Occasionally, they'd had glimmers but they were only tiny, tiny glimmers. Now they had a lot of making up to do.

How long had we waited? How many mountains had we had to climb to get here?

It wasn't in droves, letting outsiders in. It was in little bits and we still needed to orchestrate and support *both* Hayden and Genevieve when others were in our home, because *both* were easily overwhelmed by the presence of outsiders; but it was manageable. It was worth any prices we had to pay afterward.

Genevieve was the most skittish with the presence of outsiders. Hayden sometimes welcomed it. He proudly announced to me one day: "Teenage girls think I'm adorable!"

As I watched these newcomers waft through our home, I took a long look at the many charts and behavioral strategies, placed strategically throughout our home. All of them were carefully designed to keep Hayden on track, to teach him and to help him to be the person he deserved to be. All of them were designed to keep peace and sanity!

I looked at them through the eyes of our visitors. How did they appear to them? How did they see us? *We were the real thing.* We didn't *dabble* in behavioral strategies and creative, open-minded thinking. We *were* behavioral strategies *and* creative, open-minded thinking! They were to us, like breathing. In my mind, *everything* was a potential behavioral strategy.

As odd as we probably appeared, I think every visitor picked up on the love and respect that filled our home. One very pretty and sensitive girl, a close friend of Kobe's, always made a point of chatting with both Genevieve and Hayden. One day I saw her pondering all of the charts I'd designed. She looked at me, not with concern or confusion, but with respect. She said: "You know, I think all parents should do this with their kids!" I'll never forget that. She was a smart and insightful girl.

We were unique, and not just because we had autism! One afternoon an air of excitement filled our castle and the grounds outside, as Kobe's buddies strategically placed themselves on either sides of our house. Their job was to direct him exactly where to aim, as Kobe attempted to shoot a basketball from the back sundeck, over the house and into the hoop in the front yard! For two hours, with a video camera in hand, they were all there to witness and be a part of the feat. We were *definitely* a home of unique and scattered talents. (If you're wondering: Kobe never did get it right through the net, but he hit the rim twice).

Most of Sydney's "artsy" friends were musical theatre types, and they had a pretty high comfort level in our theatrical house. Amongst that bunch, like a sparkling jewel, was Michael, the young man that Sydney fell in love with. *From the very first moment he came into her life, it was pretty clear that his love and adoration for her would give him all he needed to survive even the worst that our complex family could throw at him.* To hear her really, genuinely laugh when she was with him, was one of the most beautiful sounds I'd ever heard!

Chapter 70

*O*ur castle had become a pretty happy and homey place to be. Often it felt like blue sunny skies and sun were streaming in and often we could let our guard down a little. And there was peace in knowing that our castle could be quickly armored and protected when necessary, as long as I kept my focus. But it loomed over me, and over all of us, how quickly we could spiral. Then the drawbridge would be up, the walls would get colder, sometimes to the point that moss would grow, separating us from the rest of the world.

> When that happened, my role would shift from orchestrator, to Hayden's queen, and sometimes, what felt to me like "captive wench." But at least, if we stayed inside, and if everyone was feeling safe, we could regroup and at some point, venture out again.

Reading this book must be exasperating and confusing! You must be asking: "Hey, a minute ago you said things were improving. Then you say everything could slide into a stressful mess?" That's exactly the point. *We were still a living and breathing example of chaos and contradiction!*

On one hand, we had excelled in leaps and bounds, with incredibly creative and "bang on strategies." Many had phenomenal success and continually lifted us to the next level. We were all growing and thriving, with more and more glimmers of harmony and captivating times. But still so often, there was a flip side and a price to pay.

There was either the looming presence of the *possibility* for disaster, or disaster itself. I've given you snippets of our history and our stories but a few hundred pages can give you only a taste. There were times, when even Dr. Bryson and all of his expertise and insight, and his knowledge of our family, looked like *his* head was spinning; at times he felt "one step behind." We were hard to keep up with!

But at least we were seeing what worked and more clearly, *what didn't work.* The gains we made and the increased moments of harmony made us bolder and more driven to stand firm with what we knew would work, no matter how much opposition we got from the outside world.

For all of the Hayden traumas, he made us feel incredibly loved. He was capable of such volatile, unpredictable behavior and could impact the people around him simply by walking into the room. And yet, no one could make us feel as important as he did. He could be aloof, content to stay in his own world, focusing on what was important to him; and yet he took such a *genuine interest* in each of us. Every day, he would keenly ask each of us how our day went. *He really meant it; he wanted to know.* If Kobe or Sydney, or even Genevieve had a test at school, Hayden would remember and the very first thing he'd ask when they came home was: "How was your test?" And again, he really wanted to know.

The safe world of Amity was coming to an end. The reality of high school was undeniably near. Could I envision Hayden walking through the halls of a high school, still being calm, loving and receptive? *I could not see that image.* Even in the comfort zone of Amity, he had "enemies" and looming fears that threatened him. *His mind was very simple and yet uniquely complex.* There was one special needs classmate, for example, who brought out the worst in him. At one point Hayden pinched him and tried to devise a devious prank that would get the boy expelled and out of Hayden's hair forever. When I finally got the chance to meet this young boy (another of Hayden's victims), Hayden introduced him to me saying: "This is my enemy."

How would Hayden ever survive in the world of high school and teenagers?

We did find a classroom, in a nearby secondary school that looked like a pretty good match. It was a small class, with two alternating teachers and several assistants and each of the kids had special needs of varying natures. And, Hayden's "girlfriend" Whitley was there.

Whitley....how is it that I've forgotten to tell you about Whitley? That's because she flitted in and out of Hayden's life since kindergarten, there one moment, deeply, and then completely out of his life, the next moment. It was like blinking your eyes and it was Hayden and Whitley; then blinking again and she was more like a memory.

Whitley too, had autism. She even looked like Hayden with red hair and dimples. They had the most amazing relationship I've ever seen. I mean that seriously and literally. They entered each other's lives deeply, like nothing else. They understood each other innately. It was just absolutely extraordinary! They got each other. *They played the same way, through superheroes and costumes, and the world being a flat, linear backdrop of good and evil, right and wrong.* They would play for hours and hours.

It was all about wavelength. Deep inside their mutual worlds they would connect, and then when they'd had enough of each other, they'd break away, tune each other out, and venture into their solitary worlds again. After awhile, they'd regroup and rejoin each other.

Often they overwhelmed themselves by each other's presence and I'd have to orchestrate "behind the scenes" to keep them both on track. And, Whitley could be just as stubborn and strong-willed as Hayden. Having autism, she had her own set of walls and her own body that experienced the world so uniquely. *She was and is, utterly fascinating and completely lovable.*

Together, Whitley and Hayden made the most amazing pair. But as much as they both loved being together, both were *equally happy* to let months pass by with no interactions at all. It remains the same today. In some ways *their relationship* was like an "object" that they could take down off a shelf, and play with. When they'd had enough, they could put it back up on the shelf, brushing themselves off before returning to the world that they really enjoyed the most: *their own.*

High School, even one with a protected classroom and his adorable Whitley awaiting him, was a *very* far cry from the safety of Hayden's own world. He did his best to embrace his life's new direction, but early on the "usual mysteries of Hayden" began to unfold, baffling his new teachers and staff.

They were wonderfully supportive of our concept and were receptive and helpful with the home school component; but they still had an innate insistence on pushing academics. And they insisted on Hayden venturing out throughout the hallways, to access his locker and to visit various parts of the school. To the staff's credit, it *was* confusing that what Hayden appeared to handle was different, from what was going on below the surface.

We'd lived through that before; we'd anticipated that and so we made them well-versed in the language of Hayden before the year even started. But they fell into the usual trap, and I honestly don't believe they were trained well enough to understand how complex he was, and how it was translated into behaviors that they didn't necessarily see at school.

But we saw the pattern at home, and once again, we paid the price. The step to high school was too big and their expectations were too great, even though they insisted that they grasped the severity of his limitations and the impact on our family.

At home yet again, behaviors worsened to an alarming level and we were sliding back to a place and a way of life that we'd worked so hard to move away from.

As the year progressed, the screaming, the volatile behavior and the aggression escalated. Hayden would stalk through the house aimlessly, obsessing about acquiring toys and video games. We recognized that as him scrambling to re-direct, to survive. The seriousness of his behaviors was compounded by his height, size and the fact that *he knew* he could use them to intimidate us. One afternoon when Genevieve was on the computer, he threatened her twice with a wooden stick he'd found. When I discussed it with him, he was defiant and quick to stand up and look down at me, to intimidate *me* with his size. He was then close to six feet tall.

Another day, Hayden chased Sydney around the entire house, threatening and intimidating her.

Sydney, who'd been experiencing for some time, anxiety symptoms, like a choking sensation in her throat, heartburn and tightening in her chest, had one of her worst attacks the evening she accompanied Hayden and me to a video store. Another day, for no apparent reason, other than the fact that he was overloaded, Hayden punched her in the eye.

Not all of his behaviors could be blamed on school stress, but it was a *very serious contributing factor.* There seemed no end to the levels of complexity that made up Hayden. There was so much he didn't understand and it was always such a battle keeping him occupied and entertained. *It was that constant battle between under-stimulating him and over-stimulating him.*

One day, for instance, he was in a good frame of mind so we took a risk and brought him to IKEA. He actually *asked* to have his wheelchair and did well staying calm; but by the time we got to the cashier, he'd reached his breaking point. Seeing the cafeteria, he decided he wanted *two* items when we got through the cashier. Unfortunately, the IKEA deal was "a drink and two hot dogs" which should have made him even happier, because he would get three items instead of two.

Not Hayden and the state of mind and body he was in. He flipped out because it was *more* than two items. *He couldn't comprehend that even if I ate one of his hot dogs he would then have only his two desired items.* It turned into an ugly mess. It demonstrated how rattled and unglued his sense of security had become.

⤚〰️✶⟋⟋⟋⟋⟋⟋⤙〰️

As always Hayden's horrid behaviors were contrasted by curious and lovely ones. After a couple of really grueling weeks, when I desperately needed a break from him, to my dismay he refused to go with his Sunday respite worker. He then refused to go on an alternate outing with his dad.

He said he wanted to be with me, and longingly he exclaimed: "I wish there was a twin of me; one to go with Dad and one to stay with Mom!" Nolan and I looked back at him in wonder and said: "But Hayden, then *both* of you would want to stay with Mom and then you'd *both* have to share her."

A wave of awareness crossed his face, and he replied: "Whoa, that's a problem!" *Life was just so complicated when you're Hayden.*

urious or not, we were again, in a serious place. It was time to help Hayden get deeply inside *his own head and his body*, and help him *identify and articulate* what was going on. I knew I had to present it to him in "Hayden terms and images." I did that through a small, framed mural. On the left side, was the face of *Spiderman* and on the right, the face of Green Goblin.

A door opened. Hayden was able to connect the people and stresses in his life with the underlying emotions he was feeling. *Most of them revolved solidly around the "hellish" environment of school.* It was just too much for him, and on countless levels.

Though we'd stuck to the plan of afternoon school, with no assemblies or field trips, the class room *itself* was too much. There were too many distractions and too many other kids. And *the building itself,* with hundreds of students in the hallways and classrooms around him, was too much. I could feel it. I could see it in him and in his body when he walked through the halls to his locker.

Hayden "appeared to manage;" but I could feel and see how it all weighed on him. *Too much socialness.* Even his locker and his insistence on keeping it absolutely bare, with nothing but his jacket and backpack, proved his lack of connection. You'd think he would have filled his locker with superhero security and power; but not Hayden. *The worlds of home and school were not welcome to intersect or even collide; he made that very clear.*

Life at home got worse. Often, the smallest thing pushed Hayden dangerously over the edge. The *unpredictability* of these severe behaviors was staggering. *At times, he could switch out of them, like a mood swing. Other times, there seemed no rhyme, no reason, no answer and no effective way of dealing with them.* Many occurred in the TV room, where he spent most of his time, alternating between TV and game systems.

When he became belligerent and distraught, we had few options but to physically force him into the adjoining garage. It was horrible to do, but at least in there, we stood a chance of him being distracted long enough to click into an alternate mode. Sometimes it worked. Sometimes it only escalated the situation. Nolan and I were both pushed to ridiculous levels.

This is so difficult to spell out in black and white for you to read, *but our physically removing Hayden to the garage, probably also kept him safe from us.* You just can't even imagine. You'd have a hard time finding two people with more patience, but we were pushed so far beyond anything *any* parent should ever have to deal with. And this went on for months.

And it was getting dangerous. Hayden was a big kid. Nolan was even bigger; but even with his size he could barely manipulate Hayden to the garage or anywhere. He was getting injured in the process.

It was terrible place to be. After years and years of dealing with horrendous behaviors, we'd had a wonderful reprieve where we were starting to feel just a little bit normal. We were finally able to let outsiders in, to live alongside us, *inside* our castle. *How could we maintain that with Hayden acting the way he was?* And there was no end in sight.

I'm not going to lie and make myself out to be a saint here. There were times when I was pushed so far over the edge, that I did things and said things that I later regretted. I'd have to strategize like crazy afterward, to undo the damage. I consoled myself by desperately envisioning almost every single person I had ever known and asking myself: "Would *they* have survived all that we'd gone through, and then be brought to this point and not lose *their* grip?"

This wasn't about my or Nolan's lack of ability, or lack of patience or compassion. I don't think I've ever known anyone who could have done better than we'd done. I couldn't even imagine anyone who would have lasted, for even *a fraction* of the journey we had. But this couldn't go on. Hayden needed to have changes in his life.

When I look at how well Hayden is doing today (at this moment, as I complete this book), I'm not so sure that it was a totally bad thing for him to have seen his parents so completely unglued. Though he was, and still is today, very much a victim of his body and his "wiring," he *did* have a conscience. Even back then, he had the desire to be a good person, someone he and the world could be proud of.

Our words and our actions did penetrate him enough, to make him understand that even good people who love him, and are devoted to him, could be pushed to the point of distraction. In calm times, in the aftermath, that *did* motivate him to learn more about his body and the impact of the world on his body.

Hayden learned that he didn't need to compare himself to anyone else or how *they* could handle things. He learned that he only needs to compare himself to Hayden of yesterday and Hayden of today. His body and his mind are unique and *he has*, as do those of us who love him so deeply, *the right to mold and maneuver his world around him*, to honor who he is.

That's not giving in, or letting him manipulate, or "not challenging him." That's being intelligent, realistic and respectful. That is honoring the gift that is Hayden.

Chapter 72

Could we pinpoint all of the forces that weighed so heavily on Hayden? Did it matter? Some things we couldn't alter. *Simply living in our home, with the day-to-day influx of the five of us weighed on him. Imagine what the chaos and overload of school did to him.* He deserved more; we deserved more. *We were not going to survive this.*

Dr. Bryson, Rheanna our consultant and I worked as a team, exploring every possible strategy. Finally we created something new, something radical really, and pretty extreme. Nolan was not in support and for me, it wasn't so much that it almost bordered on abusive that bothered me.... it was that as the three of us hammered out the final details, I really didn't feel in my heart that it was going to work.

It just seemed that what we needed to find was a strategy that was so completely *in Hayden's language*, on a deeply creative level, that his mind and his body couldn't help but be pulled in and altered.

We needed something that would calm him down that *didn't involve physically removing him to the garage.* The garage was clearly loosing its effectiveness because Hayden was smart, and he was desperate. He found out how to get out of the garage and then he'd come back with a vengeance, or he'd run around the outside of the house, adding fuel to the fire. And I wasn't strong enough; even

Nolan was no longer strong enough. And it broke our hearts every time we had to resort to the garage. It felt abusive.

For me, the one who was with Hayden the most....I just couldn't take it anymore. *I had to get inside his body. I had to feel what he was feeling. I had to breathe him in. I had to make myself feel what it was, that would give him some sort of inner peace....*

I asked myself: "How do I make Hayden feel like he is *enveloped* in safety?" I closed my eyes and tuned out the world and felt only Hayden and his world, and his body.... then it was like the concept simply wrapped around me and emerged:

> *How could I envelope him in safety?....I design an envelope....a superhero envelope....I literally wrap him up in superhero safety....the image was so clear and so bold. I could see it. I could feel it. I could feel Hayden wrapped up by it, enveloped....*

From there, the concept quickly took form. I reached for the tools I kept closest at hand: fabric, paints, my hands, my imagination, and my *feeling* Hayden. This time, I reached for Nolan's hands too, along with lengths of 2X4's and nails....

Picture this: our TV room and the couch where Hayden spent much of his time, the place where most of his outbursts and rampages erupted. Overhead of the couch, a wooden frame bolted solidly to the ceiling, outlined with Velcro....in a matter of seconds, "*The Spiderman Curtain*" could be attached....

The *Spiderman Curtain* completely shrouded the couch, from the floor to the ceiling. On the inside, I appliquéd the face of *Spiderman*, with webs hand-painted. As if coming from his voice, a bubble caption said: "Stress senses are tingling. I must get them under control. The world is counting on me."

The use of Velcro meant the curtain could be hung up in about ten seconds, making the entire couch shrouded from the outside world. *I knew it would have an impact. I could feel it.* Very quickly, within the first two trial runs, Hayden responded. Serious rages that *should* have been traumas, were diffused within minutes. *I wasn't surprised because I knew I was in Hayden's zone when I designed it; but I was surprised at how quickly he responded.* And, I was very surprised by the effect the *Spiderman Curtain* had *on me!*

I discovered that when *I was enveloped* inside the curtain along with Hayden, I could keep *my* presence of mind even when Hayden was amidst a full-blown rampage. *In other words, it had an amazing, calming effect, not only on Hayden, but*

193

on me. Being enveloped actually became a lovely, safe place to be and we *both* felt empowered.

Part of the magic of this strategy was that it wasn't just a distraction to help Hayden switch modes; it was a place that could calm and connect us, so that we could then look *insightfully* at what had set Hayden off in the first place. Then we could try to figure out how to address it.

What is so important to recognize, is that for a complex person like Hayden, programs and strategies have to be real. They have to be vibrant. They have to *pull him in.* The curtain and its concept was all of that:

The curtain itself was made of simple blue fabric; but it couldn't be just *any shade* of sky blue. It needed to be the color of the sky at that moment just before dusk, when *Spiderman* would likely come out to fight the criminals of the world. It had to signify the time of day that had a feeling of mystery. *Consciously or not, Hayden would feel all of that.* He would pull that into his body. And this curtain had to pull *me in*, as well, so that when I was there with Hayden, *I would be in his world.* I just really didn't expect it to calm and captivate him or me, as well as it did!

Each time, when Hayden had calmed down successfully enough, he was given a large, gold star, made out of shiny fabric. We called it "the star of success" and he would keenly pin it to the mysterious night sky. As the growing number of stars accumulated in his sky, they served to remind him of the number of times he'd been successful in using his own superpowers to calm himself down, and to understand his world and his body.

The *Spiderman Curtain* wasn't enough to end *all* of Hayden's horrid behaviors and reactions, but it *was* a dramatic turning point. It diffused so much of what we were dealing with. At least there was some level of sanity *and* we could get deeper inside his head and his body.

The thing was, he was still was a boy who was not completely safe in the world; how could he be safe in the environment of a high school? That question remained at the top of our list: what adjustments in Hayden's life now needed to be made?

Chapter 73

The concreteness of Hayden's world was constantly contrasted by the abstractness of Genevieve's. For me, it was mesmerizing but exhausting and overwhelming, shifting back and forth from her perspective to his, especially now that they were *both* struggling with the challenges of high school. Often my brain would just shut down, to the point where I felt drowsy, like being under medication. Some days I had to succumb to as many as three naps, and sometimes I literally fell asleep when talking with Genevieve.

It was just too vast a range, sweeping from her world to his. She had her need for routine but Hayden's was even more entrenched. Some of his rituals were hard to take; but many we learned to live with and quite forgot that typically families weren't bound by restrictions and "protocol." Here's one: turning off a video, meant we had to press "pause, then stop, then TV off." If we didn't follow that exact pattern, trust me; there'd be hell to pay. Here's another: each morning, when Hayden came downstairs, he'd say: "I have to go to the bathroom." If one of us (and curiously it didn't matter which one of us, as long as it was said), didn't respond with: "Okay Hayden," he'd be thrown and the morning would take a turn for the worse.

But on the bright side, our countless rituals and routines helped both Hayden and Genevieve navigate and so we respected them!

With Genevieve and Hayden it wasn't just their rituals that were contrasted; the strategies we used were generally complete opposites. That meant I had to be in two very different states of mind to conceive and implement them. *That was exhausting.* His strategies were always very vibrant and structured, with clear expectations of him. Hers were creative, playful, abstract and "pink and fluffy"; and they had to be designed carefully so that they didn't "look" like strategies.

If I were to describe how this all translated into *my* body, I would use dance terms: I *craved* to do the splitz, when the best I could do emotionally and physically, was a mediocre demi-plie. Dr. Bryson and I both knew we needed more in-home help and desperately; but we both knew the drawbacks. We'd lived through that before!

One day, frantically writing in my journal, I drew a caricature of Genevieve and then one of Hayden. I was in the middle. On her side I drew clouds and fluffiness and on his side, very bold and distinct lines. In the middle was me going just a little bit crazy.

I asked myself, and Benjamin: "How do I keep making the transition from her world to his, without being so overwhelmed, often to the point of falling asleep?" It didn't help that most often Genevieve would leave her issues until late at night. Once Hayden was off to bed, she'd spring them on me, when I didn't have a lot left to offer. Somehow, most of the time, I was almost always able to tap into hidden bits of creative power. Most of the time....

Chapter 74

At age sixteen. Kobe "pitched the game of his life." It was a showcase tournament, under the keen eyes of scouts, searching for young talent. He was "carded" by two Major League teams, which meant he was someone they'd be keeping an eye on. He was on a high; we all were. All his years of hard work and dedication were paying off. At the very least, we knew that in two years, he'd be off to the US for college baseball.

I wondered and worried: how much would his devotion to his family and especially to Hayden, get in his way? He deserved to follow his dream and I figured he *would* have the strength to leave; but how much of his heart would he leave behind? *And what about the brotherhood?* I smiled to think about a little conversation between me and Kobe years before:

> Kobe: *"Mom, Hayden doesn't love Markus with his eyes."* (*Markus was our little neighbor and friend*).
> Myself: *"Kobe, he loves Markus as a friend and you like a brother."*

Kobe, beaming back at me: *"Yes but he doesn't love Markus with his eyes. That's brother love. It's special!"*

Despite junior high, puberty and two autistic kids, we had many magical, fabulous moments. On one of my birthdays, we watched the slides from our past Disneyland trip and the entire evening was absolutely perfect! On the day before one of Genevieve's birthdays, Kobe spent almost the entire day with her, working on games and plays, to help her "make time fly" until her evening of celebration and gifts. And Sydney carved out moments and seized opportunities to connect with Hayden and Genevieve. She so naturally got inside their heads, and for her, it was more a matter of "the big picture," and how to keep us together as a family.

> But the prevailing reality was: we were slammed back into a nightmare existence. *Please do not do us the injustice of chalking this up to simply teenage hormones!* That was part of it; but only a part. Most of it was pure and simple: you think the world is a frightening and overwhelming place for an autistic child? You should see it when they become teens. The gap between them and their peers grows larger; and the expectations for them to adapt and be out and about in the world, heightens.

In response to Hayden and Genevieve's extreme angst, Kobe struggled. Often he got into fights at school, sometimes defending his siblings from kids who made comments. Frequently, he said to me: "I just feel sad and I don't know why." Routinely, he and I'd sneak out for dinner together, giving him time to try to open up about all that he was dealing with. I was shocked when I realized how much of his early years he had literally blocked out, like he had no memory of them. Sessions with Dr. Bryson helped; an anger management group helped. He had sports, he had charisma and friends which all helped; but it was like he lead *two* lives. We lived so differently from everyone else.... it was a tough life that he led.

And Sydney; she didn't suppress and bottle things up the way that Kobe did. Hers were translated more into her body....migraines, stomach and immune system issues, anxiety and low-grade depression; fear.

The signs were there; we were all in our own ways, faltering. The years of stress were too much. Strategies like the *Spiderman Curtain* brought us more deeply inside Hayden's mind and body and it helped *remarkably* to take the edge off the intensity of his aggression. But the world's expectations on him were unrealistic with what he could handle. And each of us had had too much history with him; too many traumas.

Even with "the edge" taken off, Hayden was too much. This was going to go on forever: one step forward and two steps back, at best. He was getting bigger and bigger; and the impact of high school was intensifying. Whether any of us actually said it out loud or not, we couldn't keep our eyes closed any longer. *It was upon us: we had each reached our absolute breaking point.*

Like a stack of cards, we were positioned to fall. We'd been teetering there for a long time. And then one card was pulled from below us and we fell. We collapsed. We unraveled in what seemed to happen in the blink of an eye.

It would end up being a year of our lives that could fill the chapters of a book just as long as this one.......

Chapter 75

It started with a phone call, right there on my cell in the grocery store.... the vice principal saying Kobe had been suspended from school for being caught with controlled substances. Thank God it was "only" dope, but it showed us how he'd been dealing with the stress of his life. Sydney had seen him at parties; she knew this wasn't a one-time thing. Nolan and I had to plead with his principal and school coaches, and open up intimate details about our history, so they could see Kobe for the compassionate, complex person that he was, not just some punk.

But we were stunned: he was foolishly risking his reputation at a time in his life when he was being watched by the world of baseball.

It didn't end there. Sydney plummeted. It was out of concern for Kobe, but also her own sense of hopelessness about our situation. She was burnt out; she was in a state of depression. *How could she not be, poor thing?*

At first, we didn't grasp the seriousness of Sydney's state of mind. This was our Sydney, afterall, amazing, resilient Sydney. She and I spent hours talking and pondering, getting things out. Nolan and I reached for meaningful, but quick fixes. We let her re-decorate the bathroom to feel creative and to make her home feel safe. We bought her a puppy, thinking that having someone of her own to love and take care of, would heal some of her scars.

But Sydney's new puppy was a double-edged sword. Despite our explanations to the contrary, Kobe interpreted the move as: "I screwed up so Sydney got a puppy." Yes, she gained a warm and lovable puppy; but she paid the price of a wall going up between her and her favorite brother. It only worsened her state of mind and the plight of the six of us.

It didn't really matter; all of our remedies at that point were "drops in a bucket" anyway.

A few weeks later, at six in the morning, as Nolan and I lay fast asleep, our bedroom phone rang. On the other end, was Sydney's panic-stricken and peculiar-sounding voice, from her bedroom below. She mumbled, feebly: "Mom, I need help." Nolan and I dashed downstairs, not knowing what we were going to find. Had someone broken into the house? Had she been attacked? A million thoughts went through our minds in those few seconds.

And there she was, on the floor, curled into a ball, like she couldn't move. Had she had a heart attack, a stroke? She could talk, but barely; and she couldn't feel her lower extremities. *She was so scared. We were scared.* Within minutes, her room was filled with ambulance attendants and fire fighters, all trying to figure out what was wrong with her.

Off to Emergency we went. Thank God it turned out to be an extremely severe anxiety attack, and nothing fatal. That was good news. But I knew the horror wasn't over. This was a serious breakdown, both physical and emotional. I had known this was coming; I'd felt it for months, probably the past year. I had *tried* to talk more openly to her about our history, the scars, the way that we lived. But even with me, and all of our "connectedness," it wasn't a place that she could let herself go. *And so, she put it into her body.*

For months prior, Sydney had met frequently for counseling, with both Dr. Bryson and our family doctor (who had a severely autistic child herself). It helped; but she would only let them see what she was *prepared* to let them see.

199

You have to remember that both Sydney and Kobe were extremely insightful teens, with years of seeing and experiencing the world on a very abstract level. When you live *our kind of life*, it opens up a whole world of insight and perceptiveness. It's a wonderful, powerful thing and the three of us like to interpret it as one of the "perks"; but you also learn *who* you can let in. Sometimes you really can't even let *yourself* in there to see.

And you learn to let people see *only what you are prepared to let them to see*. In Sydney's case, she had an extraordinarily sharp and complex mind, and even with skilled therapists, she knew how much to give and how much to hold back, and how to do it.

I believe Sydney *had* to hold back, because the scars were so deep, and she wasn't yet in a place in her life, where she was able to let them fester and be poked and prodded.

I think that the moment Kobe had been suspended from school, it triggered an acknowledgement in her that we were *not going to be okay,* that we were *not going to survive this*. She then started a downward descent, one that no puppy or even the coolest new bathroom could stop. On some levels, I welcomed it because I'd known for so long that there were things in her that she needed to get out, things that those of us helping her had not been able to access. This *had* to happen; I knew that, but I was scared, *really* scared.

She had hit rock bottom; we had hit rock bottom.

Sydney wasn't to blame. I think ironically, and maybe because she truly is an "old soul" and she has wisdom so far beyond her years, her breakdown ultimately, was *her way of taking care of us*. She was the big sister, the first born. That role came naturally to her. We *needed* to hit rock bottom. *She was the catalyst, not someone to blame.* In her body's wisdom, she was taking care of us.

Her body was saying to all six of us, and to everyone involved with us: *This can't go on.*

Chapter 76

One of the things about "hitting rock bottom" is that from there, you can only climb up. It sounds poetic, and it is. There is a certain beauty in it. But what *isn't* poetic, is that it's not like someone plants a seed and you instantaneously take root, and start climbing, like some wild and fanciful beanstalk that grows in green splendor, winding and reaching gloriously towards the sun.

On our slow, upward ascent, there were snags and snares all along the way. *This was a family breakdown.* We all fell apart. Emotional scars got ripped open and trodden upon. We had tiny steps forward and futile-feeling steps backward.

A breakdown, at least a breakdown like this one, takes victims in its upward spiral. Sydney was a victim because she looked like she had given up. It appeared on the surface that her actions would ultimately break our family apart. Hayden was the most victimized of all. In our hearts, and in Hayden's own heart, there was no disguising the fact that *he* was at the deepest root of all of this.

During those months, and it would be about a year, we all handled it and responded to it in different ways. *There was blame, there was denial; there was anger, there was hurt and there was sadness.*

A few days after her hospitalized anxiety attack, Sydney, barely able to pull herself out of bed each day, said the words: *"I'm done. I can't do this anymore."* I knew she was right; she couldn't. *We had to get her out of there.*

We needed two homes. It wasn't a concept that was new to me. Many times, over the couple of years leading up to these events, I'd presented it to Nolan, saying that this was all too much; that one house, *no* house, could be equipped to deal with all of us. Both Hayden and Genevieve were so deeply affected by the chaos of noise, of people and of their surroundings. And for the rest of us, the stress and the social limitations, the never-ending years of walking on eggshells, of dealing with behaviors: it wasn't healthy, no matter how many glimmering moments we shared.

The reality now was: Sydney had to get out, and fast. But she was only eighteen, and she was *not ready* to leave home. But what choice was there?

It was one of the lowest points of my life, seeing her at our door with her suitcases packed. I'd never known what it was to cry that hard. I wasn't ready for her to leave. She wasn't ready to leave and it was ripping out our hearts. *Would she even be back?* Was this short term, just until she could pull herself together, pull herself out of the deep fog of depression that now consumed her? I tried to be hopeful; but I knew the impact of our home and I also had to be realistic. Maybe she would *never* be able to come back.

> We were all crashing. Our *walls* were crashing down around us. It wasn't just because of Sydney's breakdown. That was only the catalyst. Yes, our castle walls could keep us separate from the world. *From the outside*, our fortress was as strong as ever. But there was dissention amongst us. And there was too much unlivable chaos, and we were all just too used up.

Our castle walls had crumbled from within.

I can't lie and say that I handled this well. I didn't.

Yes, we had hit rock bottom and we were slowly spiraling back upward; new leaves were shooting outward and upward, but *there were victims. I probably victimized more than anyone else*. But watching Sydney leave, and seeing so much anger in Kobe, and worrying about his future.... watching Sydney leave our home put me in a place I'd never been before: it meant, in my eyes, that all the years of hard work and devotion, of always looking to the positive, and of never giving up....ultimately left us in pieces, with my precious Sydney gone....

I no longer had my sense of direction. All that we had done to hold this family together, and here we were, dismantled. The one thing I'd fought to maintain, right from the onset of Genevieve's bizarre and stressful behaviors, years before, was to keep our family together. Now all of that was shattered.

For the first time *ever*, I felt resentment towards Hayden. I even felt it towards Genevieve, and that was so unfair because she was undeserving of blame.

And it wrenched and tormented my soul that I could feel resentment towards them.

That only made things worse. I tried to hide it, but it was from so deep within me, that I think it was pretty transparent. And I plummeted, into depression.

Chapter 77

had my own recovery to deal with and it was rough. It would take too many chapters to fill here and I'm okay with not even going there. *But we did get back on track.* Terms like "soul searching" and "re-evaluating," are insulting really, to describe how deeply inward Nolan and I had to reach, to analyze our situation. Our family had been through too much for too long, to simply reach for a temporary band-aid. Sydney had moved in nearby, with her favorite cousin for a few weeks; but she needed stability. If ever there was a time where she needed to feel a home safely wrapped around her, it was then.

It was time to be bold and brave enough to make changes that were permanent, and life altering for each of us. Our only answer *was* a second home. It wasn't a move I'd ever *wanted* to make, but I'd seen few alternatives. *I'd contemplated it for years.* How could we even do it? Who would live with whom? Would it be two revolving homes, with different family members at different times? How would two children so dependent on routine even manage it? There'd been no easy solutions, which hadn't really matter because Nolan had never been willing to even consider anything as drastic as that. He'd talked over the years about Hayden leaving and living somewhere else, but he'd never agreed to operating two homes. *Now, we had no choice.*

The plan revolved around making a safe, permanent home for Sydney, where she could live with her dad. There was no choice about that; neither Hayden nor Genevieve would have lasted a day without me. I'd stay with them and Kobe.

The second home would also be a reprieve, where I could at times go, where Kobe could go and even Genevieve, where we could take turns living with Sydney, and getting a break from Hayden. Nolan would live there with Sydney, but "straddle" the two homes and all of us.

What choice was there? At least it was a plan and it offered recovery for Sydney and a new way of living for the rest of us.

Long story short, what initially started as the concept of a nearby basement suite, ended up being an apartment, just ten minutes from our house. Things just seemed to fall miraculously in place....someone else's misfortune, a foreclosure, meant that we could actually buy a two-bedroom suite. By the skin of our teeth we were able to finance it, to make it our second home, and what we hoped would translate into a new beginning.

It was all bittersweet. As Nolan and I sat in the bank manager's office, we waited in anguish. When she announced her approval for a mortgage, I don't think the poor, confused woman knew whether to celebrate or grieve with us, when I broke down into tears.

At that very moment, they were tears of both relief and of profound sadness. This was a turning point, the most bittersweet we'd ever known.

But at least we were moving. *We were spiraling upward.*

Bit by bit, we gathered pieces of furniture and the makings for a new home, many from caring friends and family who probably didn't know whether to be impressed, saddened, confused or simply intrigued by what we were doing. As always, we were definitely stepping out of the mold and forging our own unique path.

The apartment was a breath of fresh air. Most Friday nights Nolan would switch so that I could spend the night with Sydney. I remember it *absolutely blowing my mind*, to the point where I said out loud to myself: "Do people actually live like this....where they're not in constant demand....where they don't have to constantly watch and listen and wait....where they're not braced to pounce in with a strategy....where they don't have to stick to routines and strategize or pay a high price later?" I'm not exaggerating! I absolutely could not believe it.

And nobody was screaming or biting or pinching or kicking. All of that had been my norm for so many years. At the apartment, Sydney and I would just "hang out." Sometimes Genevieve would join us and she would just glow, stress-free. She'd settle in with us when she wanted; and then retreat to her pink and fluffy world when she'd had enough.

I'm not kidding about this. My eyes are filled with tears as I write this because I absolutely couldn't believe it! *Is that what typically people did when they're at home together? Just hang out?..... I'd forgotten.*

<figure>ornamental divider</figure>

The apartment brought joyous simplicity, but also added a new level of complexity. Sydney was in a depressed and fragile state for a long time. That meant, for me, countless trips back and forth. Sometimes she was frantic when she'd call. I could hear by the tone in her voice that she needed me to be there.

And for Nolan, it was tough and heart gripping. Like me, he always looked to the positive but it *was* a juggle, and for him, the positive must have been interlaced by the unnerving. He had work, he had his home with Sydney; he had his other home with me and his other children. It was complex, and he didn't have quite the same aptitude for dealing with complexities as I did. He forged on, and adapted. *But it was tough.* It's probably too bad that he doesn't have a gift for writing. I'm sure *he* could fill volumes too.

Chapter 78

*A*s trite as it sounds, every cloud does have a silver lining. Sydney *did* recover. *She more than recovered.* Nolan and I had prepared ourselves that she might not ever be able to be around Hayden again. She had to be given that permission. Really, the abuse from him had been pervasive for most of her life. She had deep-rooted associations with him, no matter how deeply she loved and adored him. I prayed that it wouldn't come to that; but after all she'd been through, it would have been understandable.

But Sydney is Sydney, and she is one of the most quietly-determined people I've ever known. She is "old-soul Sydney" with her amazing perceptiveness and ability to explore minds, *including her own.* She just needed help and I knew exactly who to turn to: Nicola, an incredible psychotherapist, and Angelis, an extraordinary holistic physician and healer.

At the core of Sydney, her family was everything, and she worked. She worked damn hard on her own *and* with both Nicola and Angelis. Together they worked through the murk and the blackness of depression, anxiety and trauma. I like to think I had a little to do with it, because in their abstract and deep mind journeys, they were speaking my language and there was a place for me on this "team." *But honestly, most of all, it was Sydney. It was her strength, her courage and her love for her very odd and unique family.*

It was a slow process: a year of therapy and ups and downs, twists and turns, but levels of self-discovery that most people will live a lifetime and never gain. Sydney was and is incredible. *And her Michael*: he saw her at her worst, the emotional mess that she was. He only loved, respected and stood in awe of her, all the more. She would *never* have recovered as well without him.

Of no surprise, Hayden's aggression was the most prevalent and damaging force. Through therapy and hypnosis, Sydney and Nicola worked through the layers.

At one point in therapy, a pinnacle point, Sydney experienced Hayden through hypnosis, as a bear. He was malicious, terrifying and mauling her. I wasn't surprised by the alarming imagery. I'd suspected it for a long time. I'd seen it and felt it and had put those pieces together: her fascination and almost obsession with collecting teddy bears, contrasted by her intense fear of *real* bears. Even a real-life picture of a bear on a calendar had been unnerving to her.

I remembered a camping trip years before, where we'd been woken up in the middle of the night by the horrific sound of Sydney screaming, hysterically. *I'd never heard screaming like that before.*

She was frantic and could barely make the words come, to tell me that she'd had a terrible, graphic nightmare where she'd been gruesomely mauled to death by a bear. There in the dark, inside the tent, I tried to tell myself that her nightmare was just a reaction because she knew we were in a campsite, close to the mountains, where bears were known to sometimes roam.

But there was something in her voice and in her horrific screaming....I looked at where she was sleeping in our tent trailer: she was right next to Hayden, which was certainly not a place she was used to sleeping. We weren't home in the safety of our castle, each with our own safe room to retreat to. We were all tossed together in what should have been a warm and fuzzy den, like a litter of puppies.

But one of those puppies was known to be easily pushed over an edge when his personal space was compromised….as I tried to get her and myself settled and back to sleep, I knew that the bear in her nightmare, was Hayden. I could feel it.

Thoughts I'd had for so long, all made sense: her fascination for collecting bears of all sizes, colors and textures, contrasted by her fears. It was her sub-conscious attempt to make herself feel safe, and probably, to transform the image of her brother into one that was warm and cuddly. *It was her own self-therapy.* But Hayden's long-term impact was more than cuddly teddy bears could undo.

What she needed was Nicola's magic. Through hypnosis and Nicola's extraordinary expertise, and Sydney's own courage, she transformed the violent bear from her nightmare, into a friendly, calm and safe bear, lounging by a stream. *And she saw herself unharmed and safe.*

Back when Sydney and her body's defense mechanisms adopted the "strategy" of collecting safe bears, I don't think it was conscious. But Sydney has a deep and brilliant mind. Somewhere along the way, she figured out how her body had instinctively moved to protect itself, almost like a sub-conscious *master plan*. I suspected that at some point, she did recognize and acknowledge it as an actual strategy.

A few years ago, I finally just came out and asked her if maybe her fascination with collecting bears, had something to do with protecting herself and trying to undo the damage of Hayden. She smiled and said: *"Yeah, I realized awhile ago that that's what I'd been doing!"*

Brilliant, mind-exploring Sydney!

After thirteen months of living away from our home, joy of joys, Sydney was ready and counting the moments until she could move back!

Chapter 79

From the street, our house, our castle, was forest green and looked warm, but quite small. But once you stepped inside, you realized how big a house it really was. It went off in many directions. Its complex design was *completely indicative* of the six people who lived there.

Our home wasn't new or elegant, but it *was* homey and you knew immediately that kids lived there. The layout was a three level split with a big basement, making it a home where we could all be together, yet have lots of space between us. Years before, we'd gone into debt to give everyone a safe-haven bedroom of their own.

Our backyard was private and landscaped with trees, most of them purchased and planted to symbolize anniversaries and special events. Our trees and our fence blocked out most of the world around us.

Really, our castle had evolved into being the perfect "autism home."

Sometimes I'd look around at all of the charts and behavioral strategies that we were so used to seeing, and wondered what visitors thought. Anyone trained in autism, would have needed only a few seconds to see that it wasn't just that autism *lived* here; it was *embraced* here!

Inside our castle, the décor was very Asian, one of my passions because of the feeling of tranquility and of centuries past. Sydney's room, at least her room before she'd had to leave, was the most beautiful and most dramatic. It was self-designed, with dark green walls, filled with bits of fairies, Disney, Shakespeare and sentimental dried roses hanging from the ceiling. Most of those roses were from her adoring Michael. Her room felt like a secret garden.

Next to Sydney's room, was Kobe's. It shone boldly with athletic energy and pride, his shrine as he sometimes called it, filled with trophies, medallions and breathing of baseball and basketball. It exuded the warmth, strength and positive energy that were Kobe.

Genevieve's room upstairs, swirled with the uncanny "autism mixture" of chaos and bits of absolutely *everything* she'd ever had or done, contrasted with her need for order and items categorized! Spice Girl dolls, hundreds of animal figurines, her drawings and her creations....*everything* was poured into that room. It was quite a sight.

Then there was Hayden's room. It was all in soft sky blue, his comfort color and our attempt to enhance calmness. Oddly enough, when I was feeling down, tired or just in need of a few minutes to myself to be inspired, *that was the part of this castle that I was most drawn to*: Hayden's room. Go figure!

I went there often. When I did, I'd sit on his bed. I didn't *feel* all the times he'd thrashed his room. I didn't *feel* how complicated he'd made my life. I didn't *feel* the screaming or the aggression. And I certainly didn't *feel* all of the storms we'd weathered or the amazing battles we'd fought.

In Hayden's room, I felt home school. I felt "uncovering and acknowledging" the real Hayden. I felt success, sweetness and my Hayden's teddy bear hugs. I felt me, the "insightful" me, the me I'd become because of the worlds that Hayden (and Genevieve) had opened my eyes to.

I felt peace. Go figure!

O urs was a home, and it was a castle. It was a state of mind; and it was six people worth recognizing and worth protecting. Our castle was a place worth exploring, worth sharing and revealing to the world now because it had seen a lot and so there's much to tell. It was a fascinating place and an extraordinary place. That's why I'm letting you in, through my words and my images.

A nd I know there are others who live in their own castles, and they might need some help, too. That's what we want to give. But it is complex story....

.....Our home, filled with autism awareness and acceptance and our countless magical moments, *should* have been enough; but it wasn't. The walls were still too restrictive for who we'd become. But more than that, the walls had seen too much. That was even more obvious with the prospect of Sydney, after thirteen months, finally coming back home. She needed more space from Hayden. *We all did.* We needed a different layout and we needed *different walls*, walls with no tumultuous history. The fact that she was the one who'd had the breakdown, and had spent months in therapy, didn't mean all of us weren't equally affected.

This was a time to be brave, to make lasting changes and to put each of us in a new and more positive direction.

As a family, we scrutinized every aspect of what *this* house could offer and what *we knew* that we needed. There was nothing more we could do to alter this house. It was not the safe reprieve from the outside world that it had been in the past. It was as much a prison, with dungeons. And there was just too much history that was ugly.

It was time to leave our castle and find a cottage in the village.

Chapter 80

On a corner lot, not so far from our castle, our new home stood waiting. The fact that it was a corner lot was, in my mind, part of the strategy! We'd miss our quiet cul-de-sac, but I saw it as "baby steps"….no moat around us….a feeling of openness, of connectedness. We were *not going to slip* into our old reclusive patterns. Baby steps, carefully planned, strategic baby steps…*that's what works with autism*. That's what would work for us in our new direction. I could feel it!

Autism and change: those two words don't often go well together. You've read our history, especially Hayden's. An alteration like this could be treacherous, right? Or, it could be magic. As we prepared to make the transition to our new home, I focused on Hayden and my mind was continually pulled to the image of the enormous burgundy maple tree that stood in our new yard. It was right at the corner, where our two new streets intersected.

It *was* like magic under my wings. *I had my image; I had a plan. It was another epiphany.* All I needed was our maple tree, a few materials and the *perfect* moment. With autism, all too often, it's equally as much about timing as it is strategy and insight. This would be more than a baby step. This could be one of the *biggest* steps! I gathered my materials, my completed plan and tucked it away, praying the right moment would come, and soon. We had only a few weeks until the move to our cottage.

The perfect day and the perfect moment did present itself:

> It had been a rough day. School pressures for Hayden had reached a peak. With his head in my lap, sobbing and agonizing about the state of his life, his torrid past, and the uncontrollable behaviors that he struggled to combat, he blurted out: *"My past will always haunt me!"*
>
> My heart ripped open for him. *He wanted to be someone he could be proud of.* He'd proven that time and time again. Many of his behaviors we could control, and *he* could control, when realistic expectations were placed upon him. *But how could we let this poor soul off the hook?* Each of us tried to forget the past. How could we let *him* forget the past?
>
> That was *exactly* what my epiphany about the sacred and symbolic maple tree that awaited us at our new house, was all about!
>
> "Wow!" I thought, Hayden's head still in my lap, his tears spilling over his cheeks. *"This is it! This is the perfect moment! It's here!"* Carefully I revealed to him my plan:
>
> It was a photograph (a hand-drawn replica is below) of our new home, framed and matted. The focal point was the front of our "cottage" and the giant maple tree that graced our new yard. Above and below the photograph, were the words that were *carefully chosen, every, single one.* They had to be perfect, to say exactly what Hayden needed to hear and what he could relate to.

This strategy was our family's new direction. It was what I hoped
would lead to a better life in our cottage in the village:

A New House   A New Home   A New Start

*Like the big maple tree that grows in front of our new house, stand tall and proud,
every time you walk through that door! You've become an amazing child, an
amazing young man!
And we love you!*

*In our green house, we had magical times but also rough times — lots of them.
But they weren't your fault, they just happened.*

*But like that maple tree, you've grown and grown. And you've learned self control.
You've learned to be mature, but to always keep that child within.*

*As we pack up and move to our new home, we'll take everything with us —
everything but the rough times! Those are going to stay at the green house, tucked
away to gather lots of dust. We don't need them.
We're going to take only the good, only the magical!
The rest will stay in the past, as we look at the present and welcome the future!*

The passage was just under two hundred words, but every word had to be perfect. I couldn't risk a single word being lofty or offering predictions that were *unattainable*. That was the challenge, the beauty and the potential that this strategy held. Hayden *was* finally in a place in his life where he had reasonable control of his behaviors, but he needed support and expectations that were realistic. *And he needed and deserved to rid himself of the negative haunting of his past.*

These weren't just words or slick romanticizing; *this was a strategy.* He needed us to meet him halfway. *And he had to be let off the hook.*

When I unraveled my strategy, the look on Hayden's face and the expression in his eyes, told me that he *felt* every word, that *the moment* was right and that *the time in his life* was right. He was willing and wanting to make it happen.

To me, that moment felt like doors and windows opening, with sunshine streaming in, the kind of sunshine you get from a corner lot, not one tucked away and secluded!

Chapter 81

ayden vowed to do all that he could to embrace being a more stable and controlled person, if the rest of us did our part in "forgiving and forgetting" the traumas of the past. That was a concept we could welcome, understand and set into motion; *all of us but Genevieve.* Leaving the safe haven of her home was tough enough; bringing in forgiveness for Hayden wasn't even approachable.

You have to remember: Genevieve is remarkable, and she is remarkably affected by her autism. And because of that, she *did* experience the presence and the impact of Hayden on a different level than anyone else did *or could.* As I write these words, exactly five years have passed since our transition to our cottage, our time of forgiving and forgetting; but only *now* has Genevieve emerged so well in her own personal journey, that she can, in *tiny* pieces, speak about Hayden and work on undoing the past. I have to treat that respectfully now with what I write.

What Genevieve *could* contribute to our forged "forgive and forget pathway," was that she could and would acknowledge, that the Hayden of the past, was not the same Hayden *who would walk through the door to our new home.* Honestly, to respect her privacy and the complexity of her stance with Hayden, I can only fill a few lines here. But the night before we left our castle, she and I pulled together a little ceremony, where she took a bold, though tiny step forward in her acceptance of Hayden:

> A couple of years earlier, I'd been able to gently poke around in her heart, soul and body, to help her put into words and images, what "the worst Hayden trauma" had been. I thought that maybe it would help us address it. Her answer hadn't been *at all* what I was expecting. I'd fully anticipated her recalling the terrible "Captain Hook attack."

> It was then that I realized that most of the *actual physical aggression* was to her, a traumatic blur. She didn't remember many of the specifics, only that she hated him.

> The number one incident, the one that was most unnerving, she remembered in detail and it haunted her. It was held deeply in her memory and *in her body.* It was what should have been a beautiful moment, one that we had miraculously captured in a photograph: a "perfect" split second in time. *In the photograph, she was sitting on a swing, which we'd hung from a tree in a lovely, wooded campsite. There was Hayden beside her, both of them breath-taking with their red, curly hair and sweet skin, about ages two, and four and a half.* I wish I could print that photograph here; it could be in a magazine, it was that beautiful.

In that perfect split second, captured on film, Hayden kissed Genevieve's cheek.

> *How sadly ironic and yet perfectly picturesque of the complexities of these two children....despite all of the years of physical and verbal abuse from her brother, the moment that would traumatize her the most, would be a moment where he was caught up in the moment.... because he loved her....and he could feel affection....and he wanted to show love and affection, just like anyone else.... through a sweet kiss....*

214

For Genevieve, knowing that that moment had happened was traumatizing. Knowing that it was captured on film had secretly and subconsciously traumatized her for years....

What should have been, and was, one of my most prized photographs, became the focus of our symbolic, leaving-our-castle ceremony. There in Genevieve's safe haven bedroom, with a cookie sheet and matches....

Before leaving our castle, I had one little ceremony of my own left to do. It was important and in my mind, it was beautiful and empowering:

> I had two photographs. One was of the real-life, European castle I had, years before, attached to the cover of the short, original tale of *The Castle We Called Home*. The second was a photograph of our actual home, *our* real castle. Each castle had a history of its own. *Both* of them were symbols of how we lived. With the two pictures stacked together, I tore them up, into little pieces. I let the pieces mingle together to make the two castles become one.

> By the light of the midnight May moon, with only a soup spoon to dig with (everything else was packed and ready to go), I sprinkled them inches below the surface of the earth, close to the roots of the apple tree my parents had given Sydney for her very first birthday. We'd transplanted that tree from our first house, to our second and here to our third.

> *Now the apple tree was too big to move to our new home and it was one of the things we regretted most about leaving behind. But it had a job to do. We were leaving it with all of the "old stuff" and we were moving to our cottage, our cottage in the village, and to our maple tree!*

Part Two

An Honored and Altered Life

Chapter 1

Our "cottage" is open and bright. The backyard is small and very private, but it doesn't *feel* secluded, maybe because the front is so open, with those two small intersecting streets and life, activity, and our maple tree. Inside, as my niece called it, the decor is "whimsical." It tells of personalities who dare to be vibrant and exactly who they are.

The upstairs still holds the Asian tranquility, but it is set amidst rich, deep *purple* walls. It probably sounds awful, but it's glorious. Sydney's room, once again is probably the most beautiful. It's like standing *inside* a deep, burgundy rose, one of the many that Michael has given her over the years. It's safe and potent. Cuddly stuffed bears are everywhere, along with her familiar bits of Disney and Shakespeare.

Kobe's room still boasts of athletic pride but shares equally, images of rap singers and musicians. They've inspired him to discover his own capacity to write brilliant pieces of literature and songs, and to create and produce music.

Genevieve's room is an incredible mish-mash of hot fuchsia pink *and* black walls, zebra stripes and countless, fascinating objects of every description and sentiment. Lava lamps and Christmas lights glow literally night and day, month after month, pulsating and *calming* her increasingly creative mind and body. Part of her room is transformed into an art studio, where *the real* Genevieve lives, another journey that she is on....

The master bedroom is, in my mind, periwinkle: the color of that moment between the last day of spring and the first day of summer. The décor is *Camelot*. My home office has now become the secret garden of our home, a museum of fairies, theatrics, dance and things that are simply unique and beautiful. Most of them were gifts: tiny little objects that people in my life have been compelled to give me, because they were unique and beautiful. Some of them "found me," at moments when I needed something *glimmering and meaningful*, to keep my sanity so that I could then transform myself, into a person who *could* deal with

219

"crazy chaos" and still see mystery and fascination....tiny objects for my own self therapy!

My secret-garden office *is filled* with a lot of those tiny objects, the down side being that there have been a lot of times over the years when I needed them. *But if you surround yourself in uniqueness and beauty, how can that lead to anything but inspiration and depth of thought?* That's what works for me and what works for this family!

The front foyer of our new house, whispers of *Neverland* and of *Peter Pan*, our unspoken reminder to never let ourselves completely grow up. The back entrance features our "*Wizard of Oz* hallway," where there are bits and pieces reminding us that there *is* "no place like home" and that we *do* have it in us, to ward off lurking forces. We *can* click our heels three times and make magic happen. *We always have had that talent; but in this house, it's not at the expense of submerging ourselves and shutting out most of the world around us, the way it used to be.*

Gradually and still carefully, we bring more people into our home; but we choose people who fit. We choose people who have likely done some heel clicking of their own, or who are at least, intrigued by those of us who do it as a joyous part of *everyday life!*

Hayden's room is filled with *Spiderman,* his hero and his mentor. In *this* home, all of his visual behavioral strategies *stay* in the privacy of his bedroom. They are on an even *higher level*, with clever and witty usages of *Buffy the Vampire Slayer, Angel,* our two schnauzers and more. Structured into his room, these strategies are less obtrusive to the personality of our cottage; but he still *feels* them and uses them. He takes them in and he takes them to heart. They work, because they are *Hayden-specific, vibrant, carefully detailed, humorous and insightful.* And they show *love and respect.*

They are what autism strategies should be.

The *Spiderman* Curtain that was so instrumental in helping Hayden to

220

understand his body, and to deal with the pressures of the world, is neatly folded and tucked away in his closet. *We've never needed it in this house.*

Part of that is because of the "magic" of the maple tree strategy; but also because we *made changes.* We had too much at stake. This was our second chance, our new life. And we had Sydney back. We couldn't risk her going down again.

We had conviction and we had a Hayden who was so happy to have his sister back, and to have his own new lease on life. *Those were two very powerful things!*

In my mind, all of that translated into five very potent words. They became my mantra and my driving force. *And believe me, over the next few years to come, there would be times when I nearly had to scream them out, to make people listen;* but I was not going to loose my Sydney again.

I was not going to watch the rest of us crumble and falter and dismantle again. And I was not going to watch my Hayden lose his chance to become the person that he so desperately wanted to be.

Those five words were what we gave him, the moment we walked into our new cottage:

An honored and altered life!

Chapter 2

I wish I could wrap everything up with a happy, fairy tale ending. But we were not quite there yet. And there is a part that I do have to tell you, though I know it may bring tears to your eyes, because if you've read this far, you've fallen at least a little bit in love with us. I've agonized about lying and not telling you; but that wouldn't be right. There has to be honesty:

When we left our castle and started our new life in our cottage, we kept the apartment Sydney had shared with her dad; it was the second home and the outlet that we still needed to keep in place. Though

Nolan was, of course, a part of the new vein of our journey, it was on a different tract. The kids and I moved into the new house, but *he* did not. At my request, he stayed at the apartment.

How do I make this a real story if I hide this fact? I won't dwell, except to say that there was and is, and will always be, a level of love and respect. *And I will not allow Hayden, Genevieve or the impact of autism to take the fall.* Of course, the stress and the complexities shared a part. But if Nolan and I had been meant to be, we would have managed to weather all of this together. I do believe that, because for all that was heart wrenching and ridiculously stressful, there was so much that was fascinating and absolutely mesmerizing and extraordinaire! *That should have made it enough.*

Emotionally, Nolan and I were just too different. At some point that would have played out, no matter the number or "the kind" of children we had. And in our case, it wasn't just that *I had to live* so deeply in a different world for so long; it was that I chose it. It was a world of insight and of deep instinctual living that had *always* been a part of me; I just expanded on it because I had to and because I was drawn to. It became all the more like breathing to me and I loved the awareness it gave me; but as a couple, it set us even further apart.

My world, and our children's world (even without autism), had always been abstract and creative and emotional, but Nolan's wasn't. There was too much disconnection; I'd seen it happening for years. This was a move that he and I had needed to make.

All six of us were all affected; of course we were. But we survived it. We'd all seen and dealt with so much already, that we dealt with this too. Part of the reason that we could was because on many levels, "the six of us" remained intact, at least as a family. That's still true today. There *is* respect. For us there's no other way to approach life.

Chapter 3

he maple tree strategy was a living and breathing concept. Hayden took it to heart and often, when we saw him edging into past patterns, he would actually remind himself about the "new Hayden." Often, it worked for us too, especially me. When you're a parent, it's so easy to see a familiar behavior and respond with: "Here we go again...."

> But many times, that image of the maple tree in front of our new home, would rush to my mind. *I trained myself to do that.* I'd remind myself: *"Don't you dare allow yourself to slip into that pattern and don't dare let Hayden. He deserves more and we deserve more! Keep that bar raised!"* Our home became a different place, one inch, one interaction with Hayden, at a time.

Creative and *marketable* behavioral strategies slowly helped to carefully broaden Hayden's horizons. We needed to help him look at the big picture about the progression of high school and his future beyond. Those were complex tasks with lots of *deep-rooted emotions* connected to them. Dr. Bryson and I would do our work, walking together inside Hayden's head and body.

A new gentle turning point unfurled when I specifically put myself deeply into Hayden's apprehension about working towards the future. I meshed it with the characters he loved from *Buffy the Vampire Slayer* and *Angel*. The program just fell into being. It would take pages to describe here in detail; but it carefully and strategically set the tone for *a five year plan* of Hayden finally accepting concepts like being more mature, taking on bits of responsibility for his actions and of one day, having some kind of a "job." (These are all more complex than you could probably imagine).

It was called the *Angel Agency Apprenticeship.* (You can check it out, along with others at the back of this book). What appeared to be simply photos of characters from a TV show with cute captions, was actually a well thought out, intricate plan of attack. *Every* caption was *carefully scripted* to address a goal or issue in Hayden's life. Once the initial concept was conceived, the rest came easy!

I knew what Hayden's issues were and I knew what imagery he would connect to. *And,* I watched these TV shows *with him,* so I knew the characters and what Hayden drew from them. I saw how he connected with their personalities, their actions and their life stories.

> Then I had the glorious fun of transforming myself into each of the TV characters, to picture what it was that they would say to Hayden, to offer advice or motivation. Then their jargon and mannerisms came easy and I was able to make their bubble captions, as if coming from their very lips.

Hayden bought into the program, in a big way. Now *that* is child-specific strategizing!

Outside forces still raged upon us, dangerously. Most of the oppression was the pervasive force of school. Still we were confronted with terrible scenes of Hayden *hysterical* about going to school. There were times when he literally held onto the car as I tried to drive away. If I *did* continue driving, he'd follow me as I drove off, walking block after block, down the street in my direction. Each time, I slipped back, parked the van and watched to see how far he'd go.

I was horrified to discover that he showed no sign of turning back. He was unskilled and unobservant about traffic, and distraught; and so each time, I had no choice but to turn around, pick him up and bring him home. The days when I tried taking him back to school, staff was useless and ineffective in assisting.

Hayden was only expected to go to school for two hours a day, but he couldn't handle it. That's what his actions were telling us. Those nightmare scenes outside his school, when he grabbed onto the van, were beyond heart-wrenching. And I was loosing it! Time and time again I was pushed over an edge out of sheer, intense and incredible frustration; I felt like I could rip him to shreds. And at the same time, I was hurting for him.

> I *can't* lie and say that I always handled it well. There were times when I screamed and just *lost it*, to the point where he probably wasn't safe with me. *Oh my God, can you imagine what it is like to have your child hold onto your car as you're trying to drive away?* I do mean that literally. If you are a parent, stop reading and take a moment. Envision *your* child, holding on to *your* car as you try to drive away, him or her frantic and distraught. Then you'll have some idea what it was like. And this didn't happen just once. It was happening over and over.

> *And Hayden's teachers just didn't get it.* It was almost comical the couple of times when I was able to call their classroom from my car, telling them that we were there, but that I couldn't get Hayden inside. *Their feeble attempts and lack of skill was comical but sad and unacceptable.*

What was more unacceptable was that they just couldn't see how deep-rooted his fears were.

On the very worst day, when I brought Hayden back home with me, I was so far beyond being distraught and frustrated, that what I felt more than anything else, *was compassion.*

He was talking to us. His body was talking to us. There was so much anguish in him. This was *not* a lazy child trying to get out of going to school. *This was anguish. This was fear. This was a body and a mind reacting.*

I reached for the little framed mural, the one with the pictures of *Spiderman* and *Green Goblin*. It was my "soul searching through the eyes of good and evil strategy for Hayden" that had helped in the past:

*W*ith Hayden's head in my lap, he cried and he sobbed. I jotted down, onto the mural, the images as he finally accessed and put into words, through language that was *his* language, and images that were safe and made sense *to him*, the traumas of *his* life.

What came spewing from within Hayden were not the excuses or desperate attempts of a lazy, timid or manipulative boy trying to lead an easy life, that didn't involve things like school. *They were the words and images of a very deep and sincere young man, finally given the tools and the permission to acknowledge to himself and to the world around him, what his world was like and what it was to live it.*

And I was listening. I saw in his face and in his body, and heard in his

words, *that I was the one he trusted.*
That made *me* the one responsible for
relaying his message and his insight to
the world around him.

This was his life and he was telling the world what it was like to live it.

Most of Hayden's "spewing" that day
revolved around school. He explained
how for years he had watched the
other kids in his classes, and even
though he knew that most of them
had special needs, he was *very aware*
that he struggled on a different level.
With his head still in my lap, and with
exasperation, but *deep self awareness,*
he sobbed: *"My life is crap; I don't know
what's wrong with me. Everything is so
hard for me. School could burn in Hell for
all I care!"*

His words tugged mercilessly at my
heart, but I was proud of him for
finding the words and the images.
The thing is, I had seen this and had
sensed all of this for a long time. But
now the words had come from *his lips:*
that's what had been missing. Now I
finally had something concrete and
real to work from.

*And I was going to work from this.
Make no mistake about that.*

As fate would have it, Sydney was home that afternoon. She overheard Hayden's sobbing and his descriptions and his metaphors. She was taken aback by the power of his words and his level of insight. How could she or I be filled with anything but respect and compassion? When he had finished "his spewing" and had recollected himself a little, he cried and said: "High school is harder than I thought it would be.... like a mountain that's too high to climb." He said he felt like he was "a slayer and they were all demons" and that it was "Hell and he *couldn't* go back."

Sydney later told me that it made her cry to hear Hayden, but that she had needed to hear it. It filled her with a new level of tolerance, compassion and respect.

That day, Hayden and I explored deeply the range of special needs class mates he'd had over the years. I was *absolutely blown away* to discover how much of his life he had literally observed them and contemplated them, to see how *they* navigated through school and through their lives.

He didn't deny that they all had challenges; but he could see that they could handle it on a level that he couldn't. I knew in my heart, that he was right.

Of course he was right; I'd tried to make people understand that for years. He was insightful enough to see and feel that what went on in his body was on a level that not many others had.

Spiderman and Green Goblin: in Hayden's mind, he was *both*.

In his mind, *and in reality*, he was as complex as two humans, a superhero, *and* a villain.... all mashed up and thrown together!

Chapter 4

" $\mathcal{W}$ e know that as teachers, you love to teach; but in this case, it's not the goal. *We just want for Hayden to be here.*" That was our new school plan, as laid out by Dr. Bryson. It was even supported by the School District Special Education Director, at Benjamin's request. We thought: even if Hayden could manage being in school, *glued to a computer for two hours every day,* we'd be happy. *At least he'd be there.* He'd be in the presence of peers and he'd have some routine to his life. Maybe someday down the road we could expand on it....*but for now we just wanted him to be there.*

The plan was in place; but it was just too foreign for this staff. Talk about linear, in-the-box thinkers! It wasn't that they weren't lovely, caring people. But they just didn't "get it." They couldn't move beyond "teachers teach and Hayden is a high school student who should be taught." One day they marveled, at how well Hayden had done, when they had purposely strayed away from our plan and sent him to a forty-five minute art class with his class mates.

Of course *they* didn't have to deal with the brutal aftershock that his family did! Though he *lasted* forty-five minutes, *they* couldn't make the connection that he (and his family) paid a terrible price later and it set him, once again, on a simmering path of not wanting to go to school. *As usual, because they didn't see aftershock, they wouldn't acknowledge it.*

But, for God's sake, wouldn't Hayden's screaming and holding onto the van as I was trying to drive away, have been enough to tip them off?

Then they thought it was a "good coping mechanism" that Hayden had adopted, when he would lay his head on his desk and "have a little nap" when he was expected to participate in class discussions, or do seated work that was overwhelming to him.

These were not naps. This was withdrawal. This was *Nowhereland.*

I described it to them in terms that I thought they couldn't possibly miss: I asked them to visualize the universe, of Hayden floating in space, where it's just nothing; that when he was in that place, *he didn't feel connected or loved, he was just there.* I requested that when they saw Hayden with his head on his desk, that they remind themselves that he wasn't just resting, that they say to themselves: "Hayden's going to *Nowhereland*. Is that where I'd want *my* child to be?"

It didn't seem to make an impact. They didn't get it.

Hayden was actually able to speak openly to me about his "naps" at school. He *knew* he was shutting down. And he was aware that it didn't happen *just* when he was asked to participate in a class activity, or something academic like a math sheet. This is really important to note: he could articulate that sometimes he shut down even when he was "chilling on the computer."

> *That's when I knew this was a real issue.* He wasn't just manipulating, or "napping" to get out of an activity. If he was withdrawing, even when he was in the safe world of his computer games, it meant that the *environment around him* was just too draining. He let himself go there because *he needed to*. In his words, he said: "Sometimes I need to shutdown, to go into *"reboot* mode."

School staff struggled with open-ended allotment of computer time. No matter what, they couldn't move beyond using it as a reward. Again, linear, in-the-box thinking! That *wasn't* our new concept. We just wanted him there, in the school environment, focused on something positive and pleasurable.

And his teachers couldn't understand Hayden's need for routine. If their afternoon schedule changed, they'd simply remark: "Oh just have Hayden come in the morning that day." Or if there was a class field trip, they'd respond with the usual: "It's *Hayden's choice* if he would *like* to attend." On one hand, yes, they were treating him with maturity and respect, that attitude of: "If we treat him like a mature teen, he will *be* a mature teen." But for Hayden, it back-fired because he saw himself as being unable to rise to the expectations, so it made things worse.

And their comments showed that they still couldn't see that these weren't matters *of choice*. Hayden was affected by his body and environment. *If he could have attended he would have*. He didn't "choose" to have his body! And he didn't "choose" to have an attention span that made sitting through an entire movie with his class, exasperating and unnerving. This was who Hayden was. There was only so much that could be addressed by medication, therapy, modifications and his sincere desire to cope.

A couple of months later, Hayden's teachers specified a new goal on his year-end report card: *"Hayden should work towards full-time attendance"*. Unbelievable! What the hell were they thinking?

Chapter 5

O can't resist giving you another little snapshot of the bizarre life with Hayden, at least Hayden when there was too much outward school pressure on him. This is another pinnacle, an event that should have been happy, but ended up bizarre:

It was supposed to be an enjoyable Saturday afternoon....Hayden finally able to purchase a long-awaited video game system. He and I had planned our trip to the store; we had *visualized* buying the new game system and he'd been counting on it for a long time. But when the moment arrived, the underlying stress in his life caused him to flip....suddenly, instead of making his purchase and rushing home to play, *he demanded a completely different game system.*

It made no sense and *he* made no sense. He'd planned on buying this system for months!
He screamed right there in the store and lost all ability to reason.

I had no choice but to leave the store, somehow dragging him with me, all six feet of him. I was completely dumbfounded and in absolute shock. And I was angry and disappointed....*it was supposed to have been a lovely Saturday afternoon with Hayden happy with his new system, and me getting to watch Kobe's baseball game.* It ended up a bewildering trauma.

What I remember most of that ordeal was *afterward,* driving to the baseball park. I left Hayden nearby in the van while I described in intimate detail, the whole situation to poor, unsuspecting Nolan...and there I was, a well-educated mom of four, *screaming and literally kicking the concession stand at my teenage son's baseball game! I completely lost it.*

(Trust me; all I can do now is to imagine how comical I must have looked, otherwise you can't imagine how embarrassed I feel!)

The thing is: I knew *why* Hayden had reacted the way he did, I just hadn't seen it coming.

It was school; it was stress: *dark, brooding stress* that wasn't going to leave as long as he was placed in that environment. Hayden was a fifteen year old boy with a well-documented history of volatile, disruptive behavior. Despite medication, he could hardly sit still, unless he was focused on a game system. Even then, he would flick constantly from his game to TV, to a game and so on.

When he wasn't feeling centered, or at least *as centered and as grounded as someone with his wiring could be*, he spent much of his time "on the prowl," walking listlessly through life, like he didn't know what to do with himself. If he was pushed, either through over or under-stimulation, he would scream, act out and have little or no ability to reason. That was the reality; that was who he was. *That was what we had to work around.*

I was Hayden's morning home school teacher, and I was his primary therapist. So a few days later, I stepped back and took a long, hard look at who he was *during* our home school sessions and *why* he had such a *high comfort level there.* I focused on how challenging the academic component of home school was for him, even though it was pretty basic. From that perspective, I did a session as if *I was a video camera, taking us both in, and capturing how he responded and how I responded.*

I realized how much I took for granted, how much work it was for me to be constantly *reeling him in*, keeping him focused and on track. I'd done it for so long it was all just part of the process, and part of what was our special time together. Often during home school, he was funny and animated and delightful to be with. *But there was a definite art to keeping him motivated and away from the looming possibility of withdrawal.* I was skilled at seeing the signs because I'd spent most of his life, paranoid of him retreating there.

But even in the safe and controlled setting of his bedroom, sitting at his desk with me at his side and our two schnauzers snuggled up on his bed, it was a constant juggling act to keep him from being over-stimulated and even worse, under-stimulated. Even a sleeping dog was a distraction, unless I worked into our plan. I had tricks, like the one where Hayden could only touch one of the dogs at the end of each worksheet.

Seriously, how could this child be expected to survive amidst high school?

For God's sake, we were in our cottage. We'd left our castle, and *our past was supposed to stay in the past.* And yet, again Hayden was unraveling....

....In our cottage, after the first month, Hayden faltered to the pressure of his life, because he was pushed, *mostly* by the omni-present forces of school. *It was more than a falter....he was distraught....he cornered me and he punched me. I was scared....scared of his size and scared of his lack of control. I was scared for my own personal safety but I was more scared that I would shatter... and then all of us would shatter into a million pieces....I was afraid I'd lose Sydney being a part of us forever. I was afraid Kobe would be pushed to emotional extremes....*

The physical fear, joined with the family fear, was very motivating.....when Hayden calmed down that day and I pulled myself together, I vowed that that would be *the last* physically abusive incident that *that* house would ever see. *And it was.*

I had one last heart to heart conversation with his teachers. One of them finally looked at me and said: "I wish we could take a video of him so you could see him when he's here, and see how well he does..."

At that moment, it was like my blood stopped moving. It was a déjà vu moment, as I relived his past elementary school teacher saying virtually the exact same words. The confused look in these two teacher's eyes told me it was time to leave. They just didn't get it. They didn't have the capacity.

Chapter 6

fter several months of being enrolled in *no* school, we found a new classroom for Hayden. It was a resource room in regular high school, but with *insightful staff* who understood about *realistic expectations.* And this classroom was barely attached to the school: Hayden, *and his body*, basically forgot that there were hundreds of teens surrounding him. He didn't see them or feel them. In his mind, all he had to deal with was the small group of peers inside his classroom, and his lovely teacher and assistants.

We started off slow, just one hour a day. It took us over a year to work up to two and a quarter hours; but we were geared for success. Ninety-five percent of Hayden's time there was spent on the computer; but at least he was there. He knew exactly what was going on in his classroom all of the time, and in tiny bits and pieces, he interacted. He felt good about that. In his words, he was "keeping a low profile." We didn't stray *at all*, from the afternoon time slot or the fact that *all* academic work was done at home with me.

The only exception was the day he and I presented the *WWE* project that we'd worked on for months in home school. Hayden had his teachers and his peers absolutely captivated. His speech can be so difficult to understand, but he was in his zone, presenting something that was important to him. In his mind, he was an expert and with his confident expertise, they *were* captivated.

Hayden wanted this school to work. He wasn't a manipulator. He was a survivor. You have to imagine the look on his face, the first time we went to observe this classroom. He walked out the door exclaiming: "Finally! Why didn't they tell us about this class years ago?"

When he started his very first week at his new school, I offered him the incentive of a new computer game *just for attending the first day* (we were all feeling paranoid that he'd back out at the last minute). To my surprise, as we neared the school, he looked at me maturely and said: "Mom, you know that deal you made? You don't have to keep it!"

Hayden wanted this to work!

Chapter 7

*S*uccess and emergence…. if you were to ask me, in a nutshell, what were the golden keys that opened up doors for *both* Hayden and Genevieve, I would give you four terms:

1. Safety
2. Acceptance
3. Self Esteem
4. Acknowledging and Respecting the Power and Presence of *Past Associations*

These four terms are what *Effervescence* is all about. They are what *this* book is all about. And on the occasions when I'm asked to speak about my experiences with autism, they are always the backbone of *every* discussion. Sadly, I find that they're often what is *overlooked* by people dealing with autism.

First and foremost, people affected by autism need to feel safe. The world is a different place to them than it is for you and me. That is a proven and well-documented fact.

Second, they need to feel accepted, and by that I mean, accepted for who they are. I don't just mean that "we treat all people nicely." I mean that we acknowledge that though they may be "different," they have a reason and a purpose for being here. They and their autism deserve to be embraced. *From where I stand, the term autism is not a label, it is an explanation.*

If ever you want to see someone who flourished once she felt that the true "her" was embraced, pick up a copy of *Effervescence!*

Thirdly, Self Esteem is *everything!* The world is a foreign and challenging place for them, period. *How can we possibly expect someone challenged and affected so deeply by the world, to navigate and do well in that world, if they don't feel good about themselves?*

And finally, acknowledging and respecting the Power and Presence of Past Associations is critical, *absolutely critical!*

Even as I write those words: acknowledging and respecting the Power and Presence of Past

Associations, I feel my body flinching! Part of that is because to this day, as far as my two autistic kids have come, I'm still often astounded and exasperated at the associations that they make or have buried deep within them.....Genevieve, in particular! Oh my gosh! Sometimes they seem to just pop out of nowhere and they can be so incredibly deep-rooted and complex.

But what is most exasperating to me is the number of professionals *in this field* who do not acknowledge, much less understand the Power and Presence of Past Associations (this is a big issue; that's why I've capitalized it). When they are not acknowledged and not respected, these associations become a huge, frustrating and potentially damaging stumbling block. *Doors can slam shut!*

Please do not think I'm going off on a tangent here. I've lived and breathed this for a long time. This is a critical issue. If I wanted to, I could *easily* focus an entire book simply on the "Power and Presence of *Past Associations*." Maybe one day I will. It would be intense!

> But "in a nutshell," what *you* need to know about Past Associations is that someone who has autism, experiences the world so physically and so literally, that events and emotions and activities and memories are *trapped and pulled into their bodies.* They get filed away there. The further trouble is: they're not "filed away there" neatly categorized and easy to figure out.

> Those "files" *are* there, tucked away, some burrowing away, some of them smoldering. This is a complex, but very real issue. *And it isn't just a matter of behavior modification.* Maybe that's why it's so often overlooked by many therapists and professionals. It's abstract, it's complex; it can be nebulous. *But it's there.*

> Maybe you really do have to live or at least work *from the inside out*, with an autistic person, to understand this. To this day, often Genevieve's art therapist Madeleine, and I will stand back, shake our heads and say: "Oh my God, who would have thought she would have experienced it that way!"

> Madeleine recently looked at me mystified, but fascinated by some Past-Associations that she had uncovered within Genevieve; with so much love and respect she said: "I swear the blood flows differently through Genevieve's veins!"

The Power and Presence of Past Associations are part of what makes working with autism different from other disorders. It isn't just a matter of behavior modification. It's about understanding their bodies, their minds *and their histories.*

For Hayden, the issue of school is a dramatic, concrete proof of the Power and Presence of Past Associations. I can prove that in the final chapters of this book, when you get a snapshot of Hayden *outside* of the school years. Hold on just a bit.

The new school, the one where our very laid-back plan was honored, bought us precious time to keep Hayden stable. We used that time and every possible opportunity, to let him see how loved he was when he was stable. We wanted him to feel what it really was to put the old Hayden behind him.

It all snowballed. His self esteem soared, his skill levels increased, he matured and became more responsible. He had time and the ability to explore his mind, his body, the world around him and how he fit into it all.

In my mind, ultimately, I had a five year plan. In part, it coincided with the five year Angel Agency Apprenticeship. But also, it just seemed like that was how long it would take, to work at the slow pace that we needed to work. That's how long I felt it would take to undo the damage and rebuild.

Turned out I was pretty damn close. And it's amazing how quickly five years can pass!

Hayden's comfort level in this classroom was pretty high and he stayed there for a couple of years. Technically, he graduated from that school. Most of his time there was spent focused on the computer; but at least he was there. And he was blossoming, emerging and learning to feel good about who he was. *Past school associations still harbored within him, but there was growth and lots of it!*

*C*omputer and screen time is not, to someone like Hayden, or Genevieve for that matter, "filler or vegging-out time." I get *so* angry when people are quick to regard it in those terms. Of course we would have loved for Hayden to have been more active; we would have loved a lot of things. *But screen time was, and is, a time to be respected.*

Don't forget, for someone with autism, they learn differently than we do. *They need repetition and time to process.* They need to learn in ways where there is *not an overabundance of social strings attached.* Video and computer games and movies provided Hayden with that. And he *learned incredibly;* he still does. Seeing characters and stories and plots all depicted onscreen, allowed him to have that "social buffer," where he didn't have to worry about interacting *directly* with anyone, even me. He could watch and ponder onscreen scenarios. They helped him to understand more about how people interacted. He learned a lot about relationships. He learned incredibly about history and how the world has evolved.

During much of his screen time, Hayden *is* engaged, motivated and interactive. *Because he is often drawn to the darker games with superheroes and creatures and honor and dignity, he's made important connections about what it is to be a good person.* His reading skills have improved dramatically because he is highly motivated to read onscreen for directions and clues. *And he learns!* He contemplates deeply historical events like the Cuban Missile Crisis and World War One. I could take your breath away to describe his insightful comments and perspectives about the plight of man, religion….the list could go on and on. *This is not filler time! It's learning time and its recovery time.* And to him, it's also relaxation and entertainment time, just like you and I both need.

Hayden….he is the most amazing walking and talking depiction of a playful and naïve child *and* a mature young man. One Easter Sunday, after an incredibly deep debate between himself and Kobe about religion, he left the room saying: "Now where the hell is that Easter bunny?" Mature….insightful….and he still does believe in the Easter bunny!

Believer in Easter bunnies or not, Hayden has gained an incredible level of *emotional intelligence*. You'll hear that in the words to follow. These are *Hayden's words*, explaining what he considers to be *the single most important turning point in his life: video games*.

> One morning on our routine dog walk, Hayden slid into an amazing proclamation about how he knowingly "escaped reality" by playing video games. He elaborated with fascinating images of how before he discovered them, his *"mind was a tangle."* He remembered *exactly* when he discovered them, ten years prior.
>
> He described earnestly to me that there was a *"meter in his mind"* that went from hot to cold, with hot being out of control and cold being under control, like an engine in a car. *He said that if it gets hot, it's overheated and it stops working.*
>
> *To him, the role of video games was to keep his body on cold, and under control.* When he played a game, he could control himself from responding to the forces around him. Noises, the presence of people and their activities were completely tolerable to him *if* his senses were on cold, because of the influx of game-generated *coolant* in his system.
>
> *I was in awe. What started out as a casual thirty minute walk with our dogs, had transformed into a life-altering experience, where Hayden tied all the loose ends of his life together and proved to me and to himself, that he understood his body. And he was able to articulate that to me in terms that I could understand.*
>
> He recognized that *he and his body* had devised a strategy. *And it was a good strategy.* He had learned to read his body and he had learned that he could live a good life, if he used his strategy and was under control.

You have to remember that this was a boy who, for most of his troubled life, was not connected to his feelings, his emotions, his senses or the presence of people around him. During our walk with our dogs, I heard so much pride in his voice: *pride in himself for figuring it out and pride in having a family who stood up for him and respected what worked for him.*

Consciously or not, Hayden had used what tools *he felt he could handle* in life, to make his life not only livable, but exciting and meaningful. And through his efforts, his plan, he had created a way in which the world could understand him and who he was.

This was a magical moment and an incredible proclamation....it was on a beautiful summer morning....just minutes after his "I've got me and life all figured out" revelation, Hayden commented calmly: "I love sunny days. The sun is like God's heart."

Chapter 9

"An Honored and Altered Life" meant altering anything *we felt* needed altering.....even tiny details that ended up *not* being tiny, but important. Little things like *encouraging* Hayden to use his Gameboy when we were in line-ups or in restaurants or at a movie. Sure, some people thought it was weird or even rude, but at least he could function. And slowly he started making new positive associations with places. To jump ahead, at this moment, a few years later, Hayden *always* has his hand-held games in his pocket when we're out, even just to walk the dogs....but now *he rarely needs to actually use them.*

(It's pretty cute: now he has accumulated three hand-held systems that he carries around with him. His pockets are very full and his jacket is heavy, but he keeps them there "just in case." But guess what? There *is* always growth. Just last week, I was finally able to get him to decide that the two older systems can now stay at home....*there is always growth!*)

We made lots of changes: often, when we did errands, Hayden would wait in the car. Sometimes he'd come in, sometimes not. We kept expectations real. *All we wanted was for him to have the glory of feeling himself calm and feeling good about himself.*

Hayden's funny. He understands his body so well and he understands about his need for medication. Once in awhile when, for whatever reason, he gets exceptionally fidgety or compulsive, he's quick to ask: "Wow, did I have my meds this morning?"

Hayden often embraces who he is with humor and realism. He now sometimes challenges himself but honors who he is, especially when it comes to his short attention span. Frequently when I'm making expectations that are just a little beyond his comfort level, he's quick to remind me: "Mom, remember my short attention span..."

It's often a fine line between acknowledging it and using it as an excuse; but honestly, I don't think he *ever* uses it as an excuse. To him, it's an *explanation,* not an excuse. There's a difference! He's earnest and he's honest. Recently, he relayed very sweetly to me his observation that he "wasn't a multi-tasker" like me. That's something to be honored.

Here is an amazing irony or simply a piece of beautiful timing: as I write these words, the date is May 14th. *Exactly five years ago today, we left our castle and walked through our cottage doors.* Other than the one, though serious incident when Hayden cornered me and punched me, the turning-point moment when I vowed that it would be the last time, *there has been no overt physical aggression from Hayden.* We've had our ups and downs and screaming and rants; but *no* overt acts of aggression.

That is phenomenal. That is work and that is insight and growth.

And, that is because we have honored and we have altered Hayden's life. Because of that, he is growing and he is emerging. Those ups and downs and twists and turns will always be a part of his life and the challenge of living with Hayden; but he will never be that prince trapped in cold castle walls again.

There will always be some forces looming over and around him, but he has a body that is honored and understood by him and by us. We'll never turn that clock back again! And there will always be growth and further emergence.

Chapter 10

o you remember the description of the front and back entrances to our home: the "hints of *Peter Pan* and *Neverland*" and "*The Wizard of Oz* hallway?" Those weren't created just out of love for two classic tales. They were part of a strategy. This is a home that has magical capacity. *This is a home where uniqueness is embraced, where we try to only compare ourselves to us: who we were, who we are and who we want to be.* This is a home where we challenge ourselves, but also live realistically. This is *our* home.

Not so long ago, a *green lurking witch* did infiltrate the happy and pretty content walls of our new home, our "cottage in the village." It wasn't a *devastating* infiltration but it was unnerving, especially to me. It was an important reminder that green skin and old, non-insightful and conventional forces still lurked around us. It was a reminder that I still needed to be on guard.

If I were to give this chapter a title, it would be:

Witches Not Welcome:

A bit of new funding had come in for Hayden....enough for a life skills worker a few hours a week....another one of those bittersweet, catch 22's. How do you turn down funding? But I'd played this game long enough to know that funding meant "by the books, traditional, little thought or insight kind of programming." That *wasn't* the recipe for success with Hayden. It never had been; and now that we were committed to his "Honored and Altered Life" it was *even farther* from our game plan.

Maybe we'd get lucky. Maybe the director of this programming would be insightful and receptive. *I had glowing proof of what worked for Hayden and what didn't.* Maybe I could paint pictures well enough that she would see that there were ways of working *within* her guidelines, that would still be within the realm of what worked and what didn't push him over the edge, or lead to aftershock.

The director and I spent hours on the phone. She had a clear, concise image *and* what seemed like respect and understanding. The usual "take the child out in the community and do the typical activities like busy malls and rec centers," would be replaced by "Hayden working and interacting *within* the calm and conducive setting of the worker's home." Hallelujah!

....And then there we were, the programming director, the life skills worker and myself, in my living room, with Hayden nearby, anxious to meet his new "weekend buddy." The worker was bright with enthusiasm and lots of experience. But within minutes, it was obvious that she knew *nothing* of our plan. She was shocked to discover that this would not be a typical Saturday afternoon program. She had no knowledge that it was to take place in her home.

I was mystified because the director and I had spent *hours* clarifying the specifics; and yet as the three of us sat there, it was like she was hearing it all for the first time.

The director then outright questioned why I would want this program to stray so far from the typical plan....I quickly found myself *floundering to defend my reasoning* to both women....I had to rehash old traumas from the past, so that they would *understand* my reasoning....I hadn't prepared myself to be dredging up old memories and family traumas....

Bringing these two women into our hearts and into our history, meant ripping open old scars that I *had not* mentally prepared myself to be opening. *This woman knew enough of our history; I shouldn't have had to be relaying it all again and not there, in my home, where my children could have heard!*

As I listened to myself speak, I was thinking: "Wow, they must be wondering.... how is it that this family has managed to keep this child at home? How many families could have done that and how *lucky* is this young boy, that his family never gave up on him?"

In those moments, I felt traumatized, having to dredge up and stomp through the past, but at least I felt pride in what the six of us had been able to do.

But rather than being in awe, and wanting to be a part of our successful journey, this woman shook her head, quite mockingly and said: *"So are you just going to keep him at home forever?"* She then went on to ask if we had any *measurable goals* for Hayden. She asked "what our expectations" for Hayden were, *and* if we "had any expectations at all."

Can you imagine? I could hardly contain myself, I was so taken aback. *Yes, we had goals.* I had a *list* of goals, and I had lists of how we could hope to tiptoe and achieve them; but they *had to be* on terms that were realistic.

In those minutes, it wasn't just that my heart sank, realizing that she was not going to bend her rules and accommodate Hayden's needs. *I was angry! I wanted her out of my house. I wanted both of them out of my house!*

Who were they to question us?

Very graphically and *very* emphatically, I explained that *our measure of success* was not like the more "typical" special needs families that she dealt with. Hayden was an extreme case and our family dynamics were extreme. *Our measure of success was in seeing that this boy, who had shattered our family to a level that would have been for almost any other family, beyond repair, was still loved and accepted and welcomed by his family, to continue being a part of this family!*

By the time the two of them left, I was a mess. This experience hit me deeply and it took weeks to recover from.

Who the hell was she to grill and question and mock me? If she wanted to see *measurable success* and *monumental goals achieved*, she could do it by listening to Sydney now being able to laugh at the clever and witty things that Hayden said. Sydney, who only a year before was fighting for her health and a reason to get up and out of bed every day, *now* looks at Hayden with *nothing but love in her eyes.* When he walks into the room, we no longer see fear and angst in her eyes; we see pride in him, pride in herself and pride in our family.

Those, my green-skinned witch, are *measurable successes* and *measurable goals, achieved.*

When I say that you can't compare someone as complex as Hayden to anyone but himself, the green witch and her trauma is a perfect example. Yes, I get it, that she wanted to see Hayden learning to be out in the community, having a paper route or working in a sheltered workshop folding boxes. That's what my beautiful brother Erland can do. He can barely speak, but he can manage routines and he can be very social.

But autism is different; social issues are monumental. And Hayden has things over and above autism. Regardless, doing those kinds of day-to-day routines are not *the only measure of success*. Erland has been trained to do those things; but he doesn't understand life or history or concepts and philosophies, on the deep and profound level that Hayden does.

But for Hayden's insight, he pays a price. He knows the impact of his past and he knows he's limited in the future....but he has a kind of pride and personal satisfaction that my brother will *always* be miles away from ever achieving.

Which of these two loves of my life leads a more satisfying, richer life? *In all honesty, I would say Hayden.* There are colors and textures in his life that have *never* been a part of Erland's. Hayden has felt pain more deeply than Erland, because he understands about his past and his impact. He knows how hard it has been for him to fit into the world around him.

But Hayden also feels more deeply, what it is to be loved and to feel proud of himself.

Still, he needs to be protected and honored for who he is.

Believe it or not, this witch's damage that evening didn't end there. Genevieve happened to enter the room, and in a brief conversation, she and I mentioned that we were pursuing the possibility of part-time art studies later that fall. We remarked that traveling all the way downtown was, unfortunately, an issue to consider.

This woman looked at us and blurted out: "Well, Genevieve is an intelligent young woman. She can easily take transit to get there!"

I looked back at her in horror. Yes, of course Genevieve was intelligent and could learn the complex bus route. But that wasn't the only consideration! Genevieve was pervasively affected by autism, and she wasn't ready for that kind of a step. There were safety issues and emotional issues; it *was* complex. *Everything* to do with Genevieve was *always* complex.

For someone with autism, it isn't just a matter of memorizing transit routes. Trust me; no one has a memory like someone with autism. It would also be a matter of the layers and layers before, during and after that transit route *and* the art class itself, that would complicate things. *Who was this woman to make the assumption that Genevieve could handle it, knowing little about her?*

Genevieve herself didn't feel ready. Maybe down the road it would be realistic, but not then. She and her autistic mind and body, walked away from that conversation feeling: "If this woman says I'm intelligent and *can* do this....but *I don't feel* that I can do this, then how intelligent am I? What's wrong with me that I can't do this?" Genevieve did, in fact, articulate those thoughts to me later.

And this witch didn't have to deal with the fallout, the confusion and despair over the week that followed, as Genevieve's art therapist and I did.

In some ways, I know this woman's heart was in the right place. But people like her need to open their eyes and alter their interpretation, about people with disabilities, especially those with autism.

I have a tiny picture with a few sentences that I wrote, to recover from that witch's invasion. She certainly was not the first and she won't be the last. I know that. The picture is a split second captured from *The Wizard of Oz*; I keep it in my secret-garden office, and, *in my mind.* It's the image of that potent moment from the movie: the green witch hands reaching for ruby slippers....a flash of fire prohibiting her.....

These are the words that I wrote:

"It's that attitude, that presence that you have. You have no idea how hard we work and how skilled we've become at being realistic, but at the same time, still filling ourselves with wonder, acceptance and excitement for life, and all that it has thrown at us.

I can click my heels three times and make magic happen. But I'm tired of fighting the evil forces of non-insightful outsiders. Stay out until you learn and feel!
You are not welcome here until then."

Chapter 11

Years ago, I came upon a published article written by the father of an autistic child. It was well-written and heartfelt, but I felt sad when I read it. More than sadness, I felt outraged that he dared to open his article with: *"I go to bed every night and dream about what every parent of an autistic child dreams about: a cure..."* I seem to remember him referring to us as a "desperate bunch."

When I read this dad's words, I realized that I never, *ever* had even thought of using up energy hoping or praying for a cure. To be honest, it hadn't even occurred to me. *I was taken aback that he would make such a blanket statement.*

Maybe I'd just been too busy trying to get me and my family through each day to have those thoughts; or maybe I'd been too caught up in the rapture of being fascinated and in love with all four of my kids...but seriously, I've *never* gone to bed, or had a waking moment for that matter, wondering about a cure. *I do not want to romanticize autism!* It is a tough disorder. This is *not* a light-hearted tale that you've been reading! I have heard the pain in my children's cries and I've scrambled to help them, and to get help *for* them. But I've also seen the unique joy they experience in their lives. And I know the joy that they've brought me.

At this moment in time, there is no cure. What we have is this wide spectrum of children and adults affected uniquely, yet all with common threads. There is always room for growth and for emergence. Autism is part of our world and part of who they are. Some will move beyond and may even lose their "label" of autism. Some, probably most, will not. *But they will emerge on some level, if they are embraced and accepted.* I remember an interesting autistic teen that I worked with for awhile. She told me she was okay with who she was, even if it meant getting bullied once in awhile. She just wished her mom would get over it and move on!

> The term: "label of autism"….why do we get so hung up on that? I've talked to so many parents who "don't want their child to be labeled autistic." I know I'm not the "norm" because I don't understand those words. To me a perfect world would not be one where there is no autism, or where every child would eventually no longer "have it." *To me, the perfect world would be a place where the word autism is an explanation, not a label.*

So many parents say: "Make my child indistinguishable from their peers." How much of that is truly realistic? And what is the cost? Do you still leave the core of that precious person intact?

For all of their issues and challenges, both of my autistic children have made it clear that they want to grow and emerge, but that they want to be allowed to be themselves. Autism is part of who they are and they have come to accept that it is a big part of how they perceive the world and how they respond to it. Both of them have the most amazing perspectives and insights. That is something to love and accept. *Only good can come from embracing this!*

Even Temple Grandin, who unquestionably has done more than anyone on this planet to inform and teach the world about autism, is very quick to say: "If you took away my autism, it wouldn't be me anymore." A few months after *Effervescence* was published, one of the highlights of my life was a telephone conversation with Temple. She actually called me the day she read my book, to tell me how much she enjoyed it. It was an incredible honor and joy, to speak with her about the importance of always working for the future, one tiny step at a time, but still honoring who the autistic person is.

The last couple of years, I've seen such a push in the media to hear claims like: "My child is cured. He/she has recovered." Maybe it does happen for some; maybe some just learn how to hide who they really are, because they feel that they have to. Does anyone stop and ask them: "Do *you* want to be cured?" I wonder?

That thought makes me feel sad. I'd rather smile at a little "snippet of amazing":

> You're reading Hayden's story; you know about his life. He hasn't had an easy life. And yet, he remains one of the most positive and "ponderous" people I know. It's so easy for him to smile!
>
> A couple of years ago, the day Hayden had his wisdom teeth extracted, I fretted and fussed and hovered, worried about the pain and how he'd respond to it. Wisdom teeth *can* be a nightmare, for anyone! That night, I asked him how he was doing, and if he needed us to increase his pain medication, or if there was *anything* that I could do to help him out.
>
> He looked at me calmly, and simply said: "Mom, you know I've dealt with worse pain than this". I was dumbfounded and asked: "When?", because he'd never had surgery of any kind. Hayden looked back earnestly, with eyes that were letting me look right down to his soul; he replied: "You know.... emotional pain. That's much worse than this."
>
> *Wow, what a deep and pensive guy?* He was right. He'd dealt with more multitudes of emotional pain than *anyone* I'd ever known. For him, his emotional pain began even before he had the ability to recognize what emotions were. But he had survived and he had come out shining.

Hayden talks openly about the intense pain he's experienced in his life. In every one of those conversations, I can feel how grateful he is, to no longer be put into situations where he is pushed over the edge. With his wavy red hair, his dimples and his amazingly positive outlook, in his own way, he has become a precious, precious gift to the world.

I would definitely say that that is measurable success!

Chapter 12

ayden is now nineteen. He's still tough to understand and speech therapy really can't offer much more hope for improvement. Sometimes he stutters and he has to repeat the same phrase three times, either before he gets it right, or because his mind is trying to keep up with his speech, or maybe sometimes it's just like some form of self stimming. I'm not really sure....another complexity! But he speaks a mile a minute and fills every conversation with either *profound insight, or repetitious circles of ranting,* about *WWE* superstars or world politics or.... whatever. Sometimes it drives us absolutely crazy! Often he says things that are so funny and cute, that we fight back tears.

Like most people with autism, Hayden still needs time to process activities *and* time to recover from them (though interestingly enough, not as much as his higher-functioning sister). He still needs time to process what he hears and often he needs to have things repeated. Very often we need *him* to repeat what he says several times, before we can figure out what he's saying. But he does have a lot to say.

> Often Hayden stops at the dining room table and reads and ponders the headlines in the morning newspaper. It's one of the cutest things I've ever seen. (And I'm pretty proud, because basically I'm the one who taught him to read). Recently, a headline said: "Outbreak in local town claims eight seniors." Hayden exclaimed emphatically: "I know what would cause that....zombies!"

> As I tried to hide my smile and suggest that it was suspected to be from a flu epidemic, he shook his head and said: "Go ahead, doubt me. But don't come crying to me when you find out that it's true!"

Oh Hayden; just when we think you're right there with us....

The one area of Hayden's life that remains seemingly insurmountable is computers. He experiences them differently than he does video games. *The computer is like a vortex that literally sucks him in.* There is something about computers that pulls him in and he tunes everything out. I don't mean that lightly. It's a serious issue.

Add to that, the lure of internet and there is just too much freedom at his fingertips, despite all our complex attempts to limit him. Even with just the computer, we see obsessive and concerning behaviors. It's a startling contrast to his sister, who *emerges and evolves so wonderfully* through her computer and internet lifeline.

Hayden now lives a computer-free life, not that he likes it! Maybe one day we'll conquer this one for him; but it's a tough one.

By contrast, picture this image: Hayden, who still often paces and rocks back and forth, and who has the shortest attention span you could probably imagine, on a fishing trip with his dad. It's a changed guy who can now actually sit in a slow-moving rowboat, a fishing rod in his hand!

Hayden's second home, every Friday night at his dad's, has helped him to evolve and emerge. When he stays for a week or so in the summer and over Christmas, he comes back relaxed and proud, like a guy who's been on a real vacation. It's a vacation he can handle.

Hayden isn't easy to live with but he is *nothing* like the guy he used to be. He truly is a work in progress. *And he is work.* There is always that nebulous, fine line between knowing that he is doing well *because he has changed*, and the reality that he is doing well *because we are doing things right* and because he feels loved and supported. It's all about working together, meeting halfway and us, always being just *one step* ahead.

It's all about love, acceptance and fascination.

Overall, it's a pretty good life in this cottage, as long as we keep working at it. *We move slowly; we move strategically and I will now personally fight to the death anyone who challenges that!* Sometimes the rough days just happen; but really, usually they are now more *moments* than days.

One morning awhile back, for whatever reason, Hayden slipped into one of his uncooperative, non-receptive moods. I was annoyed, but mostly I was disappointed because I'd planned to spend some special time with him, working on a little comic that he'd been writing (he talks and imagines while I type). I stormed out of the room in a huff and was close to tears. It was one of those *rare* times when I really didn't care at that moment, if he slipped into playing a video game or withdrawal. (I was obviously having a rough day).

After awhile, *he sought me out* and with eyes that said: "Sorry Mom, you know that's just the way it is. No matter what, there will be times when I just get like that"....he wrapped his arms around me. He was right. He's come so far but sometimes, he just can't do it.

If he could have done it that day, he would have.

As he and I stood, his arms wrapped tightly around me, I could feel his heart beating against my ear. *What I felt was safe.* Hayden, with all his wisdom and his sweetness, this boy who had torn this family to shreds time and time again with his screaming, his biting, his pinching and kicking and all that you've read about....in those moments, *he made me feel safe and taken care of.*

He had answers for the issue at hand: it was just the way he was and we'd get through it. He was right. And I got through it because *he made me* feel safe and loved.

As I stood there with his big, bear-like arms wrapped around me, my mind flitted back to an incident a few weeks before, when he'd been close to a defiant meltdown in a video store, because the game he'd planned to rent was considered by me to be inappropriate. Amazingly, he and I had been able to work through it. When we got home, he'd looked at me and said sweetly: "Sorry about that Mom. I wasn't expecting that."

Look how far he's come! He is his own person.

Just recently, I stood back and marveled in disbelief when my wicked fear of heights happened to come up in our conversation. Hayden spouted out what was a well-planned theory that he had, of his own accord, been working on. It was about me using "reverse psychology" to overcome my fear. I just couldn't believe that one of *my fears* would motivate him to search his mind for an answer.

Look at who Hayden was and who he is now.
How is that not measurable success?
How has that not been one, <u>but a whole list</u>, of our measurable goals achieved?

The event of Hayden's "plan to address Mom's fear of heights" was even more "classically Hayden," when in the blink of an eye, after revealing his insightful plan, he switched to little kid Hayden and exclaimed: "What the hell is wrong with Daffy Duck's mind? He thinks he's so popular...."

The mysteries of Hayden!

Chapter 13

*L*ife in our home is now livable. It *is* a pretty good life, here in our cottage. In contrast to past years, when our castle walls and windows could barely contain the loud and bizarre chaos from within, often now our home is *too quiet* and *too calm*, at least by my standards. And it can sometimes be tedious because there are schedules, regiments and "recovery" time that need to be kept and respected.

But there's no longer the need for constant focus. It is an amazing home and a good place to be. There were times when our past home was both a friend and a foe. For me, I can honestly say now that our home, our cottage, is my friend.

I no longer *allow* myself to take notes everyday and document behaviors. I know it sounds crazy, but you'd be surprised to know how hard I had to work to *re-program myself* not to document, or to see every single day as therapy and emotional recovery. I'm not kidding.

Much of the time now, when I write something in a journal about Hayden or Genevieve, it's something amazing that *I can't resist* putting on paper. I'm not going to fantasize or romanticize....there are still tough, challenging, complex and often heart-wrenching issues that come up for both of them....they've both entered adulthood, for God's sake. Talk about new challenges...

But it's different. Now it's mostly just fascinating! And now that Hayden isn't raging through the world and our home, we can deal with things!

I have to interject for just a moment, and ask you to let me tell you about Jack:

> During that time when I was able to work as a special ed assistant, Jack was a tiny little teen and he was profoundly autistic. He was completely non-verbal and unable to walk. Despite his high level of self-stimming and self-injurious behavior, there was a look in his eyes that was ironically sweet and peaceful. In his own way he was captivating, and staff and typical students were drawn to him.
>
> Because I was only in the classroom for three hours a day, I didn't get to spend nearly as much direct time with Jack as I would have loved; but he and I made an immediate and deep connection. One day, unbeknown to him, I'd already arrived and was sitting across the classroom, working with another teen. Jack happened to glance my way and I saw keenness in his eyes when he saw me.
>
> A couple of minutes later, the staff and I watched as Jack somehow wriggled his way out of the restraints on his wheelchair, dragged himself across the floor and flopped himself down at my feet. The staff literally stood with their eyes wide open and their jaws dropped in disbelief. They'd never seen him do anything like that before.
>
> My heart felt like it would burst; but at the same time, Jack's actions didn't surprise me. I'd felt that force between us, every time I'd looked in his eyes. For all his profound limitations and disabilities, he somehow knew that I spoke his language, or at least that I knew enough of it that he could "talk to me" on a level that maybe didn't come as naturally to the other staff. They were an extraordinarily talented and caring group, but they didn't "live" this the way that I did. *I think he could feel that.* I know he did.

I don't pretend to have all of the answers. All I know for sure is that when my autistic children or *anyone with autism* that I've had the pleasure to meet, walks into the room, *I feel myself pulling into their heads and into their bodies.* I find myself *seeing* through their eyes and *feeling* through their bodies, at least how I suspect they might see and feel things.

I can feel my body physically shift, like there is a force pulling me in and saying: *"Step in and stay here for awhile."* To me it is second nature to want to know where they go, how it feels and what's there.

For me it feels safe; it feels a little bit like home. I lived there, or at least I was a guest there for a long time and I shared many of those threads. It's a place I like to connect with. There is a "humanity" there that I don't feel in "neuro-typicals." And it's a world where senses respond and react and experience differently.

I'm telling you specifically about Jack because he was profoundly affected by autism and yet he touched so many people. *None of us will forget him.* There was a reason for him being here in this world, just as there is for you and for me.

Jack was a precious person in my life. And I think that by pushing away all other perspectives, and simply letting myself experience *his* world on a deep level, and letting *him feel* that it was a place I loved to be, I was able to enjoy him and be touched by him, on a level that not every one in his life could. I think I was a little bit precious in his life. *I hope so.*

Chapter 14

One of the reasons our cottage is often too quiet, is that Kobe's away most of the time. Pursuing baseball, college and university, he's lived in California, Texas and now Alabama. That's a long way from the west coast of Canada. But he made the break and we all survived it, even Hayden. They're still each other's heroes; they just maintain it long distance and in between school terms, when they pick up their conversations and their video game competitions, right where they left off.

The day Kobe left, at barely eighteen, was a pretty unique autism-family moment: Hayden stayed inside, glued to his video games to fight the emotional overload that was running amuck outside on the sidewalk. Nolan was mentally preparing for the long drive to California to drop Kobe off. I was crying, Sydney was crying, Kobe was crying. I stopped for a moment to check on Genevieve, knowing full well I was in no condition to assist her anyway.

There she was, a quizzical look on her face, like she was thinking: "Wow, there's a lot of emotions flying around here....I'm not really sure what any of this means but this is really weird and kind of annoying....."

Kobe's first visit home was one of our *best* moments ever. For weeks prior to the Christmas arrival, Hayden and I argued back and forth as to who missed Kobe the most and who should get the first hug. We bartered endlessly. Hayden said that he was taller and easier for Kobe to reach. I noted that I was smaller and could sneak in between them. Of course he said he was bigger and could push me out of the way. I said I could run faster. He responded that I had "absolutely no idea how athletic he could be!" (Yes, when we think of athletic we think of Hayden.)

Finally, the day arrived. All six of us sat in the terminal, watching the monitor, looking for Kobe's image. By a stroke of luck, I was the first to see him onscreen. He looked so different with short hair and a tan, so I don't think the others really recognized him.

In what was probably my only deceitful act as a mom, ever, *I didn't tell Hayden.* I wanted to get to Kobe first, because I'd missed him so much. I leaped from my seat and started running toward him. Hayden, who has the slowest reaction time you could imagine, saw and in the blink of an eye, leapt from his seat and sprang into action!

As I dodged in and around people, I saw Hayden. With his red hair, his six foot one frame and his rather awkward run, he was quite a sight! But damned if he didn't catch up!

It's amazing how, in just a few short seconds, so many thoughts can run through your head: the funny images. At that moment, it was my Kobe coming home and I had super strength going for me; I could *push* Hayden out of the way. He'd go flying and I'd get the first hug and the first moment with Kobe!

But, that would just cause chaos and Hayden would probably push me out of the way and *I'd* go flying. And you know, Hayden had won this one fair and square. In those moments when I watched him darting past me, there was intensity in his eyes. *In his old life, we only saw intensity in his eyes when he lashed out at us. This was different. This was pure drive, determination and purpose: to get to his big brother. He had caught up because he was motivated by his love for his brother. He deserved the first hug and the first moment!* Obviously he really was right when he warned me that he was more athletic than we thought.

The brotherhood: both of them there with tears in their eyes and magic radiating between them.

According to Sydney, the observer of people, *everyone* in the terminal had seen the race and everyone had a smile. My thoughts rushed back to that dim-witted psychologist, all those years earlier, who'd accused me and specifically Kobe, of being unrealistic, thinking that two brothers (one of them autistic or not) could have a deep relationship when they were three and a half years apart! She was *so* wrong.

Just like Kobe had said when he was just a little boy: *"That's brother love. It's special!"*

....Within a couple of years, nuzzled alongside this tightly-woven brotherhood, there would be our beautiful Tamarissia. Kobe had to venture all the way down to the lone-star state of Texas to find this shining star.

And there she was: a dancer/singer/songwriter with uniqueness *and* a magical presence....likely a perfect match for our unique and complex Kobe. I have a feeling she just may be the best thing that ever happened to him. She may be one of the best things to ever happen to us. To quote a song that she and Kobe wrote together: "Life is *so* good...."

It's not that she fits in with us....*she is us!*

Chapter 15

enevieve and Hayden: "worlds apart and yet worlds the same." Here is a fabulous little snippet and one that I can't resist giving:

Awhile back, both Genevieve and Hayden wanted to check out the new "downtown apartment" of a close family friend. As it just wouldn't have worked to have both of them make the drive and the visit together, the plan was that I would take Hayden, and then Nolan would take Genevieve a bit later.

Hayden loved the very cool apartment, and when we stepped out onto the balcony, he peered over the edge and spit. I looked back at him in horror, thinking: "Since when do we spit?" I asked, with more than a little surprise in my voice: "Hayden, why did you do that?"

He looked back calmly at me and replied: "I don't care; I don't live here!"

Knowing full well that Nolan and Genevieve would be coming by very shortly, I gathered up Hayden and wrapped up our short visit. It was lucky timing as we almost brushed shoulders with them as we left (trust me: a small apartment with both Hayden and Genevieve would have been way too intrusive for her.)

Genevieve loved the very cool apartment and no doubt envisioned herself one day, an artist and living downtown in a tiny but funky apartment just like this. Apparently when she and Nolan stepped out onto the balcony, she peered over the edge and spit. Nolan looked back at her in horror, thinking: "Since when do we spit?" He asked, with more than a little surprise in *his* voice: "Genevieve, why did you do that?"

She looked back calmly at him and replied: "I don't care; I don't live here!"

Worlds apart and yet worlds the same!

Chapter 16

This current year, Nolan and I could have pressed to have Hayden do an extended year of public high school (offered to special needs students), *but Hayden was done.* He needed to move on. Instead, we opted to follow a new path, suggested by Benjamin Bryson. We were able to re-direct school funding and create what I designed and what we presented to Hayden as *"An Expansion Program."* And *this* is where I can prove what I said earlier about autism and the "Power and Presence of Past Associations":

> The plan meant that we made it clear to Hayden that this program had *nothing* to do with school. *He was done; it was history that was all behind him.* We used carefully-chosen, well-designed words and concepts. We laid out the plan and we lured him in.

> In our Expansion Program, there are four of us who work directly with Hayden: myself, two lovely women and one equally-lovely man. That marks a big step for Hayden: the first time he's ever been willing to work with a male. Each of these people is unique and has something different to offer. I found them myself and I orientated them myself; but I wasn't working on my own on this one. *God was looking over my shoulder the whole time; that I could feel.*

> In our *Expansion Program*, there's no school or building. There's Hayden's home and each of *their* homes. We include his video game time as part of the program to honor his need, *and* to use it for recovery time. We complement it strategically with bits of other activities, in and out of their homes. I can't even say "bits" anymore, because it's snowballing. Just the fact that he is welcoming new people into his life is *huge;* but add to that, Hayden is venturing out, every day, in some shape or form, into the community. And he interacts with their families and his world is opening up, slowly but impressively.

> The four of us are a team and we're working. *The plan is working.* Hayden feels like a grown-up and he is rising to the occasion. He *is* expanding, and overall, he feels good about himself!

How much of that is because we have closed that school chapter of his life? A lot; I know it is. In his *words, he had to get out of that "hell-hole." In* my *words, he had to be given permission to leave those dangerous Past Associations* in the past.

And he needed to have a new plan that had Hayden and only Hayden at its heart.

Slowly, we'll try to work on increasing his comfort level with people his age, again in tiny bits and pieces *when the time seems right.* We'll just keep expanding, slowly and carefully. As for the rough sides of Hayden: he isn't cured or fixed! He remains a work in progress. I am not naïve or inexperienced. I lived through our past and God only knows what may come along and alter his future, and throw him into chaos.

But rather than living in fear and worrying about that possibility, I prefer to see it as a dangling carrot for greatness! *I try not to focus on the fact that he may fall. Instead I focus on what can we do to make sure that he doesn't.*

He deserves more. We deserve more. It's as simple as that!

Recently, Hayden made one of his wonderful observations about something. I can't even remember exactly what it was; but I remember being astounded and so amused. I said to him, with all my heart: "Hayden, promise me you'll never stop amazing me!" With his six foot three frame, his dimples, his cleft chin and his little boy smile, he answered: "Oh ho ho ho, Mommy, I have no limit!"

I believe that to be true!

Part Three

Epilogue

When the nightmare of high school first unfolded, when both Hayden and I were so stressed and needed something shining to hold onto, I promised him that when he was done with school, I'd take the two of us to Disneyland. Well, here we are....literally, as I write these words, the final chapter of this book, my next task is to pack our suitcases. In two days we'll be on a plane.

But it won't be just Hayden and me as planned; Sydney jumped at the chance to join us. Sydney, the same Sydney who struggled and used *every thing she had in her*, to recover from the ravages of Hayden in her life....Sydney, the same Sydney who now looks at Hayden with only love and respect in her eyes, is counting the minutes until we leave.

Kobe is still in Alabama and Genevieve....well, let's just say that close confinement with Hayden is still too much for her....

But like me, Sydney can't wait to see Hayden's face on every ride and every inch of that magical kingdom. We just want to be there with *him*, there in *that* castle! For five, glorious and hopefully magical days, *that* will be the castle we'll call home....

Our cottage is our home. It's an evolving home, especially now as Kobe juggles between his home in the United States and this one, and Nolan interacts from his home and this one. And, we're adding new family members, one at a time.

But there are no moats around this home and the doors are open to possibilities, each of which we will embrace, carefully, in ways that are safe to us.

In Hayden's life, I believe that before he was even born, he and I were cast in roles that intertwined us deeply. I do believe that for much of his life he was, indeed, trapped in a castle within his mind and within his body.

He was a prince and I was his queen. It's not that way now. We don't live in that state of mind anymore, nor do we live in that actual home, that was, our family's castle. We honor who he is and we honor who each of us is. Because of our history, we are a little bit different from everyone else; but that is not a bad thing. It is us.

But before I relinquish my title as queen,
to my prince, I would like to say:

I see you in front of me, on your knee, bowing. I knight you, my
prince, with a sword, a sword endowed with our family's emblem.
Because of your heart, your soul and your wonderful sense of humor
and optimism, you have redeemed yourself of all past wrongdoings.

You and I will leave our ornate, intricately woven robes behind.
We'll put on t-shirts and jeans and live in our cottage and just be us,
a mom and her very, very loved son.

The End

Post Script

*Y*es, the five days in Disneyland *were* magical! And who would have ever thought that the two words to best describe our trip would be: "Hayden's patience?" Go figure. He was remarkable!

But then, why wouldn't he be? He was in a place where he, like everyone else, could be a kid, or an adult, or a delicious mixture of both. And some of the newer rides are like being *inside* a video game. To most of us, that would be bombarding....to Hayden, it was *soothing*! His body just works so damn differently from ours.

But he was home!

A Few Pivotal and Very Marketable Strategies.

Our Cottage, Our Maple Tree

(This is the actual image that appears within Hayden's frame.)

The Co-operation Contest
"Who will win?"

The *Spiderman* Curtain

(and its frame, attached to the ceiling)
"Enveloped in Safety"

"Spider Senses are Tingling"

To help Hayden unload and decipher
the bombarding onslaught of emotions:
Working through the opposing eyes of both *Spiderman* and Green Goblin.

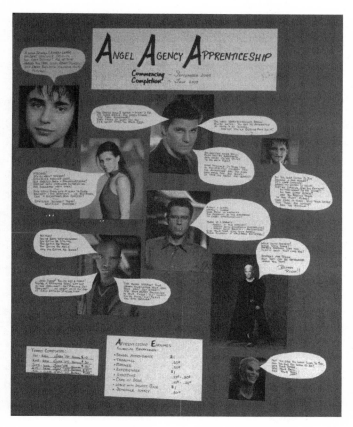

Angel Agency Apprenticeship
Finally working toward the future.

"Walk with Dignity, Walk with Pride"
Part of the Angel Agency program, to enhance being a calm and non-reactive person.

About the Author

The artistry of writing, pen to a page, words captured on a page, passion, thoughts in mind, a simple slip of paper, a journal or a book for the world to peruse....it doesn't matter, it's writing....

Muscles at peace or the body in the rapture of movement and dance, the smoothness and glory of breath....

The beauty and joy of children and of people who are real....connectedness to the world and figuring things out, of stepping back and thinking and feeling....

These are the simple components of author Simone Brenneman.

Simone is a mom of four: two sons and two daughters, each uniquely a gift to the world. Her part of the world, the west coast of British Columbia, Canada, is as vibrant and curious as her life experiences. She has delved deeply into the world of autism through the minds and bodies of her children, and others, as described in both *The Castle We Called Home* and *Effervescence*.

She works as a behavior interventionist, a writer, a dance instructor and a yoga teacher. All are absolute joys, equal to the joy of speaking and presenting about her experiences with autism and the *endless* possibilities of embracing it.

Simone's Bachelor of Arts degree in English set the stage for her writing technique; but honestly, it is the life experiences she's been blessed to have, that have been the driving and cultivating forces. *A body, a mind, a heartbeat and breath, joined with captivating family, acquaintances and life experiences....what more could any author, or simply any person, ask for?*

Please visit: effervescentclarity.com / autismembrace.com

Special Acknowledgement to Kassandra Klassen

"For capturing my images and words with your artistry, in both
The Castle We Called Home and *Effervescence*."

When "*Castle*" was finally finished, awaiting only my final "read-through," I went to pieces after reading only the first few chapters....I loved what I'd written and how I'd written it; but even as far as my family has come, parts of this book still touch me deeply....too deeply. I thought; I cried: "How can I publish this story when I can't even make myself re-read it to make sure it's flawless?"

For a few agonizing days I was convinced: "I can't do this. It's too personal. I can't publish it. Some parts are too painful and too raw." Even distancing myself as a writer, there were parts that I couldn't stop myself from re-living as I read the words.

But it wasn't the thought of years of writing and compiling all going for nothing. It was in knowing that *we have a tale to tell*, one that can change lives. *And* it was the look on Benjamin Bryson's face when I told him: "I can't do this." I'd never seen his jaw drop before.

So I did what I've always done with my autistic kids and their complexities....I closed my eyes and just "felt".....and the answer was right there; it was in Kassandra's artistry, her fabulous image of the *back of our castle*, which I'd planned to make the back cover of this book.

It all quickly became part of a process, *a behavioral strategy*, really! I made my world stop so I could focus and assemble what I needed....I diminished the image to the perfect size.... then the perfect frame practically *found* me....the frame was beautiful, almost 3D and curiously medieval looking....

And "curious"….that *is* the word….that *was* the strategy!

When I began the final journey of re-reading and preparing this book for publication, I trained myself to focus first, for a few minutes, on the framed image of the *back* of this castle….then I would re-read my story, not through the eyes of someone who lived *inside* the castle, but through the eyes of a visitor, traveling along the moat, curiously asking: *"Wow, what is this place….and who lives here?*

They must be fascinating….I want to peek in…."

That is the piece of her artistry that I love and appreciate the most.

And Acknowledgement to

Janet Shapiro, Smith Publicity, New York
For recognizing, believing and acting upon; for hearts the same.

Other Books by Simone Brenneman

Effervescence: A True-Life Tale of Autism and of Courage

*I*magine a beautiful little girl, with long curly, wild red hair, spinning in circles, completely delighted by all that she feels! She wears a long, blue dress, a replica of the one Cinderella wore to the ball. As you watch her, you get the sense that she isn't dreaming of Cinderella; in her heart and in her body, she *is* Cinderella.

Now picture the same little girl, lying on her tummy, spinning on a merry-go-round, dipping her beautiful, long red hair in the puddle of mud that encircles the merry-go-round. When it comes to a stop, she savors the wonderful sensation of the cold mud running down her face. She then submerges her entire body in the puddle, as happy as can be and entirely oblivious to the stares of the people around her.

Now picture that same little girl, in her comfortable home, surrounded by a family who love and adore her. Her mom asks a simple question, like: "Sweetie, what kind of cereal would you like?" Instantly, her beautiful face is filled with intense emotion and she screams, more like a wild animal than a child, for five minutes, or it may continue for two hours. The only thing that might interrupt the screaming is her stopping, occasionally, to frantically bite her wrist, hard enough to leave teeth marks.

Would it surprise you to learn that I have just described a high-functioning autistic child?

Now take a peak at the same child at age twelve, entering her classroom each day. Her teacher marvels to herself, as she watches this young girl navigate skillfully, smoothly and seemingly naturally throughout the classroom. Had the teacher not known her student's history of autism, she likely would never have guessed. In her own words, the only time this teacher is aware of the child's

275

autism, is when she reads the amazing stories and illustrations created by this extraordinary girl. She would then muse to herself: "There is no way a "typical" grade-seven student could write and draw like this!"

Do you get the feeling that an amazing transformation has taken place? Is the child no longer autistic? Has she grown out of it? Has she learned through behavior management to "manage" it? Was she just "a little bit autistic" and now she's "better?" There is no simple answer; autism is far too complex and diverse a disorder for it to be addressed so simply. But it is a fascinating disorder and this child's life has been an incredible journey! Her name is Genevieve.

Effervescent Clarity

By

Simone Brenneman

A Book of Short Mind and Body Journeys
for bedtime, stress-time or anytime.

Each is carefully crafted to relax, rejuvenate and re-direct your
mind and body
in just a matter of minutes.

This compilation is created through years of teaching yoga and
dance,
and living amidst the world of autism.